Historic Melrose

the archaeological implications of development

E Patricia **Dennison**

Russel **Coleman**

the Scottish burgh survey

HISTORIC SCOTLAND

in association with

SCOTTISH CULTURAL PRESS

CENTRE FOR SCOTTISH URBAN HISTORY
Department of Scottish History
University of Edinburgh

publication   Historic Scotland *in association with* Scottish Cultural Press
First published 1998

copyright   © Historic Scotland 1998
The moral right of the authors has been asserted.

editorial   Olwyn Owen

design   Christina Unwin

printing . binding   The Cromwell Press, Trowbridge

ISSN   1358 0272

Scottish Cultural Press ISBN   1 898218 51 X

all distribution
and sales enquiries   Scottish Cultural Press
Scottish burgh survey   Unit 14 . Leith Walk Business Centre
130 Leith Walk
Edinburgh
EH6 5DT
telephone *0131* 555 5950 . facsimile *0131* 555 5018

all other enquiries   ■ Scottish Borders Council
Council Headquarters
Newtown St Boswells
Melrose
TD6 0SA
telephone *01835* 824000 . facsimile *01835* 825001

■ Historic Scotland
Longmore House
Salisbury Place
Edinburgh
EH9 1SH
telephone *0131* 668 8600 . facsimile *0131* 668 8699

A catalogue record for this book is available from the British Library

British Library cataloguing
in publication data

contents

v figures
vi abbreviations
vii acknowledgements
viii foreword

1 **how to use this survey**

5 **Melrose: its site and setting**
introduction 5
geography 7
geology 8
the Ice Age 9
the post-glacial period 9
soils and land use 9
physical setting and the topography of the burgh 10

13 **archaeological and historical background**
the prehistory of the Scottish Borders 13
later prehistory 14
Melrose and the Borders in the Roman period 15
south-east Scotland in the early historic period 18
medieval Melrose and its abbey 20
sixteenth-century Melrose 32
seventeenth-century Melrose 35
eighteenth-century Melrose 40
post-script—'fair Melrose' 43

57 **area by area assessment**
introduction 57

area 1 57
Abbey Street/River Tweed/Sewage Works (east side)/The Annay fields/
Priorswalk housing estate (east side)/High Road (north side)

area 2 73
Abbey Street/River Tweed/Weirhill/High Street (north side)/High Street
(rear of properties)

area 3 81
High Street (north side)/High Street (rear of properties)/High Road (north side)/Gallows
Brae/Douglas Road/Quarry Hill/Huntly Road

the archaeological potential of Melrose a summary 93

iv

97   **historic buildings** and their archaeological potential

103   **suggested avenues for further work**   historical research objectives   103

archaeological objectives for the future   103

107   **street names**

109   **glossary**

113   **bibliography**

119   **general index**

figures

1	Location of Melrose	4	v
2	The Eildon Hills, 1980	5	
3	The physical setting of Melrose	6	
4	Aerial view of Newstead and the bridges over the River Tweed, 1984	7	
5	Melrose from the air, 1978	10	
6	Ptolemy's map of Britain, AD 167. *This version published 1730*	16	
7	J Blaeu's *Lauderdalia*, dating to the 1650s	21	
8	Site of the south gate to the abbey precincts, seen from the Market Square	27	
9	Medieval finds from the abbey—pottery jugs and urinals. The lead communion token dates to the eighteenth or nineteenth century.	28	
10	Alan Sorrell's reconstruction illustration of the abbey *c* 1500	31	
11	Charter illustration of the tomb of the second Earl of Douglas, dating to before 1544	33	
12	Leslie House, West Port, demolished in 1875	38	
13	Toll house, East Port. *Photograph 1970s*	44	
14	Chain Bridge before re-building	44	
15	View of Melrose, showing the 1849 railway line and station. *Artist unknown, probably dating to the 1850s*	44	
16	Fastern's E'en ba' festivities—the last game of handball played in Melrose. *Photographed by J Brown on 26th February 1901*	45	
17	John Wood's plan of Melrose and Gattonside, 1826	46–7	
18	The Market Square, with cross and Pant Well. *Painting by Thomas H Shepherd, 1830*	48	
19	Area location map	56	
20	Area 1	58	
21	Abbey Hotel before its demolition in 1948	71	
22	Area 2	72	
23	Area 3	82	
24	East Port and the Ship Inn before 1900	90	
25	The archaeological potential of Melrose **colour-coded**	foldout at back	

ALCPA	*Acts of the Lords of Council in Public Affairs*, ed R K Hannay (Edinburgh, 1932).
APS	*The Acts of the Parliaments of Scotland*, edd T Thomson & C Innes (Edinburgh, 1814–75).
BRA	Borders Regional Archive, Selkirk.
CDS	*Calendar of Documents Relating to Scotland*, ed J Bain *et al* (Edinburgh, 1839–1986).
DES	*Discovery and Excavation in Scotland.*
HS	Historic Scotland.
NMRS	National Monuments Record of Scotland.
NSA	*The New Statistical Account of Scotland*, ed The Committee of the Society for the Benefit of the Sons and Daughters of the Clergy (Edinburgh, 1845).
OSA	*The Statistical Account of Scotland, 1791–1799*, ed J Sinclair. New Edition, edd I R Grant & D J Withrington (Wakefield, 1973).
PSAS	*Proceedings of the Society of Antiquaries of Scotland.*
RCAHMS	Royal Commission on the Ancient and Historical Monuments of Scotland.
RIAS	Royal Institute of Architects in Scotland.
RMS	*The Register of the Great Seal of Scotland*, 11 vols, edd J M Thomson *et al* (Edinburgh, 1882–1914).
RPC	*The Register of the Privy Council of Scotland*, 14 vols, edd J H Burton *et al* (Edinburgh, 1877–).
RRS	*Regesta Regum Scottorum 1153–1406*, edd G W S Barrow *et al* (Edinburgh, 1960–).
RSS	*Register of the Privy Seal of Scotland (Registrum Secreti Sigilli Regum Scotorum)*, 8 vols, edd M Livingstone *et al* (Edinburgh, 1908).
SBS	Scottish Burgh Survey.
SHS	Scottish History Society.
SRO	Scottish Record Office, Edinburgh.
SRRM	*Selections from the Records of the Regality of Melrose*, 3 vols, ed C S Romanes (SHS, 1914–17).
SUAT	Scottish Urban Archaeological Trust.
TA	*Accounts of the Lord High Treasurer of Scotland*, 13 vols, edd T Dickson *et al* (Edinburgh, 1877–).

acknowledgements Especial thanks must go to **the people of Melrose** who gave unstinting support and helpful advice and insights into historic Melrose. In particular, we would like to mention **Mr T Little** for information, written and spoken, the loan of photographs and a guided tour of the presumed site of the precinct walls. **Mrs M Hood, Mrs P and Miss J Maxwell-Scott, Dr W Lonie** and **Mr A Crawford** all shared with us their great knowledge of the town, along with welcome coffee and biscuits on snow-blanketed days. Mr Little and Mrs Hood very kindly read some of our preliminary draft and we are grateful for their useful comments. **Mrs B Linehan**, the daughter of Dr J Curle, trusted us with her father's personal copy of his excellent book on Melrose. A postgraduate within the Department of Scottish History, **Mrs B Dalgleish**, also provided much valuable assistance.

Borders Region Archives were extremely helpful and we are grateful for the time they spent with our researchers. **Mr I Brown, Ettrick and Lauderdale Museums Service**, was also very helpful. The Centre would also like to thank **Mr J Dent** and **Ms L Dorward** of **Regional Archaeology Services, Borders Regional Council, Planning Department**; **Dr M Noel, Geoquest Associates Ltd** for discussions on his survey of the site of Melrose Cathedral; and **Mr G Ewart, Kirkdale Archaeology Ltd**, for providing information ahead of publication about the recent excavations at Melrose Abbey, funded by Historic Scotland.

Colleagues at the **University of Edinburgh** have given invaluable support and advice as always, in particular, the **Centre for Field Archaeology**. Mr D Perry and Mr S Stronach, of the **Scottish Urban Archaeological Trust**, kindly assisted with the collation of information on archaeological projects and finds in the Melrose area.

The **Royal Commission on the Ancient and Historical Monuments of Scotland** has been, as usual, very supportive; as have staff of **Historic Scotland**, in particular Mrs D Grove, Dr R Fawcett and Ms D Cameron. The staff of the **Scottish Record Office** and of the **National Library of Scotland**, at both George IV Bridge and the Map Library at Causewayside, have been very helpful; as have staff at the **Scottish Brewing Archives**, at the University of Glasgow. Editorial assistance has been provided by Mrs M Seddon and Mr M Ritchie. The index has been prepared by Mrs H Flenley. The illustrations were collated by Mr R Macpherson.

For permission to reproduce photographs and illustrations, we wish to thank the following:

figures 2, 5 & 11 are reproduced by kind permission of the **Royal Commission on Ancient and Historical Monuments of Scotland**. © Crown Copyright: RCAHMS.

figure 4 is reproduced by kind permission of **Dr Colin Martin, University of St Andrews.**

figures 6, 7 & 17 are reproduced by kind permission of the **The Trustees of the National Library of Scotland.**

figures 8, 12, 13, 14, 16, 21 & 24 are reproduced by kind permission of **Mr Tom Little** (**figure 21** from a photograph in the possession of **Mr R Wilson**, and **figure 24** from a photograph in the possession of the late **Mr J Hart**).

figures 9 & 10 are reproduced by permission of **Historic Scotland**. © Crown Copyright: Historic Scotland.

figure 15 is reproduced by kind permission of **Mr Adam Crawford.**

figure 18 is reproduced by kind permission of **Sotheby's, Victorian Picture Department.**

figures 1, 3, 19, 20, 22, 23 & 25 are based upon the Ordnance Survey 1:10,000 scale and the Ordnance Survey 1:2,500 map series, with the permission of the **The Controller of Her Majesty's Stationery Office**. © Crown Copyright, Licence number GD03032G/1997.

The area around Melrose is exceptionally rich in sites and finds from all periods of prehistory and history. These include the impressive prehistoric hillfort which overlooks Melrose, Eildon Hill North, and the important Roman fort of *Trimontium* (Newstead). Within Melrose, the famous abbey dominates both the town and its history; its ruins are among the most impressive in Britain. The first historical mention of Melrose occurs when St Aidan of Lindisfarne established a monastery at 'Mailros' (Old Melrose) sometime before AD 650, but this was destroyed by Kenneth mac Alpin in AD 839. Later, when King David I (1124–53) invited the Cistercian order to re-establish a monastery here, the Cistercians opted for a site two and a half miles further west. It was this twelfth-century monastery which grew into the later medieval abbey and beside it grew the lay settlement of Melrose. From the Wars of Independence through to the Rough Wooing of the 1540s, the abbey and adjacent settlement suffered much through the centuries. Political and religious events brought profound changes to Melrose after 1560, with the establishment of a Protestant church; and in the early years of the seventeenth century, the little township (which was by then expanding into the erstwhile abbey precincts) was formally elevated to the status of a burgh.

Historic Melrose is one of a series of reports on the historic burghs of Scotland—known collectively as the **Scottish Burgh Survey**—all of which have been commissioned by **Historic Scotland** and its predecessors. The main aim of the survey is to identify those areas of the present and historic burgh which are of archaeological interest and therefore require sensitive treatment in the event of any proposed development or other ground disturbance. It is designed primarily as a manual for the use of the local authority and archaeological curators. However, as an essential prerequisite to the assessment of the archaeological implications of development, it also describes and illustrates the geography and topography of the town, its known archaeology and history, its historic standing buildings and the origins of its street names—all of which will be of interest to the wider public, be they inhabitant, visitor or student.

Historic Melrose was prepared within the **Centre for Scottish Urban History**, under the supervision of its Director, Dr E Patricia Dennison. The Centre is part of the Department of Scottish History, University of Edinburgh. Dr Dennison and Mr Russel Coleman, of the **Scottish Urban Archaeological Trust**, are co-authors of the report. Mr Kevin Hicks, of the **Centre for Field Archaelogy**, University of Edinburgh, is cartographer and illustrator. Mr Robin Macpherson of the Scottish History Department acted as Research Assistant to the project. The research team comprised Sharon Adams, Dean Jacobs and Susan Gillanders, all postgraduates in the Department of Scottish History. The project is supervised by the Head of the Department, Professor Michael Lynch, and managed for Historic Scotland by Ms Olwyn Owen, Inspector of Ancient Monuments, who is also general editor of the series.

The research on historic Melrose was carried out during January and February 1996. The survey was entirely funded by Historic Scotland with help from the Centre for Scottish Urban History. The report has been published with financial assistance from **Scottish Borders Council** and Historic Scotland. Further copies may be obtained from **Scottish Cultural Press**, Unit 14, Leith Walk Business centre, 130 Leith Walk, Edinburgh EH6 5DT.

Historic Scotland
April 1998

the Scottish burgh survey

summary   1

1   Use the colour-coded map on the foldout at the back of this book **figure 25** and/or the **general index** to locate a particular site (normally the site of a development proposal).

2   If the site is in a **blue area**, any development proposal is unlikely to affect significant archaeological remains. No action is needed.

3   **Green areas** (light and dark green) are designated as potentially archaeologically sensitive. If the site is in a green area, it is possible that a proposal involving ground disturbance may encounter archaeological remains. Seek appropriate archaeological advice as early as possible.

4   **Red areas** are Scheduled Ancient Monuments or properties in the care of the Secretary of State for Scotland, and are protected by law. Consult Historic Scotland.

5   Use the map on p 56 **figure 19** to determine into which area of the burgh the site falls (one of Areas 1–3), and turn to the relevant area in the area by area assessment for a fuller account (pp 57–92).

6   Use the **general index** and, if appropriate, the listing of **street names** (pp 107–8) for rapid access to information specific to a site, street or named feature of the town.

step 1

As a working manual, the first point of reference is to the colour-coded map on the foldout at the back of the book **figure 25**.

The **red areas** are **protected by law**. Under the provisions of the Ancient Monuments and Archaeological Areas Act 1979 all development proposals which affect them require the prior written consent of the Secretary of State for Scotland (Scheduled Monument Consent) in addition to any planning permission required. These provisions are administered on behalf of the Secretary of State by Historic Scotland. **All applications for planning permission which affect either the site or setting of a Scheduled Ancient Monument (red area) must be referred to Historic Scotland**, acting for the Secretary of State in terms of Section 15(j)(v) of the Town and Country Planning (General Development Procedure)(Scotland) Order 1992 and Section 5(e) of its Amendment (No. 2) Order 1994. *All enquiries regarding prospective development proposals in or adjacent to red areas should be referred to Historic Scotland for advice as early as possible.*

The **green areas** are **potentially archaeologically sensitive** and may retain significant sub-surface archaeological information. *Consultation should take place with the local authority planning department, where any development proposal or enquiry involving ground disturbance is being considered*, including car parks, road schemes, environmental improvements, landscaping and drainage schemes, as well as the usual range of development and re-development proposals in built-up areas. There is no necessity for a consultation where ground disturbance is not in prospect, such as applications for change of use of a building. There may, however, be a requirement to obtain *planning permission* or, in the case of a listed building, *listed building consent* or, if demolition works are proposed within a conservation area, *conservation area consent*. In such instances, early consultation with the staff of the local authority planning department will always be helpful.

If in doubt whether consultation is necessary, please refer to the local authority archaeologist and the local authority planning department. It is important to note that sub-surface disturbance within historic standing buildings may also affect archaeological remains, and that some standing buildings may retain archaeological features within their structures. Please seek advice as required.

2

The **blue areas** denote those parts of the historic burgh which **may be archaeologically sterile** and where archaeological consultation is probably not necessary. In practice, there is rarely a hard dividing line between the green and the blue areas. If in any doubt, check the account of the relevant area in the **area by area assessment** (*see* step 2), and seek archaeological advice as appropriate.

step 2

In this new series of burgh surveys, each survey has been organised locationally, in order to assist speedy consultation on any proposed development site. In the case of Melrose, the historic core of the town has been divided into three arbitrary areas, Areas 1–3, which are shown on the plan on p 56 **figure 19**. The second step for the user, then, is to consult this plan and to determine into which area a specific enquiry falls.

step 3

Each area is assessed individually in the **area by area assessment** (pp 57–92). The commentary for each area is prefaced with a detailed plan of that area. Archaeological, historical, geographical and geological factors of particular relevance to the area are all discussed and an assessment of the archaeological potential made. For ease of reference, even if a dividing line between areas is shown as the middle of a street, discussion of the area includes any elements within the street up to the opposite frontage. The importance of an integrated approach to the historical and archaeological information is implicit in the design of this report: the history and archaeology are presented together on each page rather than consecutively.

This integrated, area-based approach has involved some repetition of information in the area by area assessment, in order that users are not required to cross-reference more than necessary when dealing with a specific enquiry. Although such repetition would not be normal in a work of interest to the general public, it was felt that it would be permissible here in order to facilitate the work of primary users: local authority planners and other curators of the archaeological resource.

historic standing buildings

historic buildings reinforces the above sections by providing basic historical and architectural information about the historic standing buildings of the town; where relevant, it also provides the area location and an assessment of the archaeological potential of specific buildings. *It should always be borne in mind that historic standing buildings may also contain archaeological remains, both beneath their floors and within their structures.* Some of these buildings may be listed and consequently subject to listed building control. Where listed buildings contain, or may contain, architecturally or archaeologically significant building fabric, the planning authority is obliged to make efforts to ensure that this is preserved and not adversely affected by proposed building works.

objectives for future fieldwork and research

Any report of this nature cannot be definitive. During its preparation, a series of archaeological and historical objectives for future fieldwork and research have been identified (listed at pp 103–5). They will be of particular interest to urban historians and archaeologists, and to those responsible for management of the archaeological resource in historic Melrose.

The **notes** to the background chapters detail *all* the documentary and archaeological sources used (*see also* the list of **abbreviations**). The **area by area assessments** are not footnoted separately but references are provided for the previous archaeological work and chance finds listed at the end of each area assessment. The report contains a comprehensive **general index** as well as a listing of **street names** giving basic historic information and, where relevant, area location. A **bibliography** and a **glossary** of technical terms have also been included.

The data accumulated during preparation of this survey and draft copies of the completed work, as well as all unpublished reports of any small-scale excavations and watching briefs, are housed in the **National Monuments Record**, John Sinclair House, 16 Bernard Terrace, Edinburgh, EH8 9NX, telephone *0131* 662 1456, facsimile *0131* 662 1477/1499.

**full reference
to this report**   Dennison, E P and Coleman, R 1998 *Historic Melrose: the archaeological implications of development*, published by Historic Scotland in association with Scottish Cultural Press, Edinburgh. (Scottish Burgh Survey 1998.)

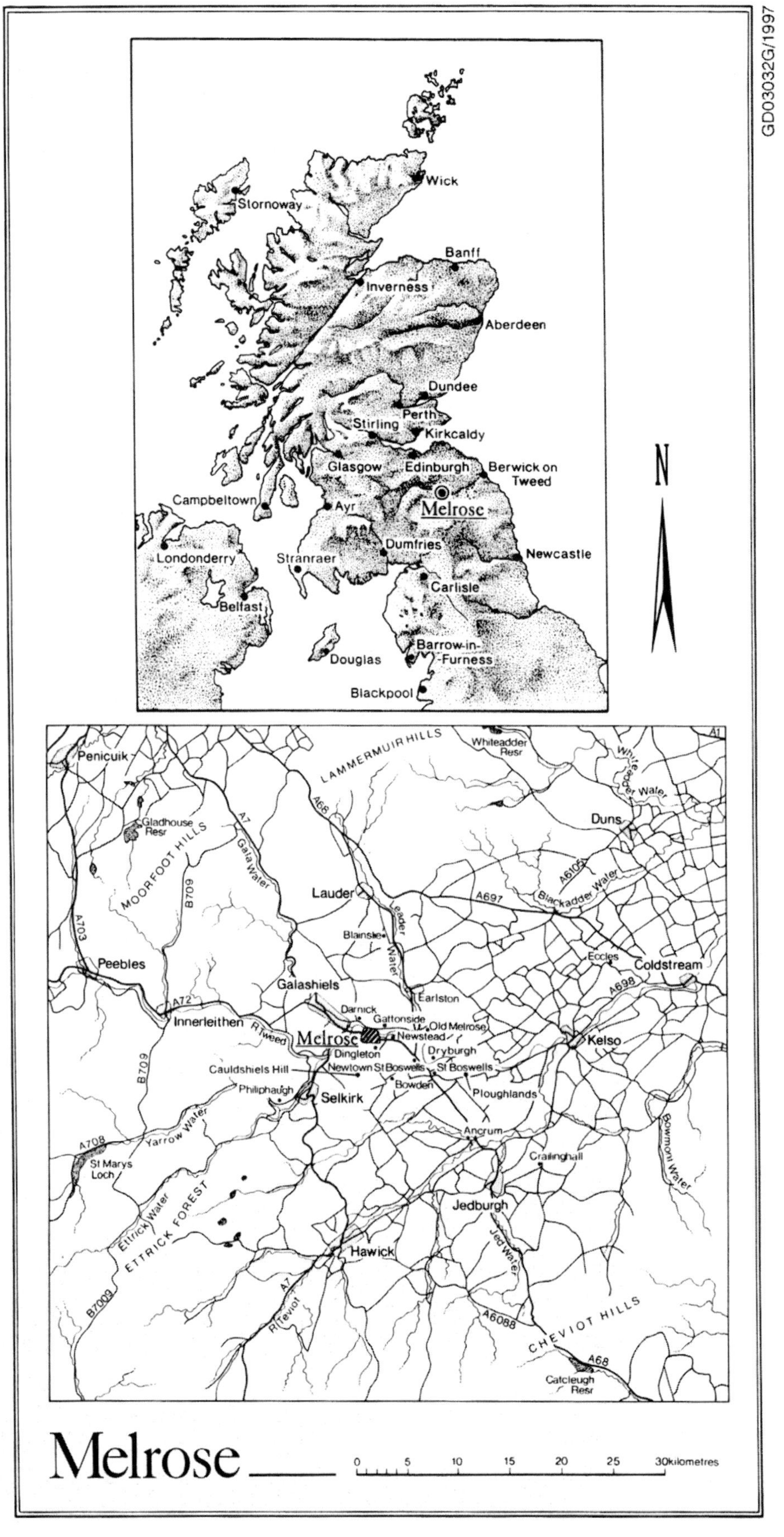

Melrose

GD03032G/1997

figure 1

Location of Melrose

Melrose is situated close to the south bank of the River Tweed as it meanders eastwards through the Borders on its journey to the North Sea **figure 1**. The Eildon Hills, which lie a little over a kilometre away to the south, provide a stunning backdrop to the setting of the burgh; from almost any viewpoint in the Middle Tweed Basin, their triple, heather-clad summits dominate the skyline, rising above the neatly ordered fields and woodlands of the Tweed Valley. These three peaks **figure 2** have long been familiar to the peoples of this area, and the name given to them, *Trimontium*, 'the place of the Triple Peaks',[1] soon became attached to the fort the Romans built close by, now the village of Newstead two kilometres to the west.[2]

Within a radius of a few kilometres of Melrose there are fine examples of a range of archaeological and historical sites **figure 3**, many of which have been subject to excavation in recent years. To the south lies the prehistoric hillfort on Eildon Hill North; to the east, the Roman fort at Newstead; to the west, the late medieval tower-houses at Darnick; and, closer to home, the great medieval abbey of Melrose itself, beside which the burgh developed. In more recent times, the three bridges over the Tweed (two road bridges, one modern, the other built between 1776 and 1780, and a railway viaduct opened in 1865) at its junction with the Leader Water, some 4 km to the east of Melrose, reflect the continuing importance of this ancient north to south route through south-east Scotland **figure 4**.

Melrose now lies within the area administered by the Scottish Borders Council, which came into being on 1st April 1996 as part of the local government reorganisation of Scotland. Prior to that, it lay within Ettrick and Lauderdale District and also within the wider Borders Region, a creation of the previous local government reorganisation in 1974, which comprised the four districts of Berwick, Roxburgh, Ettrick and Lauderdale, and Tweeddale. These had, in turn, replaced the old march areas, the East, Middle and West Marches, created in the sixteenth century to bring order to the Borders.[3] The marches eventually became Berwickshire and Roxburghshire. Melrose was formerly within the latter, the county town of which was Newton St Boswells, although the major burghs in the

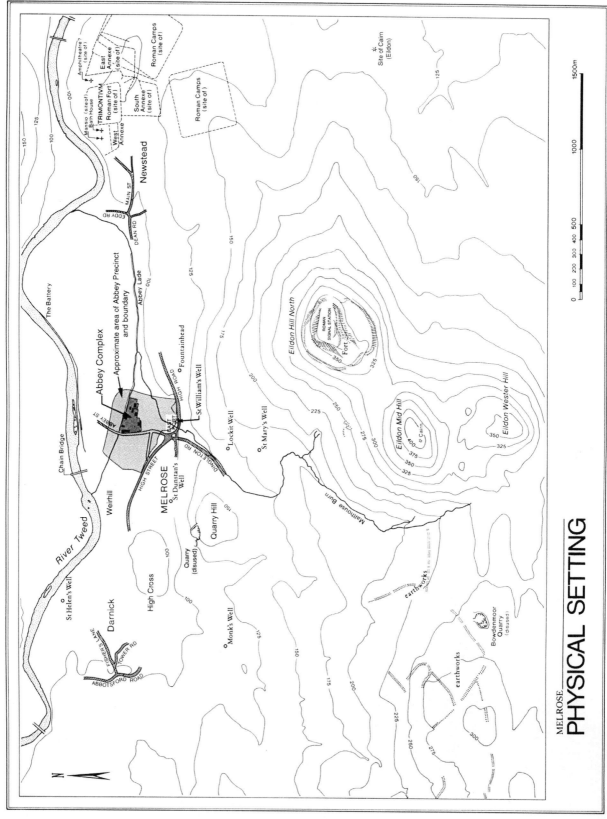

MELROSE
PHYSICAL SETTING

figure 3

The physical setting
of Melrose

figure 4

Aerial view
of Newstead
and the bridges over
the River Tweed

shire were, in fact, Hawick, Jedburgh, Kelso and Melrose. Roxburghshire was bordered by Selkirkshire and Midlothian to the north, Dumfriesshire to the west, Berwickshire to the east and the English counties of Cumberland and Northumberland to the south; it was also known as Teviotdale after the River Teviot which joins the Tweed at Roxburgh. The early twelfth-century royal burgh of Roxburgh was once one of the most important in Scotland, but was largely destroyed after a siege in 1460 and now survives as nothing more than a few grassy mounds. Similarly, Berwick, another early royal burgh, was once the principal sea-port of the region and, indeed, of medieval Scotland (although now, of course, it is in England). Its strategic importance during the Wars of Independence meant that the town changed hands on numerous occasions, and inevitably trade dwindled. Today, the population of the Scottish Borders is approximately 103,000, only 2 per cent of the Scottish total; its main centres are Hawick and Galashiels.[4] The area contains some of the richest agricultural land in Britain, but full-time male employment in agriculture fell by 30 per cent between the years 1988–1991 alone, as more and more prime farmland and upland became surplus to requirements.[5] The textile industry, however, still employs 18 per cent of the entire workforce, with electronics and tourism (Melrose won the Scottish Tourism Town of 1992 Award) helping to bring unemployment well below the Scottish national average.[6]

Despite the vagaries of political administration, the Borders have long been established as an entity in their own right, largely fashioned by geography and geology. At the heart of the area, the rolling hills of the Southern Uplands drop into the fertile lands of eastern Berwickshire during the 145 km journey of the River Tweed to the North Sea. As well as the volcanic Eildon Hills, in the shadow of which the Romans built one of their most important forts, here can be found David I's (1124–53) four Borders abbeys—at Kelso, Melrose, Dryburgh and Jedburgh; the brooding towers of Hermitage and Smailholm, a reminder of 300 years of war and border skirmishes between Scotland and England; and the sumptuous country houses of Floors Castle, Mellerstain, Manderston and Bowhill, as well as Traquair, arguably the oldest inhabited house in Scotland—some of the finest examples of their type anywhere in Scotland.

geography

From the Eildon Hills above Melrose, the Borders focus eastwards on the broad and fertile, once marshy Merse (usually taken to mean the area between Berwick and Duns) and on its capital, Berwick. North of the Tweed, the gently sloping moorlands of the Lammermuirs and the Moorfoots obscure all sight of Lothian just as the Cheviots obscure all sight of England.[7] Unlike the Lammermuirs, which terminate around St Abbs Head in breathtaking cliffs, the Cheviots stop some way short of the sea. Lying between the two, the Tweed valley is simply a northward continuation of the Northumbrian plain extending as far inland as the Lammermuirs and the Eildon Hills.[8]

Where the Tweed and its tributaries, the Gala, Yarrow, Ettrick and Teviot, have cut deep trenches into the rocks, ribbons of farmland from the Berwickshire lowlands infiltrate far into the Southern Uplands. Here, some of the highest improved land in all Scotland can be found above the woodlands of the valley sides, extending in places to heights of 360 m OD. Within this zone the towns of Selkirk, Galashiels, Melrose and St Boswells are located on valley sides above tree-lined water-courses. The qualities of the Cheviot hill sheep and the availability of water to power looms have thus concentrated much of the manufacturing of tweed and knitwear in this part of Scotland.[9]

The wider importance of this area is as a through-route to the rest of Scotland—a factor fully recognised by the Romans.[10] This broad, lowland valley controlled direct access to the heart of Scotland—northwards to Edinburgh, central and northern Scotland along the eastern coastal fringe or through one or other of the long Lammermuir or Moorfoot valleys; and westwards up Tweeddale and through the Biggar Gap into Clydesdale, the west-central lowlands and west Scotland.

geology

Tectonic movements along two major dislocations of the earth's crust, the Southern Uplands Fault and the Highland Boundary Fault, created three principal structural and physiographic divisions—the Highlands, the Midland Valley and the Southern Uplands.[11] Melrose and the Borders lie in the division known as the Southern Uplands, its northern limit being the Southern Uplands Fault, a massive fracture in the earth's crust which occurred around 408 million years ago at the end of the Silurian Period (438–408 million years ago).[12] It extends from Northern Ireland, cutting across the north of Wigtownshire at Glen App, to Dunbar. In general, the rocks lie in bands running from north-east to south-west, with the oldest rocks in the north-west and the youngest in the south-east.[13] Approximately 400 to 500 million years old, they were also distinct from the younger rocks in the Midland Valley. The oldest rocks in the region (greywacke) comprise thick series of sediments which were laid down in the centre of a deep, wide ocean that once separated Scotland and Greenland from England and Europe during the Ordovician and Silurian periods of the earth's history.[14]

The Southern Uplands belong to the Caledonian mountain chain. Formed over 400 million years ago, they were soon subjected to massive erosion by rivers and landslides during the Devonian Period (400–360 million years ago). The sediments which were formed—river deposits of boulders, sand and gravel washed down off the mountains into low lying depressions—make up the Old Red Sandstone. A gradual transition into the next great geological period, the Carboniferous (360–286 million years ago), saw red desert sandstones eventually giving way to tropical swamps, river deltas and coastal lagoons. Frequent flooding by the sea produced bands of marine limestone.[15]

The start of the Carboniferous Period in the south of the Borders region was marked by volcanic activity. The Eildon Hills are a remnant of an enormous igneous intrusion,[16] comprising several sheets of lava which invaded the underlying sedimentary rocks. Similar sheets of intrusive igneous rocks also make up Black Hill, White Hill, Bemersyde Hill and Chiefswood. The latter, an oval igneous mass some 3 km long, lying between Melrose and Abbotsford, provided a useful quarry for Melrose; stone from this ancient volcanic vent was used in the earliest phases of the abbey.[17]

Mineral and fuel deposits are rare in the Borders, so the main economically useful geological material is building stone. All the main rock types in the Borders—greywacke, slate and sandstone, with smaller reserves of limestone, cementstone, basalt and granite—

have been exploited extensively for use as building materials and road stones. Greywackes
have been used for drystone dykes, and Old Red Sandstone for centuries in buildings,
notably the Borders abbeys. Ploughlands Quarry *see* **figure 1** provided most of the facing
stones for these abbeys, but is now almost totally overgrown.

the Ice Age

From the end of the Carboniferous Period until the last Ice Age (one to two million years
ago), there is little evidence of rock-forming events in the Borders region.[18] During the Ice
Age, Scotland was completely covered by ice-caps on many occasions. In the Borders, the
last of these finally melted about 15,000 years ago. Generally, the ice flowed in a north-
easterly direction away from the high ground in the centre of the Southern Uplands (one
of the main centres of glaciation was at Moffat) towards the North Sea. Here, it met with
southerly moving ice coming out of the Midland Valley. As well as re-fashioning the
existing landscape, the melt waters from the retreating glaciers deposited vast quantities
of sediment in the lower ground, particularly in the Merse.[19] The moving ice also
streamlined the bare rock. Near Melrose and St Boswells there are 'crag and tail' features
on the hard volcanic rocks, the crag having been plucked by passing ice and the tail
formed by deposition on the leeward side, usually the north-east.[20]

the post-glacial period

Just over 10,000 years ago there was a sudden warming of the climate and within a few
hundred years the ice had completely melted. The sea level—which had fallen by about
100 metres during the Ice Age because water had been locked up as continental ice—
began to rise, as glacial melt water streams carrying huge boulders poured out.[21] Other
products of these melt waters included sand and gravel deposits which are abundant in
the region; old extraction pits are common, particularly around Peebles.[22]

The period around 5,500–3,000 BC saw highly favourable climatic conditions for tree
growth throughout Europe, with conifers the first to arrive, followed by birch and hazel.
These gave way to oak and elm, with areas of scrub gradually replacing the coniferous
forest. A climatic deterioration to cooler, wetter conditions, from about 3,000 BC
onwards, saw the decline of the elm and the rapid spread of blanket peat, heath and
grassland over previously forested areas.[23] The earliest farming communities also played a
part in this deforestation (*see* p 13).

soils and land use

The distribution of ancient monuments often provides a useful guide to the history of
land use. The majority of medieval tower-houses, for example, are found below the
150 m contour and are a good indicator of the upper limit of cultivation and settlement,
as they tended to have been built on, or even slightly beyond, the moorland margin of the
period.[24] The siting of abbeys is also a useful guide, given that most of the Merse itself
would have been ill-drained. They generally held the most favoured and strategically
important locations. To give some idea of the agricultural wealth of the abbeys and the
extent of their involvement in the wool trade, Melrose Abbey owned probably the largest
flock of sheep of any of the religious houses of Scotland—some 15,000 sheep in the
1370s.[25]

Today, the Tweed Basin is renowned for its large mixed farms, established on some of
Scotland's richest soils, with neat hedgerows of beech and thorn dividing the extensive
cornfields from the sheep- and cattle-crowded pastures.[26] On the higher ground of the
Southern Uplands and the border country of the Cheviots, the moorlands support the
sheep that supply the local woollen industry.

The siting of the abbey at Melrose afforded the opportunity to exploit a range of
landforms. The slopes of the Eildon Hills offered good soils for cultivation and orchards,

10

the uplands good pasturage, and the river valley, rich alluvial soils and meadow land **figure 5**. The river also provided salmon and trout in abundance.[27] The numerous wells and natural springs in the area, many of which have been dedicated to saints (St Mary's, St Dunstan's, St William's and St Helen's), combined with the Tweed and the Malthouse Burn, undoubtedly added to the attraction of this site for the construction of the new abbey.

physical setting and topography of the burgh

The medieval burgh is situated on gently sloping ground between the Eildon Hills to the south and the River Tweed to the north. The steep slope down from Eildon Hill North begins to flatten out around 100 m OD, the contour of which is more or less traced by the new bypass. From this point there is a gradual slope down to the Tweed around 80 m OD. There are local irregularities, however, with some high ground to the west of the burgh at High Cross (107 m OD) and Weirhill (95 m OD), and to the south-west at Quarry Hill (166 m OD). The Malthouse Burn, which skirts around the western flank of Eildon Mid Hill and then along the eastern side of Dingleton Road, flows just to the east of East Port, at which point it would have entered the abbey precinct. A number of natural wells lie both in and around the town.

The appearance of Melrose today is of a convergent street plan, with High Street, High Road, Abbey Street and Dingleton Road all converging on a triangular market place **figure 5**. Much of the town, however, is post-Reformation infill of the former medieval abbey precinct. The core of the burgh is known as the Cross, and comprises a triangular market place which occupies a small, flattish terrace. From here, the ground falls away to the north, east and west. Here was the south gateway into the precinct, a little to the south of where the Town House stands today and around which settlement was to focus. The main thoroughfare of the burgh is High Street. Just off the Cross, at the eastern approach to the town, is the East Port. The triangular block of properties defined by Buccleuch

Street, High Street and Abbey Street straddles the boundary that once separated the abbey from the town.

Abbey Street and Buccleuch Street, and all the other streets to the north of High Street, lie within the grounds of the former precinct. The boundary of the precinct is still uncertain but is thought to have followed the north side of the High Street (behind the frontage) and High Road. The western boundary is thought to lie between St Mary's School and the Melrose Rugby Football Ground, with the eastern boundary running to the east of Priorwood Youth Hostel. The northern boundary is the most contentious. It is traditionally thought to cross the fields just to the north of Priory Cottages and Priory Farm, although the abbey's lands probably extended all the way to the River Tweed. Melrose Abbey is arguably the finest of the four Borders abbeys, and its ruins are among the most impressive in Britain. Designated a Scheduled Ancient Monument, it has been in the care of Historic Scotland and its predecessors since 1919.[28] The detail of its layout and development are discussed in depth in later sections (*see* pp 57–68).

notes

1   A L F Rivet & C Smith, *The Place-Names of Roman Britain* (London, 1979), 475.
2   L Keppie, 'The Romans', in D Omand (ed), *The Borders Book* (Edinburgh, 1995), 48.
3   A Spence, *Discovering the Borders I* (Edinburgh, 1992), 4–5.
4   *Ibid*, 6.
5   *Ibid*, 10.
6   *Ibid*, 11.
7   J R Baldwin, *Exploring Scotland's Heritage: Lothian and the Borders* (Edinburgh, 1989), 13.
8   *Ibid*, 14.
9   J Whittrow, *Geology and Scenery in Britain* (London, 1992), 246.
10   Baldwin, *Lothian and Borders*, 14.
11   Definitions according to J B Sissons, *The Geomorphology of the British Isles: Scotland* (London, 1976).
12   For a survey of the geology of the Borders, see C Gillen, 'Rocks', in Omand (ed), *Borders Book*, 5–6.
13   E Edmonds, *The Geological Map: An Anatomy of the Landscape* (HMSO, 1983), 19.
14   Gillen, 'Rocks', 3.
15   *Ibid*, 6–7.
16   *Ibid*, 7.
17   Whittrow, *Geology*, 247.
18   Gillen, 'Rocks', 8. For an account of the more geological history of the Borders, *see* Gillen, 'Landscapes', *passim*, in Omand (ed), *Borders Book*.
19   Gillen, 'Rocks', 8.
20   Gillen, 'Landscapes', 14.
21   *Ibid*, 16–17.
22   Gillen, 'Rocks', 10.
23   Gillen, 'Landscapes', 18.
24   Baldwin, *Lothian and Borders*, 15.
25   M Lynch, *Scotland: A New History* (London, 1992), 63.
26   Whittrow, *Geology*, 243.
27   J S Richardson & M Wood, *Melrose Abbey* (Edinburgh, 1949), 3.
28   Historic Scotland has produced a new illustrated guidebook to the site: C Tabraham (ed), *Melrose Abbey* (HMSO, 1995).

archaeological and historical background

pp 13–54

In the historic core of Melrose, only the area within the abbey precinct has so far seen any archaeological work; and most of the stray finds that have been reported are prehistoric in date. The area around Melrose, however, is exceptionally rich in sites and finds from all periods of prehistory and history **figure 3**. A basic introduction to the early history of the area is included here, in order to provide a broader framework within which to study the origins of the medieval burgh. This includes extended sections on the great hillfort on Eildon Hill North and the Roman fort at Newstead, and an historical outline placing the Roman occupation here within its overall pattern in Scotland.

the prehistory of the Scottish Borders

The earliest settlement of Scotland occurred around 7,500 BC, when much of Scotland was covered in dense woodland which supported a rich variety of game, particularly red deer. The few Mesolithic (literally meaning Middle Stone Age) settlements known in Scotland tend to be found along the coast line and river banks. These communities were 'hunter-gatherers', who ate fish and shellfish, followed herds of woodland game through the seasons, and supplemented their diet with wild plants and berries. Their semi-nomadic existence has left few archaeological traces, although shell middens and flint tools are common finds along former river and coast lines.

The Tweed valley is particularly rich in remains of this period. The probable sites of temporary hunting camps are marked by finds of scattered stone tools collected from the ground surface. To date, more than one hundred such sites have been identified in the middle reaches of the Tweed alone, and new find spots are turning up every year.[1] These communities were using a variety of stone materials, found both locally in the river gravels and further afield, each suited to different types of tool.[2] Scrapers, blades, microliths and microburins all performed different functions and were used in hunting as well as in the cutting and preparation of meat. One of the largest assemblages of Mesolithic tools ever found in south-east Scotland has come from the fields (Monksford and Orchard Fields) around Dryburgh Mains Farm. Over the years, hundreds of flint and chert tools have been turned up by the plough here (now in the Hunterian Museum, Glasgow and the National Museum of Scotland, Edinburgh). In Melrose itself a chert core-axe and flint scraper have been found, the latter in gardens in High Cross Avenue.

Around 3,500 BC, people began to live a more settled existence in response to changes in the environment and to ideas introduced from continental Europe. Large areas of woodland were cleared by burning and trees were cut down with stone tools, livestock was kept and the land was farmed for crops. The transition was gradual, with both ways of life—that of hunter-gatherers and of farmers—probably occurring together for some time. In recent years aerial photography has been invaluable in identifying potential Neolithic sites, of which little or nothing survives above ground. At Sprouston in Roxburghshire, for example, a rectangular structure revealed as a cropmark, and a second rectangular enclosure close by, both lie in the vicinity of the major concentration of stone tool scatters in the area (*see also* p 14).[3]

Few traces of the Neolithic (New Stone Age) settlements survive, but the landscape still bears evidence of the presence of these people in the form of their ritual enclosures (including henges) and burial mounds. One of the most exciting of recent excavations was that at Meldon Bridge near Peebles.[4] This unique site, covering some eight hectares, comprises a promontory between two rivers, cut off by a massive barrier of timber posts. Pits were found throughout the interior, some filled with domestic rubbish, others with cremation burials; and traces of a possible circular building were also found. Whether this site was a settlement or a ceremonial enclosure is unclear, but it appears somewhat similar to a henge, of which only one example is known in the Borders, at Overhowden.[5]

These early farming groups buried their dead in communal stone-built chambered cairns or in barrows of wood and turf, which sometimes contained large numbers of burials. The considerable regional variation in the types and styles of these monuments no doubt reflects local traditions and perhaps the origins of the societies which used them.[6]

14

The tombs probably became a focus for ritual where elaborate ceremonies took place, perhaps in celebration of the ancestors. Two of the best examples of this little-understood class of monument in the Borders are The Mutiny Stones, near Longformacus, and Long Knowe, near Newcastleton.[7]

The most distinctive finds from this period include leaf-shaped arrowheads and polished stone axes, both widely distributed throughout the Borders.[8] Examples of the tools used in clearing woodland have been found in and around Melrose, at Mosshouses and Earlston Mains, for example, but only the one found at Langshaw is described as polished. The more elaborate axes, often found in pristine condition, were used perhaps for prestige or ceremonial purposes; they also indicate widening trade links and the growth of a social élite.

By about 2,500 BC, society was gradually changing again. Stone circles were erected, apparently incorporating an awareness of the rising and setting of the sun and moon in their design.[9] There are few stone circles in the Borders, but two examples can be seen at Burgh Hill and Ninestone Rig, both near Hawick.[10] The tradition of monumental tombs containing large numbers of burials waned in favour of a new trend for single grave burials. These Bronze Age peoples developed metal-working and new styles of pottery, and began to live in unenclosed settlements.

A number of Bronze Age burials have been found around Melrose. Typically, they comprise a small stone-lined cist beneath a stone cairn, although some cremation urns were placed in a pit. Very often the cairn has since been robbed away, leaving only the cist. Some were single, isolated burials but others were part of larger cemeteries. Cairns were often re-used, and can contain a number of later burials inserted into the flanks or top of the mound. Personal possessions, such as pottery vessels, flint blades and arrowheads, were often placed in the grave. A much robbed cairn and probable cist is situated on the south-west flank of Eildon Mid Hill, by Melrose, about 30 metres below the summit **figure 3**. Other burials have been found at Earlston, Eildon, Dryburgh and Cauldshiels Hill **figures 1** & **3**.

Discoveries of Bronze Age metalwork—both single items and hoards—are common in the Melrose area. Several examples of Early Bronze Age flat axes have been found in and around Melrose; one from the town is in Selkirk Museum. Later Bronze Age material—such as palstaves, socketed axes and spearheads—often turns up in hoards, buried either for safekeeping in times of unrest and never retrieved, or as ritual offerings. A hoard of seven axes was recently found on the lower slopes of Eildon Mid Hill; two socketed axes were found in a burn at Dingleton Mains, north-west of the Eildon hills; and fourteen more, probably a merchant's stock, were found in a river bank at Kalemouth.[11]

Evidence for Bronze Age settlement in the Borders is as elusive as for the Mesolithic and Neolithic periods. In Peeblesshire, however, groups of unenclosed circular house-platforms are common, strung out along natural terraces high up in the headwaters of the Tweed and Clyde.[12] At the excavated site of Green Knowe,[13] nine platforms were identified altogether, with one house being replaced three times. Field banks and clearance heaps nearby clearly show that these were farming communities, with a pastoral rather than an arable farming economy. These communities had perhaps been displaced from better agricultural land in the lowlands by an expanding population.[14]

later prehistory

Whereas knowledge of Neolithic and Bronze Ages settlement is rather poor,[15] by the Late Bronze Age and Early Iron Age, settlements begin to dominate the archaeological landscape. These include numerous fortified settlements, ranging from large hillforts to enclosed villages and isolated single family dwellings. The end of the Bronze Age, around 600 BC, was a time of considerable change. Iron tools begin to appear in the archaeological record. Society seems generally to have been more competitive, with the emergence of tribal groups perhaps competing for territory and natural resources,[16] although less defensive types of settlement also existed.

Hillforts are the classic component of the Late Bronze Age and Iron Age landscape, many of which lie in the Tweed basin. One of the most impressive is Eildon Hill North, overlooking Melrose. The fort as it stands today covers some 16 hectares, and is surrounded by three concentric ramparts measuring over 1.6 km in length. Traces of 296 hut platforms survive in the interior of the fort and originally there were probably many more **figure 2**. On the summit of the hill lies a small ditched enclosure, perhaps of first-century AD date, within which probably stood a Roman signal-tower. Whether or not the fort had been abandoned when the signal-tower was built has considerable implications for the relationship between the Romans and this powerful tribal grouping. Archaeological excavations in 1986 in advance of a new pathway, although limited to the western approaches to the fort, have gone some way towards answering this question. The results indicate that the site was occupied in the Late Bronze Age and again in the Roman Iron Age,[17] and that there was a substantial settlement in both periods; but there was almost no evidence of pre-Roman Iron Age settlement. Significantly, it appears that there may have been settlement on the hill top at the same time as the Roman fort at its base (*Trimontium*) was occupied **figure 3**. The function of hillforts is the subject of much debate, but they must have played a significant role during the emergence of tribal territories.[18]

Other settlement types of this period include ring-ditch enclosures, which occur in groups within the interiors of forts, and as pairs or singly within palisaded enclosures;[19] and souterrains, each comprising a curving, stone-built underground passage or gallery, roofed with either stone slabs or timbers. These underground passages were not used for accommodation but for storage purposes, probably as granaries. Two souterrains were found near Newstead in the mid nineteenth century, although no trace survives today.

Melrose and the Borders in the Roman period

It was this perhaps more fragmented Iron Age society which the Romans encountered in the first century AD. The traditional interpretation of Ptolemy's famous map of the Roman world **figure 6**, compiled around AD 167, is that Melrose and the western Borders fell within the tribal domain of the Selgovae, whose capital was thought to have been the hillfort on Eildon Hill North. The recent excavations there, however, together with re-evaluation of the historical evidence, have led to the alternative suggestion that Eildon Hill North, as well as its sister fort at Traprain Law in East Lothian, may in fact have lain in the territory of the Votadini, who seem to have been in trading contact with the Romans.[20]

The security of Roman northern England was founded on a treaty between Rome and the Brigantian Queen, Cartimandua, although she was ousted by her anti-Roman husband, Venutius, during the civil war of AD 68/9.[21] The first Roman penetration into southern Scotland may date to AD 71 to 74 when control of the northern area was returned to Rome.[22] The Flavian dynasty had by now attained power in Rome, and one of its loyal supporters was Gnaeus Julius Agricola, with whom the early Roman history of Scotland is inextricably linked. Becoming governor in AD 77, Agricola campaigned in Wales and northern England before moving into Scotland and advancing to the Tay. The following year was spent consolidating and garrisoning the new frontier zone, in particular establishing a line of garrisons in the valley between the Forth and the Clyde.[23] In AD 81 he probably campaigned into south-west Scotland, pondering an expedition to Ireland and perhaps considering routes up the west coast.[24] In AD 82 he advanced beyond the Forth—a campaign culminating in the defeat of the Caledonians under Calgacus at the battle of Mons Graupius in AD 83 (possibly somewhere in north-east Scotland).[25] This was the climax of his governorship and, shortly afterwards, he returned to Rome.

Agricola's unknown successor consolidated these advances, establishing a system of roads and forts throughout central and eastern Scotland. The nerve centre was to be the 53-acre legionary fortress at Inchtuthil on the Tay, but Inchtuthil was demolished before construction was even completed.[26] A series of military disasters in the Balkans

16

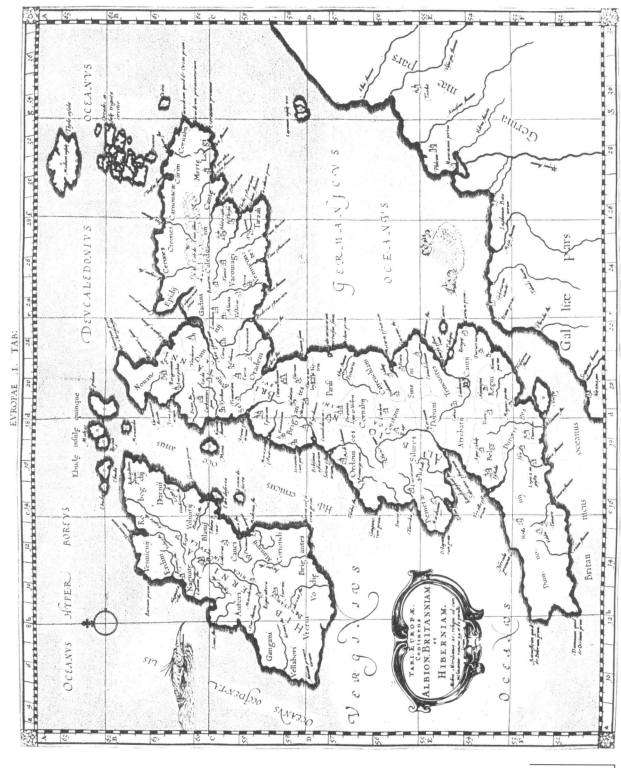

figure 6
Ptolemy's
map of Britain
AD 167. *This version
published 1730*

occasioned this dramatic shift in policy, with troops having to be redeployed from elsewhere in the Empire. Inchtuthil and all the forts north of a line from Newstead to Glenlochar were abandoned *c* AD 87 and, by the turn of the century, the Romans had fallen back as far as the Tyne–Solway line.

In the early AD 120s, Emperor Hadrian chose a line slightly further north for the construction of a massive barrier of turf and stone—Hadrian's Wall. In AD 138, his successor, Antoninus Pius, ordered his army to advance into central Scotland and begin construction of a second great barrier, the Antonine Wall. Built in the years after AD 142, the Wall stretched for some 60 km between Bo'ness on the Forth and Old Kilpatrick on the Clyde, with fortlets probably at every mile, and forts at wider intervals. New forts were established south of the Wall, many on or close by sites of abandoned forts, with some north of the Wall, up to the Tay. These forts were abandoned in the AD 160s, when the army was withdrawn to the line of Hadrian's Wall. Some were retained as outposts, in Dumfriesshire and up to the Tweed, but by about AD 180 most of these were abandoned, and Hadrian's Wall once again became the northern frontier of Roman Britain.

There was one final episode in the history of Roman Scotland. Emperor Septimius Severus and his sons, Caracalla and Geta, arrived in Britain in AD 208 to mount a major campaign in the north, specifically against two tribes—the Maeatae, probably based in Stirlingshire, Strathearn and Strathmore, and the Caledonians further north.[27] Probably accompanied by a fleet, Severus and his army advanced through eastern Scotland and up the east coast. Despite taking the title *Britannicus*, 'conqueror of Britain', Severus' celebrations were short-lived, for a major rebellion occurred in the following year. Severus died in AD 211 and his son, Caracalla, immediately returned to Rome, abandoning the Scottish conquests.[28] Hadrian's Wall was again reinstated as the northern frontier of the province, with some forts garrisoned in the Cheviots as out-posts. By the late third century AD the Picts—probably a new power grouping amongst the tribes—and others were putting increasing pressure on the northern frontier. Hadrian's Wall appears to have been garrisoned until the early years of the fifth century AD, before Britain was finally abandoned by Rome.

The most important communication link in Roman northern Britain was Dere Street (approximately the line of the A68). This ran from York, through Corbridge on the Tyne and Newstead (the Roman *Trimontium* **figure 6**) on the Tweed, to Elginhaugh on the Esk, and then on to the forts along the Forth–Clyde line. An east to west artery followed the Tweed westwards from Newstead to the Firth of Clyde at Irvine, and probably eastwards towards the mouth of the Tweed at Berwick.[29] The fort at Newstead has been the subject of extensive archaeological excavation. The first campaign was directed by a local solicitor, James Curle, in 1906–10, and was of an impressively high standard for its day.[30] Following the Second World War, Professor Sir Ian Richmond's excavations complemented Curle's pioneering work.[31] More recently, the National Museums of Scotland in partnership with Bradford University have carried out a programme of excavations (1988–93), looking at both Roman and native sites in the vicinity.[32]

The Roman complex at Newstead comprises the fort itself and associated annexes to the east, south and west; to the north, a hollow has been interpreted as an amphitheatre; and beyond these features lie several temporary camps **figure 3**. As many as ten Iron Age or native sites also lie within the area of the complex. The whole complex is a Scheduled Ancient Monument.

Newstead is the largest known fort in lowland Scotland **figures 3 & 4**. First recognised as Roman when the North British Railway cut through part of the fort in 1846, excavations over the years have shed light on its development, with four periods of occupation distinguishable.[33] The earliest phase, perhaps dating to Agricola's third campaign,[34] is represented by an unusual enclosure, measuring 4.2 hectares, with 'dog-legged' sides. This clever design allowed extra firepower to be concentrated at the gateways, the weak spot of any defensive circuit. The size of the area enclosed suggests that this early fort was garrisoned by an auxiliary unit, and finds of cavalry helmets indicate that at least one of the regiments was mounted.[35] Shortly after AD 86, the fort was enlarged to *c* 5.3 hectares, protected by a massive rampart up to 14 metres thick; and a bathhouse and guesthouse were built outwith the fort on the west side. During this period, Newstead would have been one of the northernmost outposts of the Roman province of Britain. Around AD 100, the fort was abandoned and the buildings burnt. The interpretation of events here is still the subject of debate, but they may have been burnt by the Romans themselves prior to evacuation, so as to leave little of use to the native tribes. Some of the 100 or so pits found across the site were undoubtedly dug to bury surplus weapons, armour and tools—whether in an orderly fashion or as a matter of emergency is unknown. Some of the most exciting Roman finds ever discovered in Scotland were found in these pits, including helmets, tools, agricultural equipment, weapons, horse harness, leather tents and shoes, bronze jugs, glass vessels, coins, pottery and wagon wheels[36]—most now in the National Museum of Scotland, Edinburgh.

The fort was re-occupied at the beginning of the Antonine period, and became one of only five stone-walled military posts in Scotland.[37] Two periods of occupation have been identified; in the former, the fort was defended by two outer ditches, in the latter by three. A legionary detachment and a cavalry regiment were stationed there. Once the Antonine Wall had been abandoned in the AD 160s, the Borders possibly marked the limits of the Roman province.[38]

In recent years, aerial survey has identified a number of Roman temporary camps around Newstead **figure 4**. These housed troops on the move, who camped by the fort for security and facilities. Newstead was used as a staging post on the campaign route of Emperor Severus in AD 208–210, as he marched through Lauderdale; but after his death in AD 211, direct Roman presence in the Borders probably ended.[39]

The archaeological landscape around Melrose and the Tweed valley is exceptionally rich. The increasing use of aerial photography as a survey technique in recent years has led to the identification of a huge number of previously unknown archaeological sites. Without excavation these sites are often difficult to date, but they have greatly increased awareness of the complexity of settlement patterns. A broad range of settlement types has been identified; but assessment of how many, for example, were contemporary with the Roman occupation of Newstead and the Borders is an important avenue for further research—and one which is currently being addressed.[40]

south-east Scotland in the early historic period

Major changes occurred in the political organisation of Scotland in the period after the withdrawal of the Romans. By the third century AD, the numerous small tribal groups recorded in Ptolemy's *Geography* were coalescing into larger confederacies; and, by the fourth century, these confederacies seem to have merged into an even larger grouping known as the Picts. By around the middle of the first millennium AD, the Pictish kingdom dominated Scotland north of the Forth and Clyde estuaries, attested to by a startling heritage of carved stones, spread throughout the north-east. The exception was Argyll which was occupied by the Dàl Riata Gaels, originally from north-east Ireland, whose name *Gaedil* became translated into Latin as *Scoti*. Eventually, of course, the *Scoti* came to dominate and gave their name to Scotland—but not until the mid ninth century AD, when Kenneth mac Alpin (*c* 843–58) established royal, political and cultural supremacy over the Pictish kingdom.

The four tribes listed by Ptolemy south of the Forth seem to have undergone rather less transformation. One of the most important of the Iron Age tribes was the Votadini, centred in Lothian, whose tribal capital was probably on Traprain Law and possibly they also occupied Eildon Hill North (*see* p 5). A few centuries later, Edinburgh's Castle Rock emerges as the fortified capital of the kingdom of the Gododdin, who were the post-Roman descendants of the Votadini. Their neighbours to the west, the Britons in the kingdom of Strathclyde, seem likewise to have emerged from the Iron Age Damnonii. This apparent continuity of peoples in southern Scotland—from the Iron Age, through the Roman period and into the early historic period—was broken only by the arrival of the Angles. The turbulent events of seventh-century Lothian are documented in the epic poem, *y Gododdin*, with its tales of pre-battle feasting at *Din Eidyn* (Edinburgh); and in the *Annals of Ulster* which refers to the '*obsessio Etin*', or siege of Edinburgh, interpreted as an assault on Edinburgh by the king of the Northumbrian Angles, Oswald (AD 634–42). This may have been the culmination of a process of annexation or no more than a daring raid, but it seems that the Anglian kings of Northumbria were in control of much of south-east Scotland from about the later seventh century AD. After this, the area between the Forth and the Tweed became 'border land' between the Anglo-Saxons and the Picts, but remained in Northumbrian hands until Lothian was ceded to Kenneth II (971–95) by Edgar of Northumbria in 973. The River Tweed was finally established as the frontier in 1018 following Malcolm II's (1005–34) victory at Carham on the south bank of the river not far from Coldstream.[41]

This period also saw the introduction of Christianity to Scotland. From his base at Whithorn, Wigtownshire, St Ninian is reputed to have led the first Christian mission to southern Pictland in the early fifth century AD; but monks from the monastery of Iona, founded by St Columba in 563, undoubtedly had more impact in most of Pictland. The conversion of Pictland and Northumbria was completed possibly before the end of the seventh century AD. In the Lothians, the teachings of the sub-Roman Northumbrian church (brought by the Anglian settlers) spread through the valleys that ran north and south to the Forth. Their aspirations, however, were contested to the north and west by the earlier Columban Celtic, or monastic, church. The Northumbrian King Oswald (634–642), after previous exile in Iona, was responsible for inviting the Columban monk St Aidan to found the monastery at Lindisfarne. The Columban church then founded monasteries at Old Melrose (of which only the ditched embankments survive),[42] and possibly also at St. Abbs Head; following the Synod of Whitby in 664, however, the Northumbrian church severed its close ties with Iona, and attempted an expansion into Pictland.[43] Throughout the early historic period the areas of influence of both the Columban church and the Northumbrian church changed with the shifting political allegiances.[44]

In south-east Scotland, Anglian and British placenames reflect the political history of the area during the early historic period. The Britons, speaking a British or Cumbric language were native to the area long before the arrival of the Romans; by the seventh century the placename evidence is predominantly Anglian, with traces of the older British. Pictish placenames are also present in the north of the area, but are much less common. Many placenames denote actual settlement but others are descriptive of geographical features, such as hills, moors and valleys. Indeed, the name Melrose (bare moor) can be traced back to the Cumbric *-ros* (moor).[45] Placenames catalogue the subsequent waves of colonisation; the only three primary late seventh- to eighth-century Anglian names in Scotland—Coldingham, Whittinghame and Tyninghame—all cluster along the narrow, eastern coastal strip, which is also where their early settlement sites are found.[46] Names ending in *-ington* (farm) and *-ham* (homestead) help trace the spread of settlement further round the coast and up the rivers, while names ending in *-wic* (dependent farm) are evidence of later settlement.[47] Placenames must be used cautiously but, when set alongside archaeological evidence, including aerial photography and the distribution of carved stones (the largest body of evidence for the early historic period), their value increases.

The Anglian advance into the south-east lowlands of Scotland led to the collapse of the ruling British families, but may not necessarily have been followed by extensive Northumbrian settlement. Indeed, rather few settlements of the Northumbrian Angles have so far been identified in the south-east of Scotland. At Doon Hill (NT 686755), near Dunbar, a seventh-century timber hall was discovered overlying the ruins of a sixth-century British hall. Similar sequences have been identified at Yeavering, Northumberland; two seventh-century timber halls were also discovered recently during excavations at Dunbar; and, at Ratho, near Edinburgh, a palisade alignment enclosed a sunken-featured building of sixth- or early seventh-century date, which may have been used for weaving and the dyeing of yarn or fabric.[48] Elsewhere, a multi-period site was partially excavated at The Dod, in the foothills of Teviot Dale.[49] Here, timber round houses were first replaced in stone, and were then superceded by twelve phases of rectangular buildings. Analogies with other sites indicate that the Dod was first occupied in the late pre-Roman Iron Age and continued in use through to the sixth century AD. Another site which bears a striking resemblance to Yeavering has been identified by aerial photography and has all the attributes of an important religious, ceremonial and market centre. Sprouston, a fortified promontory on the bank of the River Tweed, compromises a palisaded enclosure, within which are contained halls of varying sizes, ancillary buildings and sunken features such as buildings and barns.[50]

medieval Melrose and its abbey

It is against this background that the history of Melrose itself begins—about two and a half miles east of the heart of the modern town. Sometime before AD 650, in a secluded spot at a loop in the River Tweed within the Anglian kingdom of Northumbria, St Aidan of Lindisfarne established a monastery at a place called 'Mailros' **figure 7**. The name, meaning a bare or blunt promontory, reflects the 'desert place' setting.[51] It was settled with monks possibly from the Columban monastery of Iona. Its first abbot, Eata, was one of twelve Saxon young men taught by Aidan. One of the monks, St Bothan, gave his name to the village of Bowden and the first prior, St Boisil, is recalled in nearby St Boswells. The second prior is perhaps the best known and loved of the Melrose monks. St Cuthbert was a young shepherd in the Lammermuir Hills when he had a vision and joined the brotherhood, c 651.[52] Bede in his *Ecclesiastical History of the English People* wrote: 'Now he [Cuthbert] entered first the monastery of Melrose which is enclosed for the most part by a loop of the River Tweed, and which was then ruled by its abbot, Eata, the most meek and simple of all men'.[53] It was from here that Cuthbert went on missionary tours to the Lothians, Borders and Fife.[54] Cuthbert was to become the prior of Lindisfarne in 664; and there he died in 687, after being bishop for two years.[55] His body was returned to Melrose two centuries later, for safe keeping from Danish raids on Lindisfarne,[56] but the little monastery he had served had been destroyed by Kenneth mac Alpin, king of the *Scoti* of Dalriada, in 839.

Archaeological evidence for the major early Christian centres of the area is scant. Melrose, or Old Melrose as it became called **figure 7**, is but one of these centres, Coldingham and Abercorn being two others. At Old Melrose, all that survives today is the boundary of the monastic enclosure, known as the *vallum*. It comprises a ditch set between two banks, and can be traced practically all the way across the neck of the promontory, continuing down to the very water's edge.[57] What lay within the enclosure can only be guessed at, although excavations in other monastic enclosures have shed some light on their layout. At Ardwall, Kircudbrightshire, the first phase of use is represented by a burial ground.[58] A timber chapel was then built which was later replaced in stone, and all the time more burials were being added. Similarly at Whithorn, Wigtownshire, where excavations have been ongoing for a number of years, the earliest phases comprised a stone church and timber buildings.[59]

From this, it may be surmised that a church would have stood at the heart of Melrose, around which would have been grouped the individual huts or cells of the monks, with a cemetery nearby. Guesthouses, granaries and store rooms may also be expected, although some of these may have lain outwith what was essentially a ritual enclosure. The burning of the site by Kenneth mac Alpin suggests that the majority of these buildings were of timber, rather than of stone.

In spite of this destruction, it is known that Melrose, after being rebuilt, remained a place of sanctuary for centuries. Some maintain that the rebuilt monastery buildings were called the Red Abbey or Red House, but there is no firm evidence for this tradition.[60] It may be a reference to the colour of the stone, which may also have been used at 'Red

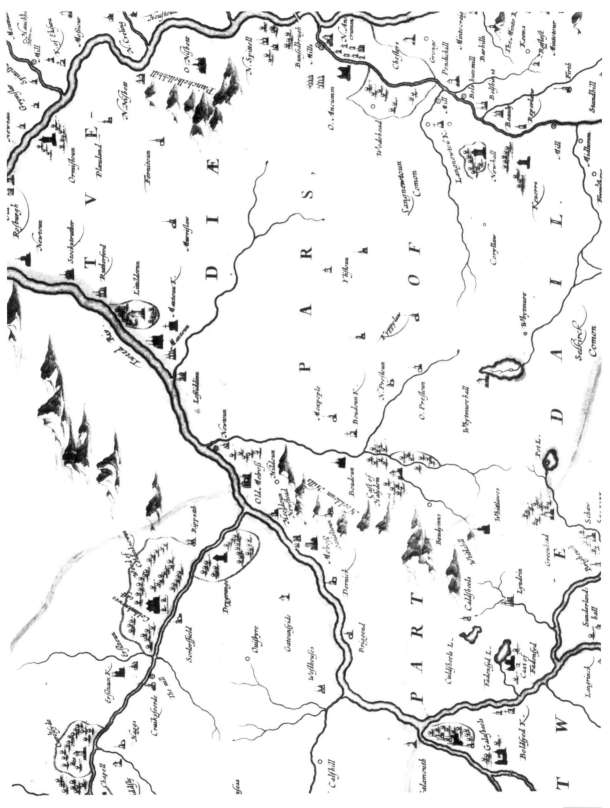

figure 7

J BLaeu's *Lauderdalia*,
dating to the 1650s.

Abbey Stead' in Newstead—a stead meaning a farm building, not a religious establishment.[61] It was at Melrose, in 1073 x 1075, that Prior Turgot of Durham, later to become the confessor and chronicler of Queen Margaret, retreated with Aldwin of Jarrow, with the blessing of Bishop Walcher of Durham.[62] An attempt by Aldwin at this time to restore the monastery for the Benedictine order failed,[63] perhaps being prevented by Malcolm III (1058–93) for failure to swear fealty to him,[64] and possibly also since the move might have appeared as a threat of assertion of Durham's right to Melrose.[65] A small chapel dedicated to St Cuthbert was established and became a centre for pilgrimage. Adam, a native of Lennox, spent twenty years here in the period around 1260 'having a full store of provisions laid up for him by those poor persons who kept flocking to him...The rich also came to him and even the king of the land [Alexander II]'.[66] In 1321, Symon, bishop of Galloway, granted a relaxation of forty days penance to all who were truly penitent and confessed, visited the chapel and made a contribution to its rebuilding, it having suffered during the Wars of Independence.[67] The following century, in 1417 x 1431, Pope Martin V granted to all who made a pilgrimage or contribution to the chapel 'a remission of penance for seven years and seven lents on all the festivals of St Cuthbert and on certain other holidays'.[68]

In the meantime, however, King David I (1124–53) invited the Cistercians of Rievaulx Abbey in Yorkshire to establish a monastery in Melrose. This was part of his major reorganisation of the church; and his reign was to see the founding of a number of Border religious houses, including Kelso, Jedburgh and Dryburgh. The king had, in 1130 x 1133, secured the status of Melrose by its exchange for the church of St Mary of Berwick to Durham.[69] The monks who arrived at Melrose some time before 1136, however, did not favour the traditional sacred site of Melrose and opted to establish their monastery about two and a half miles further west. Their reasoning behind this is unclear. Perhaps the site of the existing remnants of monastic buildings, in a loop of the Tweed, may have been considered too constrained for a potentially extensive complex;[70] and, certainly, the one that they chose was more topographically suitable. The fertility of the area had also been proven, with farmlands around the erstwhile *Trimontium* fort.[71] There was a ready supply of water power from the Tweed and the Malthouse Burn, and springs beside the site offered plentiful drinking water (*see* p 10). It was also close to a fording point which gave ready access across the Tweed,[72] and some argue that it was on the regular route from Iona to Lindisfarne, via the Clyde and the Tweed.[73] Crossing points of rivers were liable to change over the centuries, however, and the Soutra–Kelso major route perhaps offered a more suitable crossing of the Tweed for those travelling from Iona to Lindisfarne.[74] It is clear from the records that the main routeways were east–west and north–south, with the latter being more important, the area being situated as it was between Northumberland and Lothian. The *magna strata* called 'Malchomisrode', was one of the latter, its importance being reflected in the fact that it was a surfaced road. Most of the roads seem to have followed ridgeways, with their alignment based on crossings of the Tweed with the Eildon Hills functioning as a marker. Fords are mentioned in the twelfth-century record; although their sites are not specified, one may presume that there was ready access across the Tweed by the mid twelfth century for the Melrose monks to visit their lands in Gattonside.[75]

At its foundation, Melrose received 2,150 hectares of land between the Eildon Hills and the Tweed, and in 1143 x 1147 the 900 hectares of Gattonside with Gattonside Haugh and rights to pasturage, timber and pannage in the 'waste' (largely woodland, interspersed with rough grass and scrub, with rushes, willow and alder in the low-lying areas) between the Gala and Leader Waters. Although the area south of the Tweed lay outside 'waste' and came to support three main settlements, Eildon, Darnick and Melrose, the area was lightly populated with a few native landowners, tillers and foresters of the king. This environment would be developed and adapted by the Cistercians over the next centuries.[76] A ford, however, tended to attract settlement to its banks; and whether there were settlers at this new site is unclear. Since the focus of the Cistercian rule was one of prayer, the monks were unlikely to adopt a heavily populated site. There was sufficient attachment to the name of Melrose that it was transferred to the new site, and the earlier had become known as Old Melrose by at least 1285 x 1291.[77]

The first abbot, Richard, and twelve monks, who were probably chosen for specialist knowledge, such as river diversion and architectural skills, would have probably been accompanied by twelve lay brothers.[78] Initially, they may have lived in temporary wooden accommodation while they constructed their church and ancillary buildings;[79] although accommodation might have been available at Old Melrose.[80] None of these probable early wooden buildings remain in evidence above the ground. According to the *Chronicle of Melrose*, the date of foundation was 23 March 1136, which, following our modern calendar and dating system , means the year was, in fact, 1137.[81] Progress was such that the dedication took place in 1146.[82] The building of any abbey, however, was a slow process, and this one probably took much of the twelfth century, it being claimed in the Rievaulx Cartulary that the stonework had not been commenced even in 1160.[83] Recent geophysical surveys at Melrose Abbey, however, suggest that there might be evidence of earlier stone structures in the abbey complex (*see* pp 60, 65–6).

There is little to see now of the late twelfth-century church, which was largely destroyed in the fourteenth century, but archaeological investigation has given an insight into its plan. The superseding structure was architecturally very different, but in plan the church that stands today resembles the earlier church, although on a much larger scale. All that survives of the earlier church is a fragment of the west wall with the lower part of the entrance doorway, the foundations of the square nave piers and their connecting screen walls, and part of the north wall. Excavations were carried out in the early 1920s by the Ministry of Works.[84] The results, together with surviving fragments of the original church, provide enough detail to allow a reconstruction of the basic arrangement of the late twelfth-century church.[85] Based on the plan of Rievaulx, which itself was modelled on Clairvaux in France, it comprised a rectangular presbytery, two bays long. Flanking the presbytery were two single-bay chapels and cross-arms or transepts, forming an unusual stepped arrangement at the east end. Beyond the crossing, the aisled nave stretched back for nine bays to the west door. The presbytery housed the high altar, with lesser altars in the transept chapels. The monks' choir occupied the area within the crossing and into the eastern part of the nave. The remainder of the nave was taken up by the lay brothers' choir, the two choirs separated by a screen called a *pulpitum*. The night-stair connected the north transept with the monks' dormitory, to allow them to attend services at night without braving the elements. There was a similar provision for the lay brethren in the north-western corner of the nave.

The walls, both inside and out, were probably whitewashed, and the roofs of lead and of red tile. The floors of the presbytery and chapels were paved with glazed tiles, coloured yellow, green or brown, and set in geometric patterns.[86]

The other conventual buildings stood to the north of the church, an unusual location for a Cistercian establishment, perhaps determined by the water supply—the River Tweed—to the north. These consisted of the cloister, which was an open garth, probably laid out as a garden, surrounded by covered walkways. Near the east processional door to the church, the surviving walls indicate that they were elaborately arcaded and had stone benches. An east range, which partially survives, contained the sacristy, immediately to the north of the church. This was where vestments, altar frontals and other pertinents of church service were kept. Next to this was the chapter house, where the monks met every morning to listen to a chapter of the rule, discuss monastic business and make their confession. It was here, also, that important burials took place, perhaps the most noted being that of St Waltheof (*see* pp 24, 59). Other offices abutted—probably the inner parlour, where there was limited conversation, perhaps a novices' day room and a latrine block—all of which were under the monks' dormitory, which ran along the full length of the east range on the first floor.

To the north was a range that housed the domestic buildings, such as a warming room, the only room heated for monks in the complex; and a refectory, where meals were taken in silence. The refectory ran parallel to the north walk in the twelfth century, but was realigned to be sited at right angles in the thirteenth century, perhaps to accommodate more monks. Opposite the refectory was the wash room or lavatorium. Water was fed to this large circular basin, still visible in the ground, in lead pipes from a well, later called the Lockit Well, sunk to the south of the conventual buildings, at Danzeltoun (Dingleton). To the west of the refectory was the kitchen.

The lay brothers, who did many of the lesser tasks for the monastery, lived apart from the monks, in the west range. They may have been assisted by servants for more menial tasks, even though, officially, this was not in keeping with the rule. The west range was two storeys high, extending some 108 metres from the west porch of the church, and was formed of two blocks. The southern end of the northern block was the lay brothers' refectory; and a tiled fireplace in the west wall indicates the site of their warming room. At right angles at the northern end was a further block, which housed their latrines and three pits, possibly used for tanning.

To the north-east of the cloister and ranges are the foundations of the Abbot's Hall, which date from the thirteenth century. It was probably a two-storeyed building, accommodating storage on the ground floor and the abbot's private chambers on the upper. A little further west stands the Commendator's House, first built in the fifteenth century, but largely converted in 1590 (*see* p 98). To the north again ran the mill lade that fed one of the abbey's two mills (*see* p 75). It was fed from a dam on the Tweed 460 metres west of the abbey, and was partially diverted to function also as a main drain to serve the latrines of the east range and, probably, those of the lay brothers.[87] The precinct would have contained kitchen and fruit gardens, as well as one mill,[88] and it is known that there was an orchard, with a lockable postern door, but whether this was within the precinct is unclear.[89] According to local tradition, the monks also had orchards on the other side of the Tweed, on the 'sunny banks' of Gattonside.[90] Some fruit trees may have been cultivated on the south side of the Tweed, to the west of the precincts. To this day, plum trees of a very early variety still grow on this site. Only partially located by excavation are the precinct walls, but documentary evidence and remnants in cellars give a relatively clear view of their layout (*see* pp 61, 74–5).

Twelfth-century evidence indicates that Melrose was a significant house from early in its history. Its abbots were prominent in temporal and spiritual affairs. St Waltheof, the uncle of King Malcolm IV (1153–65), was the second abbot. On his death, in 1159, he was buried at Melrose and when the tomb was opened in 1171, prior to placing a marble slab over the remains, the *Chronicle of Melrose* indicates that the body and vestments were all intact. Abbot Jocelin was to become the bishop of Glasgow in 1174. He, along with Ernald, abbot of Melrose, and Osbert, abbot of Kelso, visited Rome on the affairs of William I (1165–1214) and returned with a Golden Rose for the king from Pope Lucius III. In 1189 x 1190, Ernald was elected to the cure of souls in Rievaulx. The bishop of Moray, Simon, who died in 1184, had been one of the Cistercian brethren; Reinald, a monk at Melrose, became the bishop of Rosemark in 1195;[91] and in 1202 Ralph, abbot of Melrose, was made bishop of Down, in Ireland, by John Salerno, papal legate. The latter had stayed fifty nights at Melrose in an attempt to quash disputes between the monks of Melrose and those of Kelso, with no success.[92] In 1214, Adam, abbot of Melrose, was consecrated bishop of Caithness and, two years later, his successor, William, was promoted abbot of Rievaulx. Gilbert, the master of the novices at Melrose, was elected bishop of Whithorn in 1235. Not all new appointments, however, were successful. In the same year, Hugh, formerly a monk at Melrose and abbot-elect of Dere, resigned 'no less by bodily infirmity than by the coldness of the locality'.[93] In the reign of Alexander III (1249–86), Reginald de Roxburgh, a Melrose monk, functioned as royal ambassador to Norway. One of his remits, in 1265, was to obtain the Isle of Man and 'many contiguous islands';[94] in what were, perhaps, preparatory negotiations prior to the Treaty of Perth in 1266. In 1298–9, Patrick Selkirk, the abbot of Melrose, was ambassador to the French court.[95] Such honours continued to be won by the monks of Melrose throughout the middle ages, until the abbots were probably leaving the running of the monastery to the priors. Abbot Andrew Hunter, for example, as well as being the king's confessor,[96] was the king's treasurer in 1450, a role that would leave little time for spiritual affairs in Melrose Abbey.[97]

Dispute was an aspect of the abbey's early days that also continued throughout this period. Much of the tension arose over grants of land to the new foundation. Throughout its history the abbey of Melrose was showered with gifts of lands, rentals and properties. As well as the grants received early, at or just after its foundation (*see* p 22), in 1143 x 1147 Henry, son of David I, confirmed to the monks of Rievaulx at Melrose the whole lands of Melrose, Eildon and Darnick, as well as granting Gattonside together with Gatton's Haugh (ie. Gattonside Haugh) and the rights to pasturage, timber and pannage (pig grazing) in lands between the Gala and Leader Waters. In 1159, Malcolm IV confirmed the grants of land of Hartside and the saltpan given by Patrick, third earl of Dunbar.[98] This generosity was continued into the reign of William I. In 1165 x 1174, land at the corner of the Briggate at Berwick was granted, with the services of one William Lunnok and, some time later, in 1189 x 1214, further property in Berwick was endowed.[99] In 1251, Melrose purchased more houses in Berwick, adjacent to its existing land on Briggate. By 1296, Melrose held ten properties in Berwick, the most important town in Scotland.[100] Over the centuries the abbey also came to hold property in many burghs, such as Selkirk, Leith and Glasgow, sometimes designed to provide accommodation for conventual officials when travelling on business. The abbot of Melrose, for example, found it necessary to pursue the provosts [*sic*] and bailies of Perth, in 1498, on account of theft and damage to goods in their tenement in that town.[101]

Discord had arisen between Melrose and Richard de Moreville over rights to the forest between the Gala and Leader Waters. William I decided for the monastery in 1180, when it was decreed that not only should they freely hold the disputed forest area, but also pasturage at Threepwood and a site at Comslie for a byre for a hundred cows.[102] A few years later, the king again found for the monastery against the men of Wedale, in their dispute over pasturage in the king's forest. In this latter case the jurors may have been somewhat overawed: they were required to take their oaths in front of the king and his court, 'tremblingly and reverently' on the relics of Melrose Abbey.[103] The abbey for a while also held the easements of wood, timber and pannage in Ettrick Forest.[104] In 1236, Melrose was given further extensive grants to Ettrick 'waste'. A year later, meadow land was sold to the monks by the laird of Fairnington, although the monks had already shown a proprietorial interest by ditching and banking the land.[105] It has been argued that the 'pastoral pursuits' of Melrose Abbey must have led to considerable deforestation in lowland Scotland, and, in consequence, a lack of timber.[106]

The abbey was also granted lands in the west. As early as some time before 1165, Melrose had accepted the teinds of Eskdale from Robert Avenel, who had been granted Eskdale by David I, perhaps because he, like the king, had lost his lands in Northamptonshire; and in the late twelfth century, before his death, Walter the Stewart bestowed his demesne of Mauchline on Melrose Abbey. In 1302, Robert, earl of Carrick, recognised that all the abbey's holdings in Ayrshire were free from the duties of 'forinsec' (that is, service in the host), other than their participation in defence of the realm.[107] The monastery was prepared to defend these territorial rights. In 1476, for example, the abbot and convent took action against James Auchinleck and his mother, Janet Colville, for wrongful occupation of Welwood in the sheriffdom of Ayr.[108] In 1510, Mauchline was erected into a burgh of barony for the abbey of Melrose. It could thus function as the administrative centre for the abbatial lands of Kylesmuir.[109]

Melrose Abbey and its monks were to continue to expand their holdings of land in the fourteenth and fifteenth centuries, not only in the south and west, but also in Aberdeenshire; and to receive confirmation of their previous grants of vast tracts of arable and pasture land.[110] Such extensive lands meant that Melrose was a wealthy abbey. From its outset, David I had granted the abbey a further important concession, which was confirmed in 1173 x 1177 by William I: the monks of Melrose, and, indeed, of all the Cistercian order, were permitted to trade free of toll, or trading dues, on the king's land.[111] In the 1180s, the Count of Flanders granted Melrose freedom from toll in his country. This was an important concession as Flanders was one of the most important textile producing areas and a significant market for Melrose wool.[112] By the late twelfth century, the abbot of Melrose, as many other heads of religious houses, was acting as money-lender as far afield as Northamptonshire.[113] Trading activities were such that Henry III of England (1216–72) was, in 1224, granting safe conducts through England to the men of the abbot of Melrose as they passed overseas. The following year he gave leave for the abbot to send a vessel to Flanders, laden with wool and other merchandise; and five years after, on a petition from Alexander II (1214–49), that a similarly laden ship might trade throughout England.[114] The monks of Melrose were trading in various parts of England. In the later half of the thirteenth century, for example, they were regular attenders at the fair of St Botolph (Boston, Lincolnshire), where the abbey held land.[115] By the 1270s, the Italian merchant Bagimond was depositing money, raised for papal taxes, at Melrose, although he used secular clergy as sub-collectors of this tax before transmitting it to Italian bankers. By the 1290s, however, abbots themselves were functioning as sub-collectors and banking the money with the Italians who were buying wool direct from the abbeys.[116]

A thirteenth-century assessment of the incomes of monasteries in the archdeaconry of Lothian is telling. Melrose's £54 from rentals could not match the £216 of Coldingham as this was a Benedictine foundation, with no official restriction on accepting lands and other properties. It was, however, well ahead of St Bothan's, a small Cistercian nunnery, with £5. Melrose's demesne lands brought in £18, the range of the other abbeys and priories being £4 to £50; and demesne ploughgates raised £9, in a range of £2 to £20. Income from calves and lambs and from wool and lambskins showed a very different picture. The smallest income from calves and lambs was £2 (Eccles), and the largest Melrose's £58. Coldstream had the smallest income from wool and lambskins, at £9, compared with the greatest producer, Melrose, with £86. It has been estimated that by 1300 Melrose had something like 12,000 sheep.[117] Others have argued for 15,000;[118] but the importance of the wool trade to the monastery's fortunes is obvious. The fortunes of the abbey fluctuated somewhat in the later thirteenth and fourteenth centuries, because of both political (*see* pp 29–31) and economic factors. In 1404, for example, Melrose could sell only thirty sacks of high quality wool, as opposed to its normal fifty, as wool prices had slumped.[119] But its important exporting activities continued; in 1358, for example, the abbey was granted by David II (1329–71) the whole custom of their wool, which would normally have been payable to the crown.[120] This practice became almost constant.[121]

Although its arable farming was excellent, the economy of the abbey remained largely dependent on its production and sale of high quality wool. From the later fourteenth century, the *Exchequer Rolls* indicate that the total of customs paid on hides and woolfells was much less than that paid on wool; and eventually these first two commodities faded from the record as the concentration on wool intensified. Much of this wool, in time, was produced on farms that were let out to tenants, as opposed to granges farmed by lay brothers. There is much to suggest that, in fact, there were few lay brothers remaining by 1443 (*see* p 31).

The abbey, however, had other more critical functions—as a place of spirituality and pilgrimage. It received its first appropriated church 'for the entertainment of the poor and pilgrims', perhaps in 1159, but more likely in 1195.[122] Certainly, in 1193 x 1195, following a disagreement between Bishop Jocelin of Glasgow and King William I over patronage and the rights to pasturage of 200 ewes, sixteen oxen and four cows, the king confirmed to Melrose Abbey the church of Hassendene for the reception and maintenance of poor people and pilgrims coming to Melrose.[123] But of routine life in Melrose we know little. The Cistercian life was dedicated to prayer and work and there was little contact for the ordinary monk with the outside world.

It is clear that Melrose was an abbey greatly favoured by royalty. William I, for example, spent some considerable time at Melrose between May and July 1209.[124] It was here, in the chapter house, that the Yorkshire barons swore fealty to Alexander II in 1216.[125] Alexander III chose Melrose as a strategic place to await his army in September 1258;[126] and David II (1329–71) was at Melrose in 1369/70.[127] It was to Melrose that James I (1406–37) returned from exile in 1424,[128] and it was from Melrose also that James II (1437–60) checked the power of Archibald, fifth earl of Douglas, whose predecessor and brother-in-law, the fourth earl, had been 'defender and protector' of Melrose Abbey.[129] Successive kings resided at the monastery—James IV (1488–1513), for example, based himself at Melrose for his attack on Northumbria in 1496; spent Christmas 1497 there, for which a copious supply of geese and 'birds of the forest' was required; and, two years later, received the Archbishop of Canterbury at Melrose. This occasion necessitated elaborate provisions; later in the year, when the king was again resident, supplies of wine were required.[130]

Alexander II chose Melrose as his burial place, to which his remains were brought from Kerrera after his death on 8 July 1249.[131] His body reputedly rests beside the High Altar[132] (although others have argued that the slab marks the grave of St Waltheof; *see* pp 23,24,59). Royal interments, however, were usually before the high altar in monastic churches. His grave was at one time marked by an inscribed stone, which is no longer extant. If his burial site was not changed at the rebuilding of the abbey after 1385, it should now lie to the west of the present chancel.[133] It was also here, in the south aisle of the abbey, that his wife, Joanna, was buried.[134] The heart of Robert I (1306–29) reputedly also rests in the abbey, after its travels on crusade. The king had shown great favour to Melrose in the 1320s, although the abbey and the Bruce faction had not always been on good terms (*see* p 30).

Quite what implication the comings and goings of kings, abbots and papal legates had for any possible lay settlement at Melrose is unclear. It may be expected that there would have been a small clustering of people near one of the precinct gates, as there was at the gate of the Cistercian abbey of Coupar Angus,[135] or beside the ford; but of this there is little evidence. One of the first firm pieces of evidence that there was early settlement here comes in 1303. During his invasion of Scotland, Edward I encamped at Dryburgh. One of his aides, Hugh de Audley, took a small detachment of sixty men to seek accommodation at Melrose. Hearing of his presence, John Comyn, Guardian of Scotland, forced an entry into the abbey precincts. In an attempt to save his life, one English knight, Thomas Gray, fled out of the gate, 'a la maner', which might be interpreted as 'village' or 'small township', and there seized the house outside the gate, where he took refuge until it was burned down around his head and he, too, was taken prisoner.[136] It seems, then, that settlement was clustered at the south gate to the abbey; and it may be surmised that the dwellings were simple structures of wood, if it was possible to force Gray out so easily by burning. There was probably an east gate, as well as a north, west and south gate **figure 8**. Presumably the

figure 8
Site of the south gate to the abbey precincts, seen from the Market Square

figure 9
Medieval finds from the abbey—
pottery jugs *top* and urinals *right.*
The lead communion token *above* dates to the
eighteenth or nineteenth century, *scale 3:1*

north and east gates, which might have attracted settlement, were less geologically favourable. Nineteenth-century comments that Melrose occupies the site of an ancient lake and that the Tweed had moved northwards by nearly one hundred metres in places would suggest that the north gate might have been marshy;[137] this might also have been true of the west gate, as the area of the Greenyards was not drained satisfactorily until the middle of the nineteenth century.[138]

Even though the abbey had the services of lay brothers, support from an ancillary lay settlement would be sought as the centuries passed, particularly as the original ruling of isolation for the monastery became more relaxed. Pilgrims travelling to Melrose would also require the facilities of hostelries and provisions, as would those tenants who came to pay their dues to the abbey overlord **figure 9**. All of these factors would tend to encourage the growth of the small settlement at the abbey gate.

In 1218, all Cistercian monks in Scotland were declared excommunicate. Although this was later declared invalid, the disruption to services must have had a profound effect, not only on the monasteries themselves, but also on ancillary settlements nearby.[139] Again, in 1269, the abbot of Melrose and most of his convent were excommunicated, this time for disruption over the boundary of the forest of Wedale. The bishop of St Andrews had a palace at the Stow of Wedale and some ancillary houses, which were attacked, resulting in one dead clergyman and several others wounded.[140] This, too, probably redounded on the lay people. But, whatever small settlement there was, it could not but be affected by the troubled times that were to result from the succession crisis—the Great Cause, the Wars of Independence and, after an uneasy peace, the effects of the Auld Alliance.

As a wealthy monastery and landowner, with possessions in both Scotland and England, and in a vulnerable geographical position whenever disputes between the two countries erupted, it was inevitable that Melrose would be pulled out of the political wings on to centre stage, by both protagonists. As already indicated, the barons of Yorkshire came to Melrose to swear fealty to Alexander II in the chapter house, on 11 January 1216.[141] The role of the abbey was apparently less certain to the Scottish rule when, *c* 1286, James the Stewart, hereditary Steward of Scotland and one of the six regents or guardians elected to govern for the young queen, Margaret, demanded military service from the tenants of Melrose Abbey, as civil strife threatened after the death of Alexander III.[142] In 1290, however, Edward I of England gave freedom from distraint—the seizure of their goods—to the monks of Melrose. For the following two years, his protection was given to the abbot and convent.[143] Edward's formal protection was in force in 1295,[144] but the following year the sheriff of Northumberland was instructed by Edward I to remove the servants of all those who had supported King John Balliol (1292–6), including the men of the abbot of Melrose.[145] Four months later, in August 1296, the abbot and convent of Melrose, along with those of Jedburgh, Dryburgh and Kelso, swore fealty to Edward I and appended their seals to the document.[146] Probably as a result of this, Edward I ordered restitution to Melrose of all property it had lost.[147] The abbot of Melrose, however, was ambassador to France for the Scottish Guardianship of William Wallace in 1298–9 (*see* p 24). Classified as a 'Scots enemy', Edward I gave instruction that he, along with others, including the bishop of St Andrews, should be captured on his return from Flanders.[148]

Melrose's geographical location continued to ensure that the abbey remained vulnerable as political events unravelled in the fourteenth century. How far it suited Melrose Abbey to be party to manipulation is unclear. Documentary evidence makes it clear that Melrose was to receive monies due to it from the chamberlain of Scotland, John de Sandale, on the insistence of Edward I in April 1305; along with other Scottish dignitaries, the abbot attended Westminster in September as one of the Scottish commissioners. It was at this parliament that the Ordnance for the Governance of Scotland was laid down, Wallace having been tried and executed in the previous month.[149]

During these early years of the fourteenth century, Melrose was clearly at pains to ensure guarantees for its extensive lands and franchises, by appeals to Edward I; for example, in the case of disputed land in Eskdale, it petitioned to 'let them have a writ from the English to the Scottish Chancery for remedy'. It is noteworthy that a successful appeal was made to Edward I not only to confirm all their charters of infeftment, but also to grant them timber in Selkirk forest (Ettrick Forest), since their buildings had been burned and destroyed, while at his peace and protection. This destruction may have been accidental. It does not seem that this was on Edward's instructions, as there was little point in granting the wherewithal to repair damage deliberately effected by his policies. Perhaps here there could be some evidence of displeasure by a Scottish patriot party, possibly at the acquiescence of Melrose with the English government.

In December 1307, Edward II (1307–27), king of England since July of that year, made an appeal to prominent churchmen and nobles of Scotland that they should keep the peace in the realm. Robert I had been crowned King of Scots in March 1306;

although his fortunes had been waning for a time, within less than two weeks of Edward I's appeal, the defeat of John Comyn, third earl of Buchan, by Robert I heralded the beginning of the end of concerted opposition to the new King of Scots. Such an appeal to churchmen was perhaps understandable, but the nobles who were contacted were not largely of the Bruce faction. This may be a further indication that Melrose was not pro-Bruce in December 1307.[150]

Some three years later, in December 1310, Sir Robert de Clifford, justiciar north of the Trent and warden of Scotland for Edward II, and others had been at Selkirk to treat with Robert de Brus [sic in primary documentation]. Soon after this, the earls of Gloucester and Cornwall had sought to speak with him at a place near Melrose. He failed to appear, however, since it was said that he had been warned that he would be taken.[151] Clearly, the Melrose area was still not safe for the Scottish king.

By May 1316, however, Bruce was using Melrose as a base to harry the English in Berwick;[152] and in 1322 the abbey complex was burned by Edward II.[153] The granting, by Robert I in 1326, of £2,000 for the rebuilding of the policies, suggests that Melrose was by now firmly in the Scottish king's camp; as do the grants of ferms and customs to be applied to the abbey fabric and daily sustenance of the monks.[154] The regular visits of the king[155] and his decision in 1329 that his heart should be buried there would support this. Melrose, however, remained in a vulnerable geographical position; but with the arrival of temporary peace, the regents of Edward III (1327–77) in 1328 restored to the abbey the pensions and lands seized by his father.[156] Six years later, Edward III granted his protection to Melrose and the other Border abbeys. Relations were sufficiently warm that, in 1341, Edward III visited while spending Christmas at Newcastle; and in 1348 he granted further lands to Melrose.[157]

The Scottish crown, in the person of David II, recognised in 1357 that the abbey of Melrose was 'of necessity in the peace of the English'; but deemed that it should not, as a result, lose control of its Scottish possessions. This reassurance was repeated the following year.[158] In 1358, the abbey and its immediate lands were erected into a free regality. Attempts at this time by the justiciar of Lothian and other officials to interfere in the regality of Melrose were stalled by the crown; and in February 1361 the abbey received letters from David II giving it the right to treat with the English as was thought necessary.[159] For his part, King Richard II of England (1377–99) now became more preoccupied with the situation in France. This brought relative peace for the abbey; and as late as 1378 Richard II renewed his protection of the monastery.[160] In 1381, it was still necessary for Melrose to gain permission to negotiate privately with the English. English letters of protection were issued in 1373, 1377 and 1405; but significantly during this same period of time, the monastery gained from the Scottish crown a grant of regality and exemption from customs dues.[161]

In 1385, Richard II spent the night at the abbey.[162] It was said that it was because he was so 'exasperated' that he burned it on leaving.[163] The recent Scottish invasion of England, in support of France, however, was probably the real explanation for the concerted devastation of the eastern Border region. As it was chronicled, the English destroyed everything 'saving nothing and burning down with the fiery flames God's temples and holy places, to wit the monasteries of Melrose, Dryburgh and Newbattle'.[164]

The work of rebuilding the abbey began within a few years of its destruction, probably with the active support of Richard II. Architectural evidence supports the theory that English masons were participating in the reconstruction work. Financial provision was also made in 1389;[165] and a grant of two shillings for every 1,000 sacks of wool exported by the Cistercian monks via Berwick was instituted. The revocation of this grant a year later, as the monastery attempted to export two hundred more than agreed, is indication that, although their monastery and complex had been destroyed, their wool-producing activities were still healthy. The architecture of the abbey indicates that the responsibility for building work passed to masons influenced by the European tradition; part of the south transept was the responsibility of the French master mason, John Morow. The reconstruction was to last throughout the fifteenth and into the sixteenth

figure 10

Alan Sorrell's

reconstruction

of the abbey *c* 1500

© Crown Copyright:

Historic Scotland

century; and Melrose Abbey was to re-emerge as one of the most magnificent complexes in Scotland, even though work petered out inconclusively as it approached the west end (*see* p 95) **figure 10**.[166]

Little or nothing is known of the effects of such long-term harrying and destruction on the small settlement that clustered at the south gate of the abbey; but it may be guessed that it suffered along with the monastery complex. In such circumstances, it would be unlikely that it would have expanded greatly from the early decades of the century. As a free regality, the abbey would have a measure of impact, through its regality court, on the peoples within its lands. It is possible that the abbatial court, which dealt with the temporal affairs of the abbey, had greater powers in pre-Reformation days; but how far it impinged on the locality is unclear.[167] The use, from at least 1443, of the erstwhile lay brothers' choir as the parish church would also bring closer contact between settlement and abbey. And the gradual decline in the numbers of lay brothers would, in its turn, mean that the abbey would have had to look to lay settlement nearby for assistance, not only in running their granges, but also for the more mundane services of cleaning, washing, gardening and supplying food. On-going reconstruction of the abbey complex would also have created a demand for a labouring workforce. The continued use of the abbey complex as a temporary resting place for the monarchy throughout the fifteenth century would have brought a further demand for services (*see* pp 32, 63);[168] and it may be guessed that in this century there was a growth in settlement.

The work of Dr James Curle,[169] documentary evidence from the primary sources and observation give a relatively clear picture of how and where this small settlement developed. The abbey precinct was surrounded by a stone wall, broken in four places by gates—the east, west, north and south gates. The south gate was the most important and stood astride the modern Abbey Street, a little back from where it now joins the Market Place **figure 8**. It had a chapel built at the gatehouse, or above it, as at Beaulieu. The line of the precinct wall may be located on the south side by its presence in cellars, for example at the Teddy Bear Museum and to the rear of other properties, including the Bank of Scotland. Immediately to the west of the bank, a property consisting of a house and garden had previously been two properties. The more northerly part was within the old precinct, but the southerly part was not.[170] Documentary evidence shows that, in the sixteenth century, part of the small township hugged the wall, facing southwards to the open market place and across to other properties lining the east–west routeway. It is safe to assume that this was also the morphology of the settlement in the fifteenth century. In 1422, when pronouncing a decree of excommunication, the abbot, David Binning, had canonical admonitions proclaimed three times—once in the chapter house, once in the chapel at the gate and, interestingly, at the cross before the gate.[171] Here is clear evidence that a cross had already been set up in the market square of Melrose. Other crosses, or possibly markers, stood near the township. The High Cross, for example, to the west of Melrose centre and another marker on the present golf course, the 'Haly Sing of St Waltheof', were religious spots, offering first views of the abbey to pilgrims. If the cross in the open space before the south gate of the monastery was a secular cross this would be clear indication not only of trading activities at the gate of the monastery, but also of an established trading settlement. Melrose, although still perhaps more of the nature and size of a village, was probably already displaying certain urban characteristics.

sixteenth-century Melrose

Although various abbatial disputes in 1485 x 1506 marred the peace of the monastery,[172] nevertheless the work of its reconstruction continued until sometime after 1505. King James IV (1488–1513) granted drink silver to the masons working there, for example, in November 1502[173] and just before Christmas 1504.[174] The *Treasurer's Accounts* at the turn of the century indicate that James IV was resident at Melrose on a number of occasions, for example in 1502 when he received the French ambassador (*see* p 66). The docu-mentation also gives some small detail of the types of occupation of the local people. Tree fellers, wheel wrights, coal quarriers, metal workers, fishers and masons were all at work,[175] as well as the expected farmers and food producers. In a letter to Pope Julius II in April 1507, however, King James IV noted that 'the lands of Melrose are on the border and so exposed to war and to banished Scots during peace that resources formerly ample will not meet bare necessities'. To the Cardinal of St Mark, he wrote that the abbey of Melrose was 'occupied by banished men and outlaws in time of peace'.[176]

This view was perhaps confirmed some nine years later. The disastrous battle of Flodden had been fought in 1513 and James IV, with nine earls and many others, was dead. In September 1516, the Lords of Council decided that the Lord Governor (John, duke of Albany, nephew of the deceased king) should 'pas with ane honest company to Melros, and fra thin to Jedburgh and forthir as it sall be thocht necessar for gud reule to be maid apon the bourdoris and for the expulsioun of thevis and putting of the kingis lieges to rest and quiet'.[177] The next years were ones of continued strife for the Borders. One of the closest skirmishes to home for the town was the battle of Melrose in 1526. This was fought in the presence of the young king, James V (1513–42), when Archibald Douglas, sixth earl of Angus, who had been married to the Queen Mother, defeated Walter Scott of Branxholm and Buccleuch,[178] who was reported to be attempting to free the teenage king from Angus. The king was not to gain his freedom for another two years.

During James V's personal reign, Melrose was one of the many ecclesiastical establishments that was to suffer from the financial exactions of the crown. In 1533, for example, the abbey paid merely £159 in part payment of its tax of £380.[179] The following year, a similar partial payment was made.[180] Six years later, in the July of 1540, the abbot of Melrose paid only £159 of its imposition; but on this occasion he and the 'place' of Melrose were discharged of their remaining dues.[181]

There is evidence of a certain relaxation of the strict Cistercian rule for the monks. The abbots, however, had acted increasingly as temporal lords for some time (*see* p 24). The decree, in 1534, of the abbots of Coupar Angus and Glenluce that the practice of the Melrose monks of possessing private property was unsuitable reveals the distancing from the original rule.[182] An investigation by the abbot of Charlieu, on behalf of the Cistercian General Chapter, had already found that the monks were in receipt of portions for food and pensions for clothing, as well as private gardens for their own use. In their own

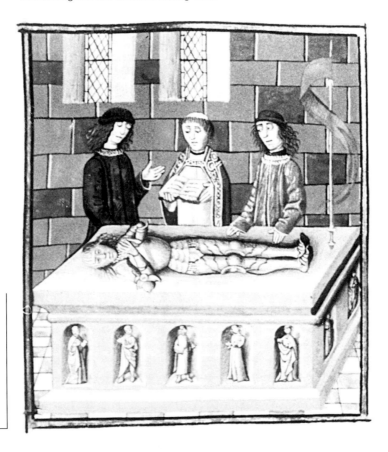

33

defence, the monks argued that such practices, which were, in effect, illicit indulgences, had been common practice for over a hundred years.[183] In 1536, there were still at least thirty-two monks at Melrose;[184] although as witness to the decline of the order, the last abbot, Andrew Durie, was forced to resign, to be replaced by a commendator (and his administrator) in 1541. The nominal commendator was James V's eldest illegitimate son, James Stewart, an infant.

A year later, in 1542, the laird of Buccleuch entered Melrose Abbey and took all the king's sheep, saying not only that he would keep them in part recompense for the sheep the king had taken from him, but also that he would keep the land on which they were to graze.[185] Melrose was merely a pawn in the local politics of the region; but later in the year, the defeat of the Scottish army at Solway Moss and the subsequent death of James V on 14 December was to leave the abbey and township with a worse legacy: the 'Rough Wooing'.

Henry VIII of England (1509–1547) was intent on uniting the crown of Scotland with that of England by the marriage of his son Edward with the young Queen Mary (1542–67). When negotiations failed, he determined to beat Scotland into submission. There followed seven years of devastation, much of its main toll falling on the Border region. Melrose was to suffer greatly in this war of attrition. In 1544, the abbey was burnt by the English under Sir Ralph Eure (Evers) and the tombs of the Douglases, the erstwhile defenders of the abbey, desecrated **figure 11**.[186] This was not a suddenly conceived plan. For some considerable time letters and discussions had been under way to burn Melrose.[187] The following year, in 1545, it was 'raced' by the forces of the earl of Hertford, numbering, it was claimed, 15,000 men.[188]

The town must have suffered as much as the abbey during the years of battering, although there is little or no evidence in the records of the effects on the townspeople. Little seems to have been done to repair the devastation to the abbey; there was perhaps little point. English troops were not easily ousted from the Borders, being, for example, in Jedburgh in 1549,[189] backed by a fifth column of 'assured Scots' who were bribed or bullied into taking an oath of allegiance to the king of England.[190]

Unsurprisingly, in 1549, the abbey was stated to be in great and urgent need of money.[191] Peace with England, agreed in 1551, did not signal any upturn in the abbey's fortunes. Still by 1556, the monks were warning that 'without the kirk be repairit this instant sommer God service will ceise this winter'.[192] The following year, sixteen monks received an assignation for their living, the rents amounting to £63 'for repartion and bigging of the place being ruinous' and £200 from teinds to the 'bursour' or master of works for application 'quhair maist neid is'.[193] In 1555–6 James Stewart, the commendator of Melrose and Kelso, granted a feu charter in return for funds 'towards the repair and rebuilding of the abbey of Melrose destroyed by the English'. This was signed by the commendator, the sub-prior and eleven monks.[194] There is charter evidence of many such instances,[195] which would suggest that there was, at the very least, intent to effect repairs; as would a precept of sasine by the commendator to infeft one John Hunter in a husbandland of land, which specifically excluded the fishings on the Tweed and 'stone quarries and stone necessary for the…monastery of Melrose'.[196] A complaint by the monks in 1556, however, reveals that some of these monies were diverted to other uses; and lead from the roof of the abbey was being sold off.[197]

Political and religious events were to bring profound changes to Melrose after 1560, with the establishment of a Protestant church. The old order, however, did not change overnight. In 1536, twenty-nine monks, including the abbot and sub-prior, had subscribed a charter, although a further three, at least, were identifiable at the time. Their numbers appear to have fallen after the 1545 destruction and probably at the Reformation there were seventeen monks left;[198] although some claim that there were even fewer monks than this, there being only twelve left as early as 1556.[199] The surviving members of convent became pensioners,[200] a number of them continuing to live in Melrose and perhaps joining the new Protestant ministry. The first known ministers were James Pont, given the charge in 1562; John Watson in 1568; John Wilson in 1569; and, in 1584, John Knox, nephew or great-nephew of the famous John Knox.[201] The community of monks may have become extinct shortly after 1590, with the death of John Watson, pensioner of Melrose;[202] although it is possible that one remaining monk lived till 1609, when he was functioning as the bailie of Melrose regality.[203]

In 1581, the newly organised Melrose parish was created, with parishioners still worshipping in the outer church or choir. It is known that on 25 April 1573 the regality court of Melrose was held within the abbey kirk.[204] Clearly, parts of the church were still able to function, in spite of the damage it had suffered over the decades. The English, however, were not the sole desecrators. The commendator, James Douglas, son of Sir William Douglas of Lochleven, later the earl of Morton, with Alexander Colville, commendator of Culross, as coadjutor and administrator (during the minority of Douglas)[205] took action against Sir Walter Scott of Branxholm in February 1570 for committing a 'spuilze at the place of Melrose'.[206] In the June of that year, he was recalled to court for the removal of lead from 'the place and kirk of Melrose'.[207] He had dismantled the 'inner queir, uter kirk, the stepile, an croce kirk of the same'. His defence was that he was merely removing them to save them from the English![208] He was not the sole culprit. In June of the same year, letters of arrestment were raised by the commendator and 'convent of our said abbey of Melrose' against those who had violently taken the 'haill leid of the kirk and place of' Melrose, with the intention of, amongst other things, taking it to the port of Leith to export out of the realm. The majority of the perpetrators were local, such as Thomas Scot, tailor in Jedburgh, but not from Melrose.[209] James Douglas was himself, moreover, happy to pillage the abbey ruins to build the Commendator's House in 1590.

The thirds of benefices accruing from Melrose show it still to have been a wealthy abbey in 1562–3.[210] This was due to its extensive land holdings, the dispersal of which increased after the Reformation. Rentals and duties of Melrose to the sum of £1,060, for example, were bestowed by the Queen Regent, Mary of Guise, on the three sons of George, Lord Seton. These grants from lands in Ayrshire, Carrick and Nithsdale were ratified by Queen Mary when she came to power;[211] and further gifts and pensions were, for example, granted by James Douglas, commendator in 1579.[212] The dissipation of abbey lands continued into the seventeenth century.[213] Such grants of temporal lordships could lead to prolonged dissension, as in the case of Francis Stewart, fifth earl Bothwell, and the commendator of Melrose, James Douglas,[214] but the net result for the church was that its days of landed wealth were over.

The town, after the disruption of the Rough Wooing of the 1540s, saw something of a return to normality in the personal reign of Queen Mary. In September 1566, a justice ayre was convened at Melrose to meet 'thair majesteis' (Mary and Henry, king of Scots, Lord Darnley)[215] and pass from there to Jedburgh.[216] A similar order went out in May 1567 to meet with Queen Mary on 15 June.[217] This ayre was to seek the pacification of the lordship of Liddesdale, a notoriously troublesome area of the Border region, to the south of Melrose, which was possessed by James Hepburn, fourth earl of Bothwell. He had been the husband of Queen Mary for less than a fortnight, and had previously been granted feu of a large part of the old abbey lands.[218] On the date set for the ayre, however, Mary and her husband were not in the vicinity of Melrose as both were involved in the fateful battle of Carberry. The ongoing presence of troops and constant warfare must have affected the townscape; but of this the records tell us little.

It seems that Melrose still did not have the privileges of a burgh in the latter decades of the sixteenth century (see pp 35–6). In September 1564, letters to 'baronis, landit men, gentilmen and utheris', concerning order in the middle marches, were sent to provosts and bailies of Jedburgh, Selkirk and Peebles. The missive for Melrose was directed to the abbot.[219] The town was still, undoubtedly, only a small place, probably much the size of Gattonside. One building known to have been built, or rebuilt, at this time was the Black Bull Inn, next to the abbey's main gate. The original lintel of the doorway bears the initials 'IN' and 'ID' and the date 'Ye 2nd of May 1573'.

In 1576, the tenants and farmers of Gattonside and Mosshouses defaulted on the payment of rentals. Two interesting factors emerge from this case. These tenants and farmers numbered only 'three score householders', which would suggest a population of somewhere in the region of only 270 in the two settlements (using a multiplier of 4.5 per household). The excuse was that they were not paying as they had lost some sixteen score of acres by the rising of the Tweed.[220] Clearly, the river was still shifting its banks; in consequence, there was little likelihood of the township of Melrose spreading out to the banks of the Tweed.

There was soon, however, a significant development in the townscape. In April 1589, for example, a tack was issued by James, commendator of Melrose, to John Scott, the town's notary public, and John Scott, his son and heir. They were to be infeoffed of a 'yard within the abbey walls sometime pertaining to the deceased dean Thomas Mein, monk'. There were adjacent occupied properties to the north, the south-east and the west.[221] The bakehouse yard, which stood within the precinct or 'mantill wall', near to the mill, and the mill itself were set to tack.[222] John Knox, the minister from 1584, was given tack of a dwelling and garden in the north-east of the precinct, close to where Dene John Watson had his 'roume', with 'the auld ruinus wallis one the east syd of the closter on the vest'. The commendator, significantly, retained the stones for his own use.[223] The colonisation of the erstwhile abbey precincts had already begun.

seventeenth-century Melrose

In the early years of the century, the little township was elevated to a burgh. Although there is mention of it being a burgh of barony in 1605, there is no firm evidence that this was so. In 1609, Melrose was erected into a burgh of barony for John Ramsay, first Viscount Haddington.[224] This elevation was, in effect, a gift from King James VI (1567–1625) to Viscount Haddington, who was one of his favourites; and thus the lands and barony of Melrose, together with the abbey, were constituted a free lordship and barony in his favour.[225] By 1618, he had resigned his lordship to his relative, Sir George Ramsay of Dalhousie, at which time the latter was granted the barony with the title of Lord Ramsay of Melrose. Within a few weeks, he, in turn, resigned the barony to Thomas Hamilton, Lord Binning,[226] who in 1619 became the earl of Melrose and eight years later opted, as a greater honour from the crown, to use the title of earl of Haddington.[227]As the earl of Melrose, he received a new grant, in 1621, which raised the burgh to the status of a burgh of regality. He had now, as burgh superior, full powers to create a provost, bailies and councillors, and to hold markets and levy customs from those using it.[228]

The town had had a cross from at least the previous century where markets were held (*see* p 32). If not a secular cross, it is possible that it became so after the Reformation. Although the town did not have burgh status, it is clear that the regality court tried to enforce a monopoly at the Melrose market. One John Hastie, in 1608, for example, was 'condempnit' for selling food outside the town and not presenting it at Melrose market.[229] The Haddington coat of arms, perhaps replacing an earlier abbatial one, was placed on the seventeenth-century market cross.[230] Whether this was placed on the cross soon after Viscount Haddington became burgh superior is unclear. One tradition believes that the old cross was destroyed in 1604 and replaced in 1642.[231] The date 1645 on the capital may be an indication of replacement or, perhaps, the date of alteration (and possibly repair work at the same time). A plot of ground, called the Corse Rig or Cross Ridge, had its rentals diverted for maintenance of the market cross. The Corse Rig is sited on the way to Newtown St Boswells via the Bogly Burn, and is the next field but one west of the Wairds Cemetery.[232] The market cross, as well as being the site of the market, also functioned as the place for public proclamations. In 1657, for example, after a complaint by the inhabitants of Melrose and Danzeltoun to the bailie, it was announced at the cross, 'that none pretend ignorance thereof', that 'no persone...shall suffer or permitt thair horses or utheris thair bestiall to goe upon thair nichtbouris cornes aither grein or rype naither by nicht nor by day'.[233] To further ensure that the populace was kept fully apprised of important news, proclamations were also made at the kirk door.[234]

The records indicate that Melrose market had some difficulty in attracting all within its hinterland to attend. In October 1660, the Saturday weekly market was 'almost altogether decayed...be reason of the haile inhabitants of [the] paroch who aucht and sould bring their cornes to [Melrose] market doth carrie them to other mercats in the cuntrie'. All those within the lordship of Melrose who lived in the parish, or the sheriffdom of Roxburgh and Berwick, or who were vassals of the earl of Haddington were, therefore, obliged to bring any goods for sale to the Melrose market on 20 October and, thereafter, for three consecutive Saturday markets. Only if goods failed to sell at this point were they to be sold elsewhere.[235] James Mertoun, tailor in Melrose, feued the custom of the market from October 1661 to October 1662; and James Elleis did likewise the following year. Payments respectively of £5 8s and £4 13s 4d for this right are clear indication that the annual profits on the market tolls were slight.[236]

On occasion, markets were also held at the Weirhill. Whether this was because there was congestion at times at the small market place of Melrose is unclear. On the occasion, in 1616, that the market was known to have been held at Weirhill, victuals ('viveris') were being sold. Perhaps there is here indication that the food market needed more space than the small market place could offer; or that the medieval market was traditionally held outside the town. Certainly John Sandilands, an indweller from Kelso, had been accustomed to sell food at the Weirhill market for the previous twenty years. On 1 August 1616, however, a group of men, including some from Melrose, 'insolently destroyed tua barrellis full of aill, with quheit breid and uther viveris...they strak and dang him doun undir thair feit...and brusit him with thair handis and feit', even though he was a cripple. Failure of proof, however, meant the case was dropped.[237]

Melrose also had the right to three fairs by 1660, at least. In 1695, a formal ratification of a fair on the second Tuesday of May, to last for two days, was approved by parliament.[238] Fairs are known to have been held on the Greenyards; but the traditional site of the Lammas, or Scare Thursday Fair (or Keir or Scarce Thursday Fair), was at the foot of the Eildon Hills, on the site of the present golf course.[239] If the fragment of the last will and testament of Gibbie Hatley of Gattonside, dated 1547, is to be believed, the Scare Thursday Fair was already in existence in his time.[240] It has, certainly, traditionally been accepted as an 'ancient' fair.[241]

The weights used at the market and fair were held in the tolbooth. It also functioned as the town gaol and as a meeting place for courts. When, for example, thieves and 'lymmars' (villains) called 'Egyptians' (often meaning 'gypsies') arrived at Gattonside, a justice court to deal with the problem was held in Melrose tolbooth.[242] The tolbooth stood in the High Street, and the building had a forestair. In 1682, there was some concern over security. On 4 March of that year, it was decided that the keys to the tolbooth should not be taken out of the town 'but left in some honest mans hands'. Nine days later, a new padlock was put on the door, although all knowledge of the taking away of the old lock was denied.[243] Two years later, however, there is evidence of a John Aitken being 'apprehended on suspicion of breaking Melrose tolbooth', which suggests that the security problem had not been solved.[244]

While the tolbooth and market cross were the most important secular buildings in the town, the parish church remained the religious focal point. By 1618, a decision had been made to form a parish church from the partial ruins of the old abbey. Architectural evidence suggests that the western archway of the crossing had already been blocked;[245] it was in the original abbatial aisle, or nave (as opposed to the lay brothers' aisle where the parish church originally functioned), that the new, barrel-vaulted, parish church was constructed. According to the *Old Statistical Account*, it was only around 1649 that the statues in the abbey were demolished.[246] It was estimated that there were some 2,000 communicants in the parish in 1634, from 1627 being under the pastoral care of John Knox's successor, Thomas Forrester, renowned for his anti-episcopalian views.[247] The interior of the church was modified on a number of occasions, in order to house the parishioners. On 12 March 1643, one Robert Pringall applied to build the first loft in the church (raised seats for the use of particular families or craftsmen);[248] and, from this time, a number of lofts were built in the church. On 30 October 1669, the weavers were given permission to build a loft 'providing they go no further then the north end of Thomas Lythgows loaft that no person be wronged yrby'. On 7 January 1683, 'the masons in Neusted desyred the priviledge of building a loft in the east end of the church'. Permission was granted.[249]

As well as the maintenance of these buildings, Melrose also had a school to look after. The original probably stood on the site of the present Station Hotel before being transferred to Little Fordell, on the west side of Abbey Street.[250] There was a schoolmaster by at least 1608; he was William Coke, who had 'bluid drawin' in an incident with one John Rogear. In 1617, Alexander Wishart was the master; and in 1623, Robert Brown.[251] It is clear that the public school, supported by the church and heritors, was to be the only school. Some time before February 1669 an unnamed woman attempted to set up a school; but the kirk session ruled that 'no woman school be for reading in the town of Melrose'. Later in the year, in a further attempt to prevent rival schools, it was enacted that 'no schules be kept in Melrose, Daneltione, Darnick and Newstead besides the publick schuile under pain of ten marks'.[252] A year later, a new school building was erected, with monies bequeathed by the bishop of Lismore and Argyll, David Fletcher, once minister at Melrose. This needed regular upkeep; in 1672, for example, 'ane sneck to the school door and oyr things needfull' were bought.[253] The Session seems to have been relatively diligent in its maintenance of the school and helping to support poor scholars. Some instances, however, suggest that occasionally funds were not readily forthcoming. In 1657, Mr James Strang, the schoolmaster, took out a decreet against all the elders of the parish of Melrose for their failure to collect the stent from their regions of the parish.[254] Some pupils boarded with the schoolmaster; they seem to have shared a bed. In March 1668, Patrick Lukup was paid for 'putting of a bed bottome to the common bed of the school'.[255] How many children boarded and how many walked to school is unclear. Certainly the school had a large catchment area, extending over Newton, Eildon, Newstead, Darnick, Bridgend, Gattonside, Westhouses, Appletreeleaves, Longhaugh, Threepwood, Newhouses, Blainslie and Danzeltoun, as well as over other properties in private hands, such as Old Melrose.[256]

The ford remained the main crossing point of the Tweed for most people. At some time, the Turf Ford was paved. This paving was not broken until the twentieth century, when Gattonside sewage pipes were inserted. The well in the square and its source of

38

supply also needed maintenance. The supply had been from an old well on the road to Bowden, but from *c* 1656, the source was the Marion Ker fountainhead in Dingleton. It was named after a widow who had a croft in that area of Danzeltoun.[257] The flood dykes, revealed after the scouring of December 1994 and the drought of the summer of 1995, may have been of medieval origin.[258] Originally an earth wall, it was referred to as 'the water wall in defence of the Annay'.[259] If their origin is of a medieval date, these, too, would have required a measure of upkeep.

Houses now lined the street which was once the main entrance into the precinct. It later became called 'The Bow', and then 'Abbey Street'. The street pattern remained otherwise little changed: major settlement was around the market place, stretching only short distances westwards along the road to Darnick, eastwards towards Newstead and southwards to Danzeltoun. One well-known house, with a date stone of 1635, was perhaps the most westerly building at this time. It stood, with gable projecting into the street, opposite the King's Arms. Sometimes called the West Port, it was a two-storeyed thatched house, built of rubble and harled on top. It was here that General Leslie stayed in 1645, on the night before the battle of Philiphaugh **figure 12**.[260] Two charters, contained in the Melrose Regality Records, define clearly typical burgage plots in the town. In 1556, John Clennan and his wife Agnes Watsoun were infeoffed of 'a tenement with pertinents before the front door of the monastery of Melrose, between the tenement of the deceased John Watson on the south and the tenement of John Lorimer on the north, having the High Street on the west and the garden of the monastery called the Prenteyse yairdis on the east, the said tenement containing twenty ells and twenty inches in length and seven ells seven inches in breadth'.[261] A Scots ell was approximately one fifth smaller than the English ell, which was a variable measurement, being the length of an arm. In tailoring terms it became accepted as one and a quarter yards. This ell used in Melrose was probably about a yard; so the plot was very approximately 61 feet 8 inches in length and 21 feet 7 inches in breadth. A plot of this size was needed because life in Melrose town was still essentially rural,[262] the backland of the plots being used for growing produce and rearing animals. It also housed the midden or cess-pit, and sometimes also a well. This rural nature was reinforced by the grant, along with the tenement, of 'an acre and half a rood of arable land lying in Quarelhill [*sic*] at the west side thereof and a garden outwith the walls of [the] monastery, with pasturage for two cows in the commonty of Danzeltoun and a horse in the green yaird and Weirhill'. When George Hall inherited, on the death of his uncle in 1573, a tenement 'before the front gate of the monastery' and on the south side of the High Street between the land of the deceased John Noitman on the west and the land of the deceased James Turnbull on the east and the lands of Quarrelhill on the south and the said High Street on the north, a further grant of agricultural land was also made. He received 'an acre of arable land of the Quarrelhill and pasture for two cows in the commonty of Danzeltoun and of a horse or heifer in the Green Yaird and Veirhill from 1st April yearly till harvest, and for the remainder of the year where the animals of the monastery were in use to pasture, with rights of peat etc'.[263] Such grants continued into the seventeenth century.[264] The Quarrelhill was the Quarry Hill, still extant, to the south of the by-pass.

Melrose was described in 1618 as 'tour fortalice and manor place containing and comprehending thainn the abbay place and monasterie of Melrose with the hous biggingis yairdis orcheardis doucawis and utheris lyand within the precinct and boundis thairof'.[265] When King Charles I (1625–49) *de novo* granted the lands, lordship and barony of Melrose to Thomas, earl of Haddington, Lord Binning and Byres, Melrose town was detailed as 'the monastery and precinct of Melrose' and 'thirty-one tenements and portions of land'.[266] These thirty-one tenements were not all necessarily occupied and are an indication of the smallness of the town. Using a multiplier of 4.5 per household, this would imply about 140 townspeople. The fact that proclamations from the market cross could be heard by all inhabitants is further evidence of how small it was.

In 1691, when assessments were made of parishes and burghs in order to raise a hearth tax, Melrose was calculated to have ninety-four hearths. Of these, however, the earl's house had ten hearths, indicating a very substantial property; the house of Langshaw and its various offices had twelve hearths; another two properties had five hearths; two properties, including that of the minister, Robert Wilson, had four; four properties had three hearths and four had two. This means that thirty-two properties had only one hearth. If one assumes 4.5 persons in each of the forty-six properties, this would suggest a population of only about 200. By comparison, Gattonside, which had no formal privileges as a burgh, had eighty-four hearths; but given that it did not have two such grand houses as the earl's house and the house of Langshaw, which accounted for twenty-two of Melroses's hearths, Gattonside was significantly larger than Melrose. Two properties here had four hearths, one had three and two had two hearths, which means that there were seventy-one properties altogether—and it was more than half the size again of Melrose. Darnick and Newstead were also relatively substantial settlements, with fifty-nine and sixty-four hearths respectively. In the case of Newstead, this accounted for fifty-seven properties, again making it a larger settlement than Melrose; and in the case of Darnick, forty-four properties. Darnick was, therefore, much the same size as Melrose and, like Melrose, also had some substantial properties, one with eight hearths and two with five, one of these two tower houses surviving to this day. Danzeltoun, however, had only eleven hearths, which were in ten properties.[267]

The town of Melrose occupied only a fraction of a large parish which amounted to thirty-six square miles in area. Yet a series of seventeenth-century indicators of the income, wealth and assessments for taxation of Melrose and the surrounding hinterland clearly indicate that it was not a wealthy town dominating lesser settlements around it. A petition of 1622, raised by Thomas, earl of Melrose, in an attempt to force payments due to him also gives an insight into the standing of Melrose compared with its neighbours. The feuars of the town and lands of Melrose and within the abbey were liable to pay £8; the feuars of Darnick and Bridgend, £8; likewise the feuars of Gattonside and Westhouses; and the feuars of Newstead were also rated at £8.[268] According to the valuation of the parish in 1643, the feu duty of the 'wairds and acres' of Melrose were assessed at £40, with Little Fordell and the precinct at £100. The feu and tack duty of Newstead was £411 0s 4d, and the feu duty of Gattonside and Westhouses was a staggering £1404 13s 4d.[270] By 1707, the parish valuation was £20,185 4s 6d, of which Newstead accounted for £742, whereas Melrose was a mere £426.[270]

The records indicate that there were poor people to be maintained throughout the parish. Regular payments were made by the Kirk Session. In 1679, for example, ten shillings were given to the poor fatherless children of Gattonside and eight shillings to those in Melrose.[271] Four years later, sixteen shillings were donated to 'a woman in philiphaugh whose nails wirs as bird claws'.[272] On 5 December 1690, a list of the registered poor was drawn up, nineteen in all—twelve came from Melrose, two from Gattonside, one from Westhouses, one from Eildon, two from Darnick and one from Langhaugh.[273] The purpose of the list was to ensure that only the poor of their own parish were being maintained, not 'vagrant and sturdie' beggars from elsewhere. The last seven years of the seventeenth century were ones of foul weather and ruined harvests. By 1699, there were sixty-one names on the official list of the destitute; and in the following year measures were taken to carry away outsider cripples to the next parish, at a cost of 1s 6d each. The Register of Disbursements, however, shows that a wide variety of aid was given between 1690 and 1702—grants included a book and paper to a cripple in Darnick; help towards the payment of a 'chirurgeon for mending a poor thing's leg'; and 'cloathes for the poor daft lad in Ladhopemuir'.[274]

Poverty, however, could be exacerbated by external factors. On occasions, troops were billeted in the town; on 13 April 1651, for example, the Kirk Session records refer to the quartering of English soldiers in the town.[275] In November 1678, one division of Lord James Douglas' regiment was quartered in Melrose. It was recommended that the townspeople allow some 'trust' [credit] to the soldiers until their pay arrived—probably not a very popular recommendation with the inhabitants. In the following January, however, it was agreed that the soldiers' accounts would be settled by the king's commissioners before the regiment was disbanded.[276]

Another visitor, perhaps equally feared, was the plague. In the summer of 1636, plague hit the borders of England and threatened Scotland. In an effort to contain it, all markets and fairs in Duns, Kelso, Selkirk, Hawick, Coldstream, along with Melrose and others were expressly forbidden. The following year in May, they were again abandoned, but by June, Ancrum, Spittal and other neighbouring areas were affected. Throughout that summer various acts restricted movement in the Borders. Jedburgh and Crailinghall were hit in January 1638; and, by March, legislation specifically laid down that no one was to pass to the border with England.[277] Ten years later, in October 1648, there were no collections of kirk money, for fear of the plague; from 21 January to 2 March 1649, the Session did not meet for the same reason; and by 25 March no collections had been made since the plague began.[278] Disruptions to regular town life and loss of the market meant hardship.

The records indicate that a number of trades were being pursued by the townspeople. These, too, would have been damaged by the enforced lack of movement. The weavers were the most highly organised, receiving their seal of cause from the earl of Haddington in 1668. As an incorporated body, they were then entitled to control quality within their craft, lay down rules over training of apprentices, appoint their own officers and raise funds for their own welfare.[279] Those who were involved in the supply of food included millers, fleshers, fishermen, brewers, vintners, bee keepers and inn keepers. Masons, wrights, carpenters, boxmakers, tailors, cordiners [shoemakers] and calsay men [pavement makers] are all referred to in the contemporary records. Merchants and notaries were an important element in society, as was the town herd, the town clerk, the schoolmaster, the town piper and the town jailor. A number of the inhabitants worked as servants to the larger houses; and Melrose had its ubiquitous quota of prostitutes.

eighteenth-century Melrose

Melrose moved into the eighteenth century as a small market town, supporting a modest level of manufacturing. It still held its Saturday market, although it was said in 1743 that it 'was not much frequented'. There were also four fairs, at Martinmas, Lammas, on the last Wednesday in May and on the Thursday before Easter.[280]

Although there were a few writers to the signet in the town and a few merchants by the end of the century, the majority of the occupants still pursued humbler occupations, as in the previous century.[281] One interesting outlet was carrying on 'searching for coalls in Darnick', but the records give no indication whether this was successful. In all probability it was not, as in 1733 the minister announced that there would be a house collection 'to encourage the search for coal'.[282] Candle-making was also under way in the town, and Melrose was one of the four centres engaged in the industry in Roxburghshire. In the 1790s, the town was paying an annual excise in the region of £12 to £13. When this is compared with Hawick's £32, Jedburgh's £58 and Kelso's £186, it is obvious that this was not a thriving industry.[283] There had also, by the middle of the century, been some immigration of workers from Galashiels, bringing their manufacturing skills. These were mainly Anabaptists, who swelled the ranks of the 350 Burghers, Antiburghers, Relief Church members and Methodists.[284] The greatest proportion of the population, however, still attended the established church, even though there was some upset in the town in 1785, when the minister, Frederick MacLagan, was charged with debts to the Kirk Session,[285] as well as adultery.[286] Three years later, perhaps in consequence, it was the schoolmaster, not the minister, who was asked to give some thought to a Sabbath school, which was, indeed, opened. There had also been a suggestion that there should be a 'school of industry for young indigent girls by spinning'. Whether this was ever opened is unclear; as is how long either of these two schools functioned.[287]

The town's weavers, for a while, brought considerable renown to Melrose, exporting linen as far afield as London and abroad. In 1755, 33,282.5 yards were manufactured, at a revenue of £2,575 10s 11.25d. Ten years later, however, only 32,300.625 yards were produced, for £2,495 14s 9.25d. In 1774, the output had dropped further, to 20,789.75 yards, at an income of £2,051 16s 7.25d; and in 1784 a mere 17,792 yards was woven, bringing in only £1,845 12s 4d. There were fears that the town would lose 'its name and business'; the decline was blamed on the promotion of woollen manufacturing, at the expense of linen. Nearby Galashiels had invested a considerable sum in plant and machinery for wool manufacture, which was drawing away customers from Melrose. Women were, moreover, paid more highly in the woollen industry. The linen manufacturers could not compete, and thus the workforce was declining as well; once work was undertaken in the woollen industry, it was claimed, hands were spoiled for linen. Added to this, the price of Dutch flax had risen beyond the means of the Melrose manufacturers.[288]

In spite of the competition from Galashiels, Melrose was initially able to hold its own in the woollen industry. By 1776, there were 140 looms in Melrose, compared with forty at Galashiels. It has been argued that all of Melrose's looms were for woollen goods.[289] It seems, however, that an interest in linen must have continued to some extent in the town; in 1778 Selkirk was refused a linen stamper as linen was sold only at two fairs and both of these were attended by the Melrose stamper.[290]

It was also maintained by the 1790s that the bleachfield, an essential for the linen industry, which was on the west side of Weirhill, was decaying through lack of water in the dry seasons and its ancillary buildings were in a state of disrepair.[291] The bleachfield had been established in 1748 by the minister, James Brown, and he had done much to encourage the linen industry.[292] In the latter years of the century, however the bleachfield once more came into its own. In 1787, for example, 715 pieces of cloth were bleached; in 1789, 2,917; and in 1791, 1,232. The introduction of cotton looms was a further boost to the town's economy,[293] and Melrose, like many other towns, was to witness a rapid conversion to the cotton industry.[294] How far child labour was utilised in Melrose's mills is unclear. In 1797, after an inspection of the Lanark cotton mills, the minister offered this 'humane information', that children of nine years and over might profitably be employed in the mills. It seems that three years later, parents were put under some pressure to 'get some children put up, in particular those of nine years or older'; but the records do not indicate the success of this project.[295]

The small prosperity that this brought prompted the assessment at the end of the eighteenth century that the townspeople were better fed and clothed than ever before; and that, although consumption and rheumatism were prelavent in the 'lower classes', due to the coldness of the winters, most people were healthier, as a result of the introduction of inoculations and improvements to drains.[296] In order further to alleviate their condition, in

1790 the townspeople established a Friendly Society, to which an annual subscription was made as insurance against ill fortune resulting from sickness and death. The whole community benefited also from agricultural improvements; from the levelling of old rigs and the enclosing and draining of land, as well as the introduction of new farming techniques and crops. The initiative of three Melrose lawyers brought Melrose to the forefront in this process, with the consolidation and enclosure of the Annay, Weirhill and other erstwhile run-rig lands.[297] Analysis of the Valuation Books of the County of Roxburgh for 1788, however, indicates that Melrose and its environs remained a relatively modest settlement. The feuars, as opposed to the householders, of Melrose were assessed at £426, compared with £89 5s for Bridgend. Darnick, however, was assessed at £522; Gattonside and Westhouses at £600; and Newstead at £642.[298]

There was no change in the town plan in this century. The main thoroughfare passed from east to west, with cottages near to the East Port, by at least the middle of the century. The West Port (*see* p 38) still defined the western limit of the town. Houses remained small, usually of only one or two storeys, with thatched roofs. There was a certain dilapidation of some properties in the early decades. In 1720, for example, the elders of the town met to discuss the weavers' houses which were 'fallen down'.[299] These were of the smaller type of houses in the town, being single storeyed of harled rubble and thatched. There were two rooms, one each side of the central entrance, and one of these housed the loom. Loft accommodation above provided extra sleeping accommodation and storage space.[300] There is evidence of some improvements in the townscape during this century. The sundial built in 1762 onto the window sill of a house near the East Port, which could be viewed only by those inside, is evidence of a level of sophistication in some dwellings.[301] In 1791, the joint oldest lodge of Freemasons moved from Newstead to Melrose.[302] Two buildings remained in Abbey Street—Abbey House (still standing; *see* p 98) and, until the 1950s, *no* 12, the town's first post office. They were indicative of the new, albeit modest, improved middle-class housing of the later eighteenth century and of a growing prosperity.

The school proved more of a problem. By 1704, the schoolhouse was in need of repair and 'like to fall'.[303] The following year, on learning that the costs would be £364 Scots, plans to add a new upstairs and a chimney were dropped. Repairs were still needed in 1710 and two years later the heritors decided 'to set up the roof and to cover it sufficiently with thatch and divots'.[304] By 1713, further measures had to be taken to make the school habitable;[305] and a collection was made throughout the parish the following year. By 1723, a decision was made to finance major refurbishment of the school; and, a year later, it was agreed to supply 'two sufficient floors, put in windows, timber and glass, two stairs within the house and partitions needful with doors, to make up the chimney, to convert the door designed for a stair without to a window, lay hearthstones, cast the house within and without with lime and to plaster the windows of the said schoolhouse, to cleanse the grounds of it, to lath and thatch the roof'. In spite of these efforts, by 1763 the school was again in need of repair, so a collection was made to repair the session house and convert it into a school. Soon after this a chapel in the south aisle was converted into a public school;[306] but by the end of the eighteenth century, there were eighty scholars at the school and the master had a house and garden at its old site.[307]

The overall impression, however, is of a small town, dominated by the ruins of the abbey. When Daniel Defoe visited in 1724, his main interest was in 'the ruins of the once famous abbey of Melrose'.[308] Heron, in 1799, noted merely 'the magnificent remains of Melrose Abbey, the finest of any in Scotland'.[309] Robert Burns, visiting in 1787, commented on 'that far-famed glorious ruin'.[310] It is also clear that, even for local people, there was an increasing awareness of the need to maintain their parish church and provide for adequate light. The building of lofts was blocking light, and agreements were made that extra windows should be broken into the church walls.[311] It seems, however, that good intentions did not materialise fully into actions. In 1776, a visitor to Melrose wrote of his impressions on entering the parish church:

*On opening the doors it is not to be expressed the disagreeable scene which
presented itself; this place is filled with lofts in the disposition of which
irregularity alone seems to have been studied; some are raised on upright beams
as scaffolds, tier above tier, others supported against the walls and pillars, no
two are alike in form, height or magnitude; the same confusion of little and
great, high and low, covers the floor with pews; the lights are so obstructed that
the place is as dark as a vault; the floor is nothing but the damp earth;
nastiness and irregularity possess the whole scene. The fine workmanship of
the pillars whose capitals for flowers and foliage exceed all the rest of the
building; the ribs of the arches and ornament of their intersections are scarce
to be seen in the horrid gloom which possesses the place. What idea
concomitant to religion can dictate filthiness and confusion in a house of
worship, I know not...Many of the old churches of Scotland I have seen
filthy and foul...but for uncleanliness this place exceeds them all.*[312]

postscript—'fair Melrose'

The concern for the state of the abbey and parish church was one of the first signs that
growing prosperity was to encourage a new approach to the townscape. At the beginning
of the new century, a report on the 'sufficiency or insufficiency' of the fabric of the parish
church highlighted its dilapidated state. Numerous repairs were essential; but it was
suggested that 'if instead of...repairs the heritors think proper to build a new church we
are of the opinion that the whole of the modern church in filling up arched windows, the
pillars in the inside supporting the arch over the church, the arch itself and the buttresses
placed against the pillars of the east end (all modern) may be taken away with perfect
safety and thereby the old ruin will be restored to its former elegance and grandeur'.[313]
The heritors adopted this last option and in 1810 the congregation transferred to the new
parish church on Weirhill. All that now remains of this new parish church is the tower
that abuts the south side of the twentieth-century church (*see* p 100).

Equally important for the town was the restoration work on the abbey, begun in 1822
under the supervision of Sir Walter Scott, with the advice of his builder, John Smith of
Darnick. When Dorothy Wordsworth visited in 1803 she commented that the abbey ruins
were 'unfortunately...surrounded by insignificant houses'.[314] These were the remnants of
the dwellings that had begun to line Abbey Street from the sixteenth century onwards.
The Abbey Hotel **figure 21** also stood within the precincts, to the right of the entrance to
the abbey. Most of these were cleared by the twentieth century, enhancing the setting of
the abbey ruins.

The writings of Scott also added to the interest of the town, and Melrose soon became
a major tourist attraction in the Borders. Visitors were assisted by the new turnpike road
system and the fact that Melrose was on the main stagecoach route between Edinburgh
and Jedburgh. A daily stage left in each direction from the George Inn (now the George
and Abbotsford Hotel), departing for Edinburgh at 9.30 am and for Jedburgh at 2 pm.[315]
In 1826, the toll house was built at the East Port, for the collection of dues **figure 13**. A
nineteenth-century painting shows the roadway barred by a gate, which would be opened
on payment of toll for the use of the road.[316]

In the same year the Chain Bridge **figure 14** was built by Redpath, Brown & Co,
physically connecting Melrose and Gattonside, the two settlements that had been
intimately linked for centuries. Payment had to be made here, as well; consequently and
not surprisingly, the ford continued to be used, with a box of stilts at each side of the river,
to assist pedestrians. Even until about 1929, the refuse cart trundled over it through the
water.[317]

The town was to become even more accessible in 1849, with the arrival of the railway.
The station, the platform of which is still to be seen lining the newly constructed by-pass
road, had been constructed over the previous two years **figure 15**. According to an account
of 1861, 'a considerable street known as Dingleton Wynd occupied the situation...covered

44

figure 13
Toll house, East Port.
Photograph 1970s

figure 14
Chain Bridge
before rebuilding

figure 15
View of Melrose,
showing the 1849
railway line and
station. *Painting
probably dating to the
1850s, artist unknown*

figure 16

Fastern's E'en ba' festivities—the last game of handball played in Melrose. *Photographed by J Brown on 26th February 1901*

by the railway station'. Its clearance, along with that of the east side of Abbey Street, 'compelled many inhabitants to resort to the neighbouring villages'.[318] In spite of this, the town was growing. John Mason, visiting in 1826, noted that the town had about 500 inhabitants and that the houses were 'in general good…and more…have lately risen or are now rising'.[319] By 1845, there was a population of 689;[320] by 1851, 964 and by 1861, 1141. An assessment in this last year was that 'the town [had] witnessed an influx of the middle and higher classes, with a diminution of the poorer and industrious ones'.[321] Whatever the truth of a lessening of industriousness in the town, there was still time for the annual 'Fastern's E'en Ba'' festivities **figure 16**. The windows of houses were barricaded, shops put up their shutters and at one o'clock the ball was thrown up at the market cross and 'football-playing on a most indiscriminate and unlimited scale [was] the order of the day'.[322]

Harmony Hall, a Regency dwelling of three storeys, is one of the many comfortable villas erected in the town to accommodate the growing number of substantial families. Built in 1807, it was named after the Jamaican plantation of the owner, Robert Waugh. The manse, built in 1813 to a design of John Smith, Abbey Park, constructed *c* 1820, with its classical stable block, and Prior Bank were, along with Harmony Hall, all sited within the old abbey precinct. Smaller residences, such as Rosebank in Dingleton Road, built in 1814 to a design of John Smith for James Curle, the Baron Bailie Depute, also appeared; and the many detached and semi-detached villas that spread westwards up High Cross Street are standing reminders of the popularity of the town as a place of residence **figure 17**. Perhaps most renowned, approximately two miles west of the town, the farm called Cartleyhole was purchased by Sir Walter Scott in 1811; this he converted into a substantial residence, Abbotsford.

There were other tangible signs of increasing comfort. In 1813 x 1814, a private venture led to an improvement to the water supply to the town, with water fed from the south of Gallows Hill to the Pant Well in the market square **figure 18**.[323] By the middle of the century, it was sufficiently out of repair that there was a great loss of water through leakage. As a result, the Water Company shut the well, opening it only at stated hours in the morning and evening. As might be expected, this occasioned 'a good deal of dissatisfaction'.[324] Within less than a month, more than £12 had been subscribed for the erection of a new well, although the collectors were instructed to 'wait upon those who had not yet contributed'.[325] In October of that year a new 'public desideratum' was in

46

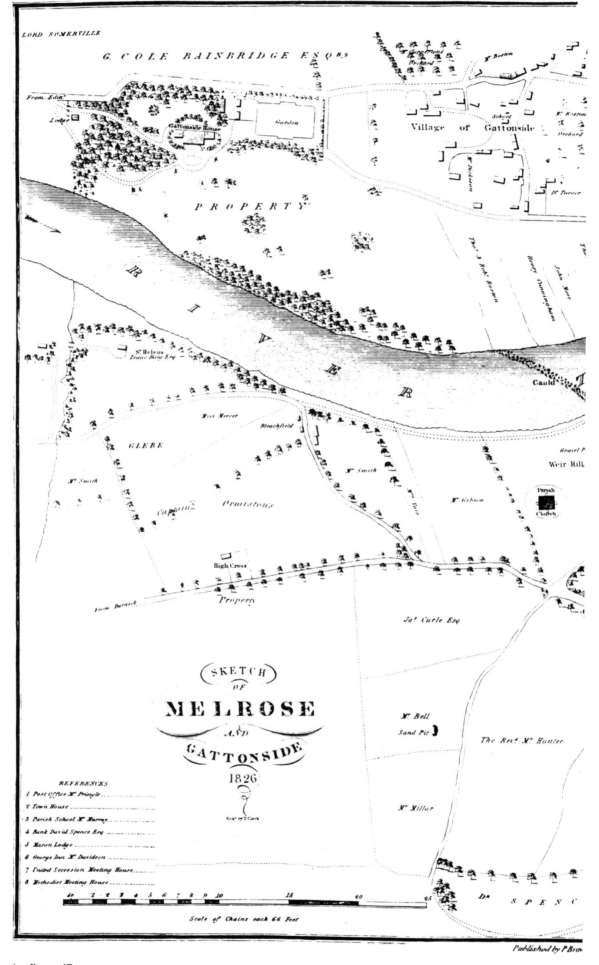

figure 17
John Wood's plan of Melrose and Gattonside
1826

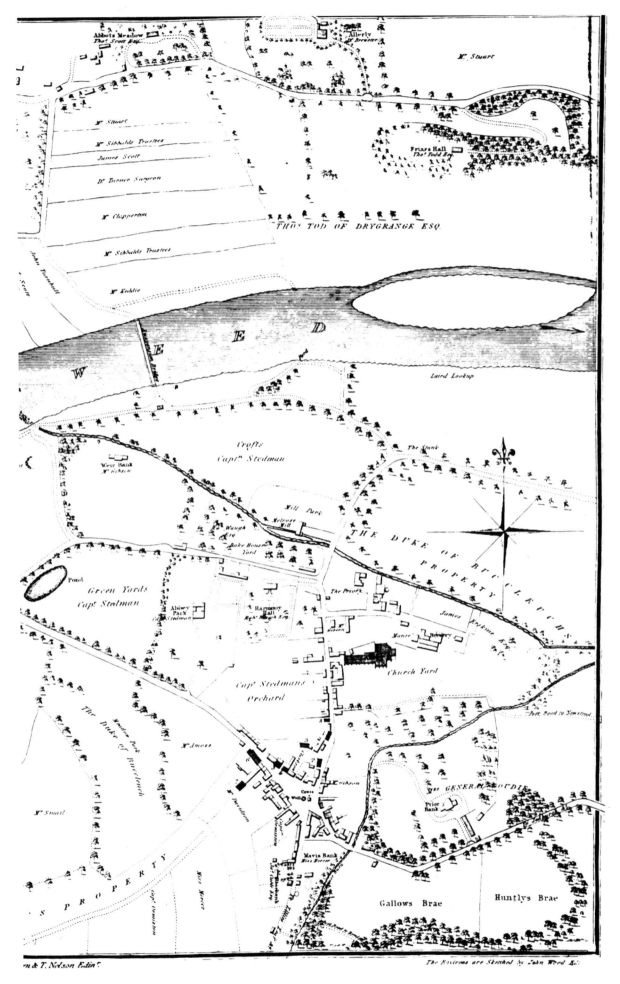

48

figure 18

The Market Square,
with cross and
Pant Well. *Painting by
Thomas H Shepherd,
1830*

place. It was deemed to be 'of handsome and massive proportions, standing fully five feet high, upon a square iron base, with a stone foundation'. With 'four stern and masculine countenances, with open mouths [on the] upper part of the fountain [and] elegant mouldings...down the sides', it had a drinking trough with cup attached by a chain to the north and a water jet to the south. The *Border Advertiser* reporter felt that this 'elegant fountain' would 'form no inconsiderable addition to the many attractions which 'fair Melrose' presents to the tourist and visitor'.[326] Although both of these water supplies were replaced, they are familiar sights in a number of contemporary illustrations. They both stood close to the market cross, which, according to these same illustrations and from John Wood's map of 1826 **figure 17**, had probably been moved from its original site right outside the abbey gates some time earlier. The market cross then stood on an octagonal stepped base supporting an octagonal shaft. In 1822, the superior of the town and parish, the duke of Buccleuch, whose family had acquired the barony from the earls of Haddington, contracted John Smith to build a new Town House in Abbey Street. This still remains, largely in its original state (*see* p 100).

The century would see the arrival of banks, an enlarged school with seventy to eighty scholars and a subscription library.[327] By 1886, there were six hotels[328] and about thirty inns (*see* pp 98–9),[329] which catered not only for sight-seeing visitors, but also for those who came to the town's three fairs and, by 1861, its 'capital weekly market' held on Mondays for the sale of stock and grain at its corn exchange.[330] Melrose had established itself in the role that it fulfils to this day—as a town that attracts visitors not only to its abbey and its splendid setting at the foot of the Eildon Hills, but also to its Greenyards, once the common green for the townspeople, and now the home of Melrose rugby.

notes

1 For an archaeological survey of the prehistory of the Borders, *see* S Halliday, 'The Borders in prehistory', in Omand (ed), *Borders Book*, 23.

2 C Wickham-Jones, *Scotland's First Settlers* (London, 1994), 62–4.

3 Halliday, 'The Borders', 25.

4 G Ritchie & A Ritchie, *Scotland: Archaeology and Early History* (Edinburgh, 1991), 43.

5 Halliday, 'The Borders', 26.

6 T Darvill, *Prehistoric Britain* (London, 1987), 63–4.

7 R Feachem, *Guide to Prehistoric Scotland* (London, 1977), 42, 58.

8 Halliday, 'The Borders', 24.

9 Darvill, *Prehistoric Britain*, 75.

10 For a survey of stone circles in Britain and of regional types, *see* A Burl, *The Stone Circles of the British Isles* (London, 1976).

11 Ritchie & Ritchie, *Scotland*, 81.

12 Halliday, 'The Borders', 30.

13 Ritchie & Ritchie, *Scotland*, 86.

14 Halliday, 'The Borders', 30–31.

15 Darvill, *Prehistoric Britain*, 103.

16 *Ibid*, 133.

17 For a full account of the excavations, *see* O A Owen, 'Eildon Hill North, Roxburgh, Borders', in J S Rideout, O A Owen & E Halpin, *Hillforts of Southern Scotland* (Edinburgh, 1992), 21–71.

18 Ritchie & Ritchie, *Scotland*, 94.

19 Halliday, 'The Borders', 32.

20 *See* J C Mann & D J Breeze, 'Ptolemy, Tacitus and the tribes of north Britain', *PSAS* cxvii (1987), 85–91.

21 W S Hanson & G Maxwell, *Rome's North West Frontier: The Antonine Wall* (Edinburgh, 1983), 33.

22 *Ibid*, 33–4.

23 *Ibid*, 39.

24 L Keppie, *Scotland's Roman Remains* (Edinburgh, 1986), 8.

25 *Ibid*, 11.

26 Hanson & Maxwell, *Antonine Wall*, 43.

27 *Ibid*, 16.

28 *Ibid*, 18.

29 L Keppie, 'The Romans', in Omand (ed), *Borders Book*, 45.

30 An account of the excavations was published as J Curle, *A Roman Frontier Post and its People: the Fort of Newstead in the Parish of Melrose* (Glasgow, 1911).

31 The results of this second phase of work were published as I A Richmond, 'Excavations at the Roman fort of Newstead, 1947', *PSAS*, lxxxiv (1949–50), 1–37.

32 For an interim report of this work, *see* R Jones *et al*, 'The Newstead Project', University of Bradford, Archaeological Sciences 5th Annual Report (1990–1).

33 Ritchie & Ritchie, *Scotland*, 135–8.

34 W S Hanson, *Agricola and the Conquest of the North* (London, 1987), 97.

35 G S Maxwell, *The Romans in Scotland* (Edinburgh, 1989), 90–91.

36 Keppie, 'The Romans', 50.

37 Maxwell, *The Romans in Scotland*, 179.

38 Keppie, 'The Romans', 50–1.

39 *Ibid*, 51.

40 R Jones *et al*, 'The Newstead Project'.

41 Ritchie and Ritchie, *Scotland*, 151.

42 C Thomas, *The Early Christian Archaeology of North Britain* (Oxford, 1971), 35.

43 A P Smyth, *Warlords and Holymen: Scotland AD 80–1000* (Edinburgh, 1984), 118–9.

44 *Ibid*.

45 J R Baldwin, *Exploring Scotland's Heritage: Lothian and the Borders* (Edinburgh, 1997), 16–17.

46 W F H Nicolaisen, *Scottish Place-Names: their study and significance* (London, 1976), 71–6.

47 Nicolaisen, *Scottish Place-Names*, 73–83.

48 D Perry *et al*, 'Excavations at Castle Park, Dunbar: 1988–90' (SUAT unpublished site report, forthcoming); and A Smith, 'Neolithic, Bronze Age and Early Historic Features near Ratho, Edinburgh', *PSAS* 125, 115–7.

49 C Morris, 'The early historic period' in Omand (ed), *Borders Book*, 54–5.

50 *Ibid*, 59.

51 W J Watson, *History of the Celtic Place-Names of Scotland* (Edinburgh, 1926), 496. Nicolaisen, *Scottish Place-Names*, 6, suggests, rather, 'bare moor'.

52 Smyth, *Warlords and Holy Men*, 33.

53 *Bede's Ecclesiastical History of the English People*, edd B Colgrave & R A B Mynors (Oxford, 1969), 430–1.

54 W Croft Dickinson, *Scotland From the Earliest Times to 1603*, 3rd ed, ed A A M Duncan (London, 1977), 40.

55 *Bede's Ecclesiastical History*, edd Colgrave & Mynors, 433.

56 C Innes *et al* (edd), *Origines Parochiales Scotiae*, 2 vols (Bannatyne Club, 1850–5) i, 280.

57 RCAHMS, NMRS NT 53 SE 21.

58 Ritchie & Ritchie, *Scotland*, 146–7.

59 P Hill, *Whithorn and St Ninian: the excavation of a monastic town* (Stroud, 1997), 26–40.

60 *NSA*, iii, 58.

61 We have benefited from discussions with Mr T Little on this point.

62 F Groome, *Ordnance Gazetteer of Scotland*, 6 vols, (Edinburgh, 1885), v, 21.

63 Cowan, I B & Easson, D E, *Medieval Religious Houses: Scotland* (London, 1976), 51.

50

64 W E Kapelle, *The Norman Conquest of the North: the Region and its Transformation, 1000–1135* (London, 1979), 267.

65 R L G Ritchie, *The Normans in Scotland* (Edinburgh, 1954), 45.

66 *The Chronicle of Melrose*, ed J Stephenson (Felinfach, 1988), 96.

67 J A Wade, *History of St Mary's Abbey, Melrose* (Edinburgh, 1861), 95.

68 Groome, *Gazetteer*, v, 21.

69 A Lawrie (ed), *Early Scottish Charters, Prior to 1153* (Glasgow, 1905), 79; A A M Duncan, *Scotland: The Making of the Kingdom* (Edinburgh, 1989), 146.

70 A local tradition is that there were too many midges at Old Melrose.

71 We have benfited from discussions with Dr W Lonie on this point.

72 *SRRM*, iii, 387.

73 Ritchie, *Normans*, 41.

74 We have benefited from Dr W Lonie's views on this.

75 J Gilbert, 'The monastic record of a Border landscape, 1136–1236', *Scottish Geographical Magazine*, ix (1983), 12.

76 *Ibid*, 4–7.

77 *Chronicle of Melrose*, 33.

78 We have benefited from discussions with Mrs Muriel Hood on this point.

79 S Cruden, *Scottish Medieval Churches* (Edinburgh, 1986), 67.

80 *Inventory of the Ancient and Historical Monuments of Roxburghshire* (RCAHMS, 1954), 265.

81 *Chronicle of Melrose*, 7.

82 Cowan & Easson, *Religious Houses*, 76.

83 J C Atkinson (ed), *Cartularium Abbathiae de Rievalle* (Surtees Society, 1889), 455. Cf Lynch, *Scotland: A New History* (London, 1991), 206).

84 The results of these excavations have never been published, but the primary records, drawings and correspondence can be viewed at West Register House, Charlotte Square, Edinburgh.

85 A description of the first church can be found in J S Richardson & M Wood, *Melrose Abbey* (Edinburgh, 1949), which has been updated by Historic Scotland with new illustrations and reconstructions; *see* Tabraham, C, *Melrose Abbey* (Historic Scotland, 1995).

86 The remains of tiled floors at Melrose are one of only two examples left in Scotland, the other being Glenluce, Galloway. For an account of these, *see PSAS*, lxiii (1928–9), 282–310.

87 Tabraham, *Melrose Abbey*, 14–17.

88 According to the 'Melrose Rental', the abbey had two mills, as well as Langschaws mill and Newton mill (Innes, *Origines Parochiales*, i, 286). Only one is definitely known to have stood within the precinct, although a fulling mill may also have stood within the precinct.

89 *Chronicle of Melrose*, 94.

90 We are indebted to Mr A Crawford, the late Mrs P Maxwell-Scott and Miss J Maxwell-Scott for their views.

91 *Chronicle of Melrose*, 11, 16, 17, 18, 22, 23, 26, 30.

92 *Ibid*, 331; Duncan, *Scotland*, 417.

93 *Chronicle of Melrose*, 38, 46, 61.

94 *Ibid*, 102.

95 G W S Barrow, *Robert Bruce and the Community of the Realm of Scotland* (Edinburgh, 1976), 134.

96 We have benefited from discussion with Mrs Muriel Hood on this point.

97 *ER*, v, 369.

98 *RRS*, i, 157, 195.

99 *RRS*, ii, 188, 189, 311.

100 W B Stevenson, 'The monastic presence: Berwick in the twelfth and thirteenth centuries', in M Lynch, M Spearman & G Stell (edd), *The Scottish Medieval Town* (Edinburgh, 1988), 100.

101 *Acts of the Lords of Council in Civil Causes*, edd G Neilson & H Paton (Edinburgh, 1918), ii, 212.

102 *RRS*, ii, 274; *Chronicle of Melrose*, 20.

103 *Chronicle of Melrose*, 23.

104 Duncan, *Scotland*, 364.

105 *Ibid*, 459.

106 J Gilbert, *Hunting and Hunting Reserves in Scotland* (Edinburgh, 1979), 236.

107 Duncan, *Scotland*, 149, 180, 381.

108 *Acts of the Lords Auditors of Causes and Complaints*, ed unknown (London 1839), 45.

109 G Stell, 'Urban Buildings', in Lynch, Spearman & Stell, *Medieval Town*, 61.

110 *RMS*, ii, no 142; iv, no 1819; vii, no 149, no 1915; viii, 127; ix, no 64.

111 *RRS*, ii, 238.

112 Stevenson, 'Monastic presence', 109.

113 *CDS*, i, 33, 40, 70, 71.

114 *CDS*, i, 156, 162, 198.

115 Stevenson, 'Monastic presence', 110.

116 Duncan, *Scotland*, 429.

117 *Ibid*, 424, 429.

118 A Grant, *Independence and Nationhood: Scotland 1306–1429* (London, 1984), 62.

119 *Ibid*, 80.

120 *Selections from the Records of the Regality of Melrose*, 3 vols, ed C S Romanes (SHS, 1914–17), i, p. xliv.

121 *ER, passim*; eg *ER*, v, 32.

122 Duncan, *Scotland*, 457. We have benefited from discussions with Mrs Muriel Hood on this dating.

123 *RRS*, ii, 359.

124 *RRS*, ii, 103.

125 Groome, *Gazetteer*, v, 23.

126 *Chronicle of Melrose*, 92.

127 *RRS*, vi, 522.

128 *The Scalacronica of Thomas Gray*, trans. H Maxwell (Glasgow, 1907), 260, 299.

129 M Brown, *James I* (Edinburgh, 1994), 52, 134–5.

130 *ER*, xi, 32, 234, 260.

131 A H Dunbar, *Scottish Kings* (Edinburgh, 1906), 91.

132 Groome, *Gazetteer*, v, 25.

133 We are grateful to Mr T Little for this information.

134 Groome, *Gazetteer*, v, 26.

135 E P Dennison & R Coleman, *Historic Coupar Angus* (SBS, 1997).

136 *Scalacronica*, trans. H Maxwell, 4. We have benefited from discussions with Mrs Muriel Hood on this point.

137 J A Wade, *History of St Mary's Abbey*, (Edinburgh 1861), 136.

138 We are grateful to Mr T Little for this information.

139 *Chronicle of Melrose*, 53.

140 G Chalmers, *Caledonia* (Paisley, 1887), iv, 826; vii, 192.

141 *Chronicle of Melrose*, 48.

142 G W S Barrow, *Scotland and its Neighbours in the Middle Ages* (London, 1992), 32.

143 *CDS*, ii, 106, 130, 131.

144 Groome, *Gazetteer*, v, 23.

145 *CDS*, ii, 175.

146 *CDS*, ii, 187.

147 Groome, *Gazetteer*, v, 23.

148 *CDS*, ii, 271.

149 *CDS*, ii, 445, 457.

150 *CDS*, iii, 5.

151 *CDS*, iii, 39.

152 *CDS*, iii, 93.

153 Groome, *Gazetteer*, v, 23.

154 *RRS*, v, 547, 565.

155 *RRS*, v, 154.

156 *CDS*, iii, 173.

157 Groome, *Gazetteer*, v, 23–4.

158 *RRS*, vi, 191, 202. *See also* A A M Duncan, 'The *Acta* of Robert I', *SHR*, xxxii (1953), 20.

159 *RRS*, vi, 248, 255, 267, 282.

160 Groome, *Gazetteer*, v, 24.

161 Duncan, '*Acta*', 21.

162 J H Dawson, *The Abridged Statistical History of Scotland* (Edinburgh, 1855), 958, argues the event took place in 1384.

163 Groome, *Gazetteer*, v, 24.

164 Richardson & Wood, *Melrose Abbey*, 29.

165 *Ibid*, 30.

166 Cruden, *Medieval Churches*, 167.

167 *SRRM*, ii, p. vii.

168 Brown, *James I*, 40, 52, 53, 135, for example.

169 J Curle, *A Little Book About Melrose* (Edinburgh, 1936), 1–22. We are indebted to Mrs B Linehan for the loan of Dr Curle's (her father's) personal copy of this book.

170 Curle, *Little Book*, 12.

171 *Liber Sancte Marie de Melros*, 2 vols, ed C Innes (Bannatyne Club, 1837), i, 505, no 516.

172 Cowan & Easson, *Religious Houses*, 76.

173 *TA*, ii, 346.

174 *TA*, ii, 470.

175 *TA*, i & ii, *passim*.

176 P Hume Brown (ed), *Letters of James IV* (SHS, 1953), 64, 65.

177 R K Hannay (ed), *Acts of Lords of Council in Public Affairs, 1501–54* (Edinburgh, 1932), 18.

178 Dunbar, *Scottish Kings*, 229.

179 *TA*, vi, 145.

180 *TA*, vi, 228.

181 *ALCPA*, 491.

182 Richardson & Wood, *Melrose Abbey*, 32.

183 We are grateful to Mrs Muriel Hood for this information.

184 Cowan & Easson, *Religious Houses*, 76.

185 *Hamilton Papers*, 2 vols, ed J Bain (Edinburgh, 1890), i, 344.

186 *Ibid*, ii, 569.

187 *Ibid*, ii, 454, 457, 464.

188 D Laing, 'A contemporary account of the earl of Hertford's second expedition to Scotland and of the ravages committed by the English forces in September 1545', *PSAS*, i (1851–4), 277.

189 *TA*, ix, 312.

190 M Lynch, *Scotland: A New History* (London, 1991), 206.

191 SRO, GD 32/2/2 Elibank Papers, 20 July 1549.

192 Richardson & Wood, *Melrose Abbey*, 34.

193 *ALCPA*, lvi.

194 *Laing Charters, 854–1837*, ed J Anderson (Edinburgh, 1899), 167, no 642.

195 *Ibid*, 167, no 642; 168, no 643; 173, no 668, for example.

196 SRO, GD 111/vi/3, James Curle Writs, 3 February 1557.

197 *SRRM*, iii, 158.

198 Cowan & Easson, *Religious Houses*, 76.

199 M Dilworth, *Scottish Monasteries in the Late Middle Ages* (Edinburgh, 1995), 49.

200 *SRRM*, iii, 192.

201 *Fasti Ecclesicanae Scoticanae*, 10 vols, ed H Scott (Edinburgh, 1915–81), ii, 168, 187.

202 John Watson is last found witnessing a charter in May 1590: RMS, v, *611*, no 1796.

203 Dilworth, *Scottish Monasteries*, 79.

204 SRO, GD 150/1472, Morton Papers, 25 April 1573.

205 *RSS*, vi, 138, no 701.

206 SRO, GD 150/1464, Morton Papers, 16 Feb 1569/70.

207 SRO, GD 150/1467, Morton Papers, 26 June 1570.

208 C A Strang, *The Borders and Berwick: An Illustrated Architectural Guide to the Scottish Borders and Tweed Valley*, (RIAS, 1994), 175.

209 SRO, GD 150/1467, Morton Papers, 26 June 1570.

210 G Donaldson (ed), *Thirds of Benifices, 1561–1572* (SHS, 1949), 25, 30, 35, 38, 41, 44; J Kirk (ed), *The Books of Assumption of the Thirds of Benifices, Scottish Ecclesiastical Rentals at the Reformation* (Oxford, 1995), 193, 207–11, 243, 257–61, 260, 264.

211 *RSS*, v, part i, 192, no 818.

212 *RSS*, vii, 331, no 2017; 335, no 2033, for example.

213 *Laing Charters*, 200, no 791; 298, no 1206; 369, no 1519, for example.

214 *APS*, iii, 596, for example.

215 *RPC*, I, 481.

216 *RSS*, vi, part ii, 228, no 3117.

217 *RPC*, I, 516.

218 *RPC*, ii, 558. The monks of Melrose would later claim that many of their dealings with James Hepburn had been committed under duress as 'he said...he should exile us from the place of Melrose, take away the keys to our chambers, and shortly burn and mark us with hot keys on our cheeks' (R Gore-Brown, *Lord Bothwell* (London, 1937), 126).

219 *RPC*, i, 283

220 *RPC*, ii, 569.

221 SRO, GD 1/452/1, 10 April 1589.

222 *SRRM*, iii, 316–17, 354–5.

223 *SRRM*, iii, 332–3

224 G S Pryde, *The Burghs of Scotland: A Critical List* (London, 1965), 64.

225 J Balfour Paul (ed), *The Scots Peerage*, 9 vols (Edinburgh, 1904–14), iv, 300. *RMS*, vii, 51, no 139. *APS*, iv, 461.

226 SRO GD 224/997/19, Buccleuch Muniments, 15 September 1618. SRO GD 45/16, no 2786/2787, Dalhousie Muniments.

227 *Scots Peerage*, iii, 98; iv, 310–11

228 *SRRM*, i, p.xlvii. RMS, viii, 37, 77.

229 *SRRM*, i, 77.

230 *NSA*, iii, 61.

231 Groome, *Gazetteer*, v, 22.

232 We are indebted to Mr T Little for this information.

233 *SRRM*, i, 145

234 *SRRM*, ii, 230.

235 *SRRM*, i, 313.

236 *SRRM*, ii, 44.

237 *RPC*, xi, 193.

238 *APS*, ix, 501.

239 We are indebted to Mr T Little for this information.

240 We are indebted to Mr T Little for showing us a transcript of this will and testament.

241 Groome, *Gazetteer*, v, 23.

242 *RPC*, II, vi, 16.

243 *SRRM*, iii, 1, 56.

244 *RPC*, III, ix, 165.

245 *Inventory of Ancient and Historical Monuments of Roxburghshire*, (RCAHMS, 1956), 281.

246 *OSA*, iii, 573.

247 *Fasti*, ii, 187.

248 SRO CH2/386/1, Kirk Session Records, 12 March 1643.

249 SRO CH/386/2, Kirk Session Records, 30 October 1669; 7 January 1683.

250 We are indebted to Mr T Little for this information.

251 J Gilbert, *Melrose. Its Kirk and People, 1608–1810* (Melrose, 1991), 11.

252 SRO CH/386/2, Kirk Session Records, 14 February 1669; 19 November 1669.

253 SRO CH/386/2, Kirk Session Records, 30 June 1672.

254 *SRRM*, i, 161–2.

255 SRO CH/386/2, Kirk Session Records, 22 March 1668.

256 Gilbert, *Melrose*, 13.

257 We are indebted to Mr T Little for this information.

258 We are indebted to Dr Lonie for this information.

259 We are indebted to Mr T Little for this information.

260 Groome, *Gazetteer*, v, 22.

261 *SRRM*, iii, 227.

262 For a discussion of the lifestyle of the typical dweller around Melrose, *see* M H B Sanderson, 'The farmers of Melrose', in M H B Sanderson, *Mary Stewart's People* (Edinburgh, 1987), 103–119.

263 *SRRM*, iii, 249.

264 SRO GD 224/997/16, Buccleuch Muniments.

265 SRO GD 224/997/19, Buccleuch Muniments.

266 *RMS*, ix, 25.

267 SRO E69/21/1.

268 *RPC*, xiii, 759.

269 Borders Regional Archive, R/CS/1/4, Valuation Roll of the Shire of Roxburgh, 1643.

270 BRA R/CS/1/15, Valuation Book, 1707.

271 SRO CH2/386/2, Kirk Session Records, 1679.

272 SRO CH2/386/2, Kirk Session Records, 18 March 1683.

273 SRO CH2/386/2, Kirk Session Records, 7 December 1690.

274 Gilbert, *Melrose*, 18.

275 SRO CH2/386/1, Kirk Session Records, 13 April 1651.

276 *RPC*, III, vi, 66;113.

277 *RPC*, II, vi, 303; 311; 429; 431; 445; 473; vii,1;14.

278 SRO CH2/386/1, Kirk Session Records, 25 March 1649.

279 SRO GD 111/vi/16, James Curle Writs Seal of Cause in favour of the weavers.

280 A Milne, *A Description of the Parish of Melrose*, (Edinburgh, 1743), 57.

281 BRA R/LR/1/1, Lieutenancy records for the Shire of Roxburgh, fo 115.

282 Gilbert, *Melrose*, 18.

283 Hood *et al*, *Melrose. 1826* (Melrose, 1978), 17.

284 *OSA*, iii, 567.

285 SRO CH2/386/5, Kirk Session Records, 18 April 1785; 22 October 1785; 24 January 1786.

286 *Fasti*, ii, 188.

287 Gilbert, *Melrose*, 13.

288 *OSA*, iii, 254–56.

289 D Bremner, 'The industries of Scotland, their rise, progress and present condition', in N Murray (ed), *The Scottish Hand-Loom Weavers, 1790–1850* (Edinburgh, 1978), 2.

290 W Elliot, 'The age of reason? 1690–1780', in J M Gilbert (ed), *Flowers of the Forest: Selkirk: A New History* (Galashiels, 1985), 99.

291 *OSA*, iii, 564–6.

292 *Fasti*, ii, 188.

293 *OSA*, iii, 564–66.

294 Bremner, 'Industries', 5.

295 Gilbert, *Melrose*, 13.

296 *OSA*, iii, 568.

297 Hood *et al*, *Melrose. 1826*, 7. *See also* R A Dodgshon, 'The removal of runrig in Roxburghshire and Berwickshire, 1680–1766', *Scottish Studies*, xvi (1972), 131.

298 BRA R/CS/1/16, 98.

299 SRO CH2/386/3, Kirk Session Records, 28 February 1720.

300 Hood *et al*, *Melrose. 1826*, 35.

301 D MacGibbon & T Ross, *The Castellated and Domestic Architecture of Scotland from the Twelfth to the Eighteenth Century*, 5 vols (Edinburgh, 1887–92), v, 406.

54

302 *TSA*, xxviii, 248.
303 SRO CH2/386/3, Kirk Session Records, 1704.
304 Gilbert, *Melrose*, 12.
305 SRO CH2/386/3, Kirk Session Records, 1713.
306 Gilbert, *Melrose*, 12.
307 *OSA*, iii, 569.
308 D Defoe, *A Tour through the Whole Island of Great Britain*, ed P N Furbank & W R Owens (New Haven, 1991), 339.
309 R Heron, *Scotland Delineated 1799* (Edinburgh facsimile, 1975), 287.
310 Groome, *Gazetteer*, v, 27.
311 SRO CH2/386/3, Kirk Session Records, 2 August 1719.
312 Quoted in Gilbert, *Melrose*, 30.
313 Gilbert, *Melrose*, 32.
314 Hood *et al*, *Melrose. 1826*, 33.
315 *Ibid*, 26.

316 We are indebted to Mr A Crawford for this information.
317 We are indebted to Mr T Little for this information.
318 Wade, *St Mary's Abbey*, 139.
319 J Mason, *Border Tour, 1826* (Edinburgh, 1826), 121.
320 *NSA*, iii, 67.
321 Wade, *St Mary's Abbey*, 139.
322 J E McLachlan, 'The Story of Fastern's E'en', *Borders Magazine*, viii (1908), 86–8.
323 We are indebted to Mr T Little for this information.
324 Border Advertiser, 24 June 1859.
325 Border Advertiser, 15 July 1859.
326 Border Advertiser, 7 October 1859.
327 *NSA*, iii, 71.
328 Groome, *Gazetteer*, v, 23.
329 *NSA*, iii, 75.
330 Wade, *St Mary's Abbey*, 135.

area by area assessment

pp 56–95

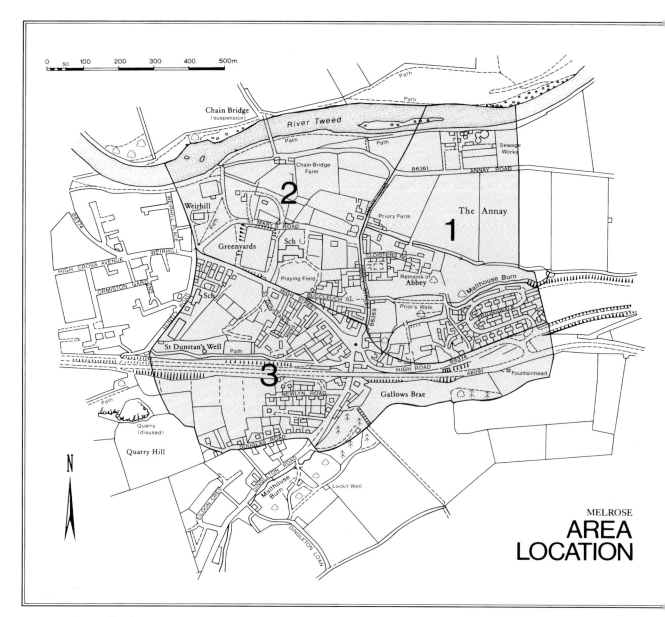

figure 19

Area location map

The medieval core of Melrose has been divided into three areas **figure 19**. The abbey precinct is contained within Areas 1 and 2—the eastern half, which includes the abbey itself, within Area 1 (**figure 20**); and the western half within Area 2 (**figure 22**). The historic (medieval) core of the town is contained within Area 3 (**figure 23**).

The north bank of the River Tweed provides an easily recognisable natural boundary to the study area. The southern, eastern and western boundaries are more arbitrary, and are marked by Douglas Road and Gallows Brae to the south, Weirhill to the west and The Annay to the east. Within the study area, the presumed course of the wall around the abbey precinct, which no longer survives, and Abbey Street divides the three areas.

area 1

Abbey Street / River Tweed / Sewage Works (east side) / The Annay fields / Priorswalk housing estate (east side) / High Road (north side) **figure 20**

description

Area 1 contains the ruins of the abbey, which are open to the public. Designated a Scheduled Ancient Monument, the abbey has been in the care of Historic Scotland and its predecessors since it was gifted to the state in 1919 by the duke of Buccleuch. At the heart of the complex is the church. To the south of the church is the graveyard **A**; to the north, unusually, the cloister **B**. Other than the church, all of the buildings that once

---

archaeological potential and future development

the abbey

Area 1 is clearly the most archaeologically sensitive area of Melrose. The eastern half of the abbey precinct contains the abbey church and cloisters. The exact boundaries of the precinct, and the location of the buildings ranged within it, are still unclear, but documentary sources have enabled the approximate course of the boundary, and therefore the limits of the abbey grounds, to be traced. The area of the scheduled ancient monument (coloured red on **figure 25**) has recently been extended to include a much greater proportion of the abbey precinct than previously. There has been relatively little modern development within the eastern part of the former precinct; any house or garden here, therefore, might overlie, or contain within its fabric, the remains of earlier medieval buildings or features associated with the abbey. There are currently no development proposals for this area.

The ruins now visible were largely exposed in excavations in the 1920s by the then Ministry of Works. Although a fascinating assemblage of finds was retrieved **figure 9**, now on display in the Commendator's House **D**, few records were kept of this work. Much of the abbey complex is now visible only as wall foundations defining buildings and sometimes individual rooms **figure 5**. Evidence of their occupational history and internal arrangements, such as floor levels and drains, lies unexamined beneath the turf. In 1996, a detailed geophysical survey (a non-invasive technique for detecting buried features) of the main abbey complex was undertaken. The results of this survey not only complement the visible remains but have also identified hitherto unknown buildings, and are incorporated in the account of the buildings which follows.

The original twelfth-century church was largely destroyed in the fourteenth century, and the superseding structure was architecturally very different. Nonetheless, in plan the fragmentary church that survives today resembles the earlier church, albeit on a much larger scale. All that survives now is a fragment of the west wall **L** with the lower part of

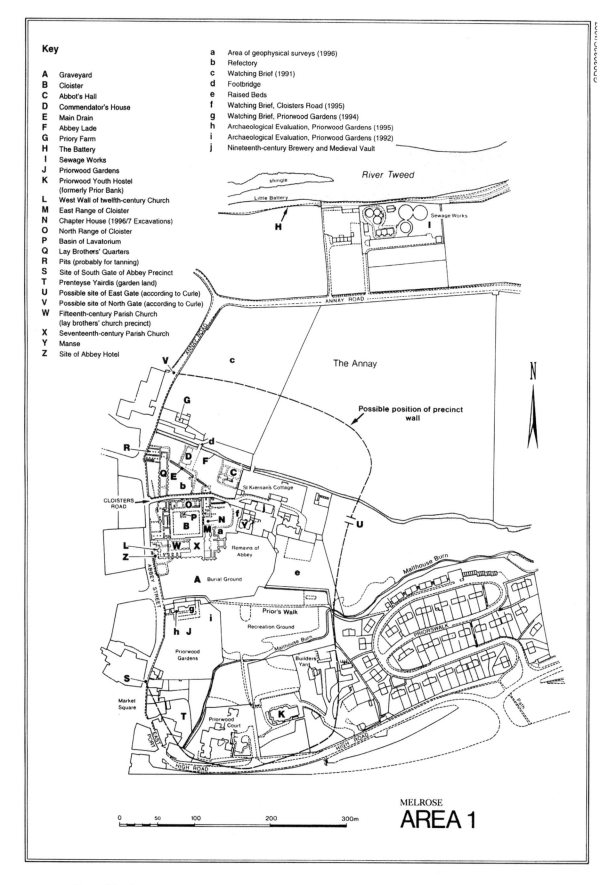

Key

A   Graveyard
B   Cloister
C   Abbot's Hall
D   Commendator's House
E   Main Drain
F   Abbey Lade
G   Priory Farm
H   The Battery
I   Sewage Works
J   Priorwood Gardens
K   Priorwood Youth Hostel
    (formerly Prior Bank)
L   West Wall of twelfth-century Church
M East Range of Cloister
N   Chapter House (1996/7 Excavations)
O   North Range of Cloister
P   Basin of Lavatorium
Q   Lay Brothers' Quarters
R   Pits (probably for tanning)
S   Site of South Gate of Abbey Precinct
T   Prenteyse Yairdis (garden land)
U   Possible site of East Gate (according to Curle)
V   Possible site of North Gate (according to Curle)
W Fifteenth-century Parish Church
    (lay brothers' church precinct)
X   Seventeenth-century Parish Church
Y   Manse
Z   Site of Abbey Hotel

a   Area of geophysical surveys (1996)
b   Refectory
c   Watching Brief (1991)
d   Footbridge
e   Raised Beds
f   Watching Brief, Cloisters Road (1995)
g   Watching Brief, Priorwood Gardens (1994)
h   Archaeological Evaluation, Priorwood Gardens (1995)
i   Archaeological Evaluation, Priorwood Gardens (1992)
j   Nineteenth-century Brewery and Medieval Vault

River Tweed

shingle

Little Battery

Sewage Works

ANNAY ROAD

The Annay

Possible position of precinct wall

N

St Kiernan's Cottage

CLOISTERS ROAD

Remains of Abbey

Burial Ground

Malthouse Burn

Prior's Walk

Recreation Ground

PRIORSWALK

Malthouse Burn

Priorwood Gardens

Builders Yard

Path

Market Square

Priorwood Court

EAST PORT

ABBEY STREET

HIGH ROAD

HIGH ROAD

MELROSE
AREA 1

0   50   100   200   300m

figure 20

Area 1

ranged around the cloisters survive only as wall foundations. Cloisters Road now separates the northern end of the main complex and some of the more outlying buildings and features, such as the Abbot's Hall **C**, the Commendator's House **D**, and also the abbey museum, the main drain **E** and lade **F** (sometimes referred to as the Mill Lade and sometimes as the Abbey Lade), from the cloisters in the south. Cloisters Road is partly private, providing access to housing at Abbey Place.

At the western edge of the area, Abbey Street marks the division between Areas 1 and 2, although the original abbey complex clearly extended out into, under and beyond Abbey Street. Beyond the Mill Lade, the character is essentially rural. On the opposite side of the lade from the Commendator's House is Priory Farm **G**, from which point fields slope gently down to the Tweed, interrupted briefly by Annay Road.

Along the south bank of the Tweed, long stretches of stone walling, known as The Battery **H**, lie at varying distances back from the river's edge, and represent former flood defences. In the north-eastern corner of the area is the sewage works **I**.

To the south of the abbey graveyard **A** lie Prior's Walk and Priorwood Gardens **J**, the latter a National Trust for Scotland property. East of the gardens, Prior's Walk opens out onto a grassed, children's play area.

In the south-west, the backs of the properties that front onto East Port mark the boundary of Area 1 and the approximate line of the abbey precinct boundary. Lined with trees, the Malthouse Burn cuts through here on its journey from the slopes of Eildon Mid Hill to join with the Mill Lade and ultimately the Tweed itself. East of the burn is a large block of modern maisonettes; to the west, gardens attached to properties on the East Port/High Road frontage.

A narrow lane runs up the hill from the footbridge over the burn at Prior's Walk to High Road. To the east is a modern housing estate; to the west are several Victorian villas and, behind them, Priorwood Youth Hostel **K** and grounds.

---

archaeology

the entrance doorway, the foundations of the square nave piers and their connecting screen walls, and part of the north wall. The results of the 1920s excavations, together with the surviving fragments of the original church, provide enough detail to allow a reconstruction of the basic arrangement of the first church. Based on the plan of Rievaulx, which itself was modelled on Clairvaux in France, it comprised a rectangular presbytery, two bays long. Flanking the presbytery were two single-bay chapels and cross-arms or transepts, forming an unusual stepped arrangement at the east end. Beyond the crossing, the aisled nave stretched back for nine bays to the west door. The presbytery housed the high altar, with lesser altars in the transept chapels. The monks' choir occupied the area within the crossing and into the eastern part of the nave. The remainder of the nave was taken up by the lay brothers' choir, the two choirs separated by a screen called a *pulpitum*. The night-stair connected the north transept with the monks' dormitory, to allow the monks to attend services at night without braving the elements. There was similar provision for the lay brethren in the north-western corner of the nave. The walls, both inside and out, were probably whitewashed, and the roofs of lead and of red tile. The floors of the presbytery and chapels were paved with glazed tiles, coloured yellow, green or brown, and set in geometric patterns.

The chapter house **N** was excavated in 1921, and again in 1996/7 (*see below*), the results of which have demonstrated the high archaeological potential of the abbey area. In 1921, three stone coffins were discovered beneath the floor **figure 9**, close to the doorway. Three fragments of a monumental tomb, perhaps from the shrine of St Waltheof, were recovered. These finely dressed and moulded pieces, with traces of gilding with gold leaf, are now on display in the nearby museum. An even more intriguing find was that of a cone-shaped lead container, thought to be the casket containing the heart of King Robert I. His dying wish was that his heart be taken on Crusade, and thence returned to Scotland to be buried at Melrose. It is likely that the heart was moved from a more suitable location (at the high altar) to the chapter house when the church was rebuilt during the fourteenth

historical background

the history of the abbey

King David I (1124–53) invited the Cistercians of Rievaulx Abbey in Yorkshire to establish a monastery in Melrose. This was part of his major reorganisation of the church; his reign was to see the founding of a number of Border religious houses, including Kelso, Jedburgh and Dryburgh. The monks who arrived some time before 1136, however, did not favour the traditional sacred site of 'Mailros' (Old Melrose) and opted to establish their monastery about two and a half miles further west. The name of Melrose was transferred to the new site, and the earlier was known as Old Melrose by at least 1285 x 91. One reason for this decision (*see* p 22) might have been the fertility of the ground in this area and the ready accessibility of a ford. Fords are mentioned in the twelfth-century record, and, although their sites are not specified, there was probably ready access across the Tweed at least by the mid twelfth century for the Melrose monks to visit their lands in Gattonside (*see* p 22). A ford would have tended to attract settlement to its banks. Whether there were already settlers at this new site is unclear, but the monks were perhaps unlikely to adopt a heavily populated site, given that the focus of the Cistercian rule was one of prayer.

    The first abbot, Richard, accompanied by twelve monks and lay brothers, would perhaps have lived initially in temporary wooden accommodation while they constructed their church and ancillary buildings; although accommodation might have been available at Old Melrose. None of these buildings remains in evidence above the ground.

history

archaeology

century. The casket was re-discovered in the 1996 excavations and has since been re-buried at Melrose for the third time.

    Only the western end of the chapter house is visible today. The 1996 geophysical survey **a** successfully traced the eastern end, complete with buttresses, and subsequent excavation revealed a sequence of three successive chapter houses from the initial twelfth-century building, through a thirteenth-century rebuilding, and culminating in the fourteenth-century chapter house. In the latter two phases, the chapter house had an elaborate, decorated tiled floor. Immediately to the north of the chapter house, but south of the latrine block, was the south wall of a building, aligned east to west. The inner wall of the cloister ambulatory, or walkway, was revealed, as well as a network of drains that criss-crossed the cloister itelf. Some negative cut features were also identified here, representing a possible pit and ditch (*see below*).

    The Commendator's House **D** is a 1590 conversion of an earlier fifteenth-century building. Evidence for the original ground plan was probably destroyed when cellars were inserted, but the external features, such as the foundation posts of the timber gallery and the stair tower, may survive beneath the present ground level.

    North of Cloisters Road, the wall footings of the refectory block **b** were identified, while to the south of the tannning pits **R**, a short stretch of wall was detected. Between the Abbot's Hall **C** and the Commendator's House **D**, another previously unknown building was discovered, together with an extensive surface, probably a courtyard or floor. Throughout the survey area, numerous other anomalies could be paths or drains. Without excavation, none of the above can be treated with any certainty, but the results have undoubtedly added to our present understanding of the layout of the abbey, and of the archaeological potential of the site.

    The course of the precinct wall has been plotted using late sixteenth-century documentary sources, which record properties being within or outwith the mantle (precinct) wall. A recent watching brief **c** on a pipe trench in the field to the north of Priory Farm, however, has cast some doubt on the course of the northern section of the wall. In the 1920s, although no records could be located, a number of trial trenches were dug in these fields and the rubble core of a wall uncovered. If the observations were

According to the *Chronicle of Melrose*, the date of foundation was 23 March 1136/7; the dedication took place in 1146. The building of any abbey was a slow process, and this one probably took much of the twelfth century. It was claimed in the Rievaulx Cartulary that the stonework had not been commenced even in 1160. There is little to see now, other than the west wall of the twelfth-century church **L**; but archaeological investigation has given an insight into its plan (*see* pp 57, 59, 66).

The other conventual buildings stood to the north of the church. This was unusual for a Cistercian establishment, perhaps determined by the water supply, the River Tweed, to the north. These buildings included the cloister **B**, which was an open garth, probably laid out as a garden, surrounded by covered walkways; the surviving walls, near the east processional door to the church, indicate that they were elaborately arcaded and had stone benches. An east range **M**, which partially survives, contained the sacristy, immediately to the north of the church. This was where vestments, altar frontals and other pertinents of church service were kept. Next to this was the chapter house **N**, where the monks met every morning to listen to a chapter of the rule, discuss monastic business and make their confession. It was here that important burials took place, perhaps the most noted being that of St Waltheof (*see* pp 24, 59). Other offices abutted, probably the inner parlour, where there was limited conversation, perhaps a novices' day room and a latrine block, all of which were under the monks' dormitory, which ran along the full length of the east range, on the first floor.

To the north of the cloister was a range **O** that housed the domestic buildings; these included a warming room, the only room heated for monks in the complex, and a

history

refectory, where meals were taken in silence. The refectory ran parallel to the north walk

archaeology

accurate, the wall should have been exposed in the recent pipe trench, but was not. It is unlikely that the wall would be further north, but it could be slightly further south.

The building of a wall enclosing the abbey grounds was a considerable undertaking and must have taken some time to complete. It is likely that the wall replaced an earlier boundary. This was the case at Dunfermline, where archaeological excavations revealed the stone wall to have replaced an earlier ditch, or possibly a natural stream bed, some time in the late thirteenth or fourteenth century. Precinct walls rarely survive in an urban setting as they provided a useful quarry for the townsfolk, but imposing sections can still be seen at St Andrews and Arbroath. No trace survives of the wall in this area of Melrose, but it is likely to be preserved buried beneath the fields to the north and east of the abbey. Further south, it may extend out under East Port/High Road itself, and further west it may have been incorporated into the fabric of the properties that front on to East Port and The Square.

There are thought to have been four gateways into the abbey precinct, and three of these lie within Area 1: the main south gateway at the south end of Abbey Street **S**, around which the town developed **figure 8**; the eastern gateway, which stood in the field to the east of Abbey Place **U**; and the northern gateway, which lay to the north of Priory Farm cottages on Abbey Street **V**. Nothing visible remains of any of these structures, but they may survive below street level. Structural elements of the south gate may also survive within the properties either side of Abbey Street, or towards the rear of those that front onto The Square. Fine examples of monastic gatehouses can be seen at St Andrews, Arbroath, and Dunfermline.

The layout within monastic precincts in Scotland is little understood, and Melrose is no exception. A range of ancillary buildings would have been sited here, such as an infirmary, almshouses, at least one mill, storehouses, barns, stables, brewhouses and kilns. Water meadows, pasture fields, orchards and gardens would have provided food for the table and for the many visitors to the abbey, and an elaborate network of drains and paths would have linked the various parts of the precinct. The archaeological potential for these outer areas is difficult to predict. Recent archaeological work in Priorwood Gardens **J**, however, has shown that deep (over one metre thick) deposits of garden soil have accumulated here,

in the twelfth century, but was realigned to be sited at right angles in the thirteenth century, perhaps to accommodate more monks. Opposite the refectory was the wash room or lavatorium. Water was fed to this large circular basin **P**, still visible in the ground, in lead pipes from a well sunk to the south of the conventual buildings, at Danzeltoun (Dingleton). To the west of the refectory was the kitchen.

The lay brothers, who did many of the menial tasks for the monastery, lived apart from the monks, in a west range **Q**. It was two storeys high, extending some 108m from the west porch of the church and was formed of two blocks. The southern end of the northern block was the lay brothers' refectory; a tiled fireplace in the west wall indicates the site of their warming room. At right angles at the northern end was a further block, which housed their latrines and three pits **R**, which may have been used for tanning.

To the north-east of the cloister and ranges are the foundations of the Abbot's Hall **C**, which date from the thirteenth century. It was probably a two-storeyed building, with storage space on the ground floor and the abbot's private chambers on the upper. A little further west stands the Commendator's House **D**, first built in the fifteenth century, but largely converted in 1590 (*see* p 98). To the north again ran the Mill Lade **F**, which was fed from a dam on the Tweed 460 m west of the abbey, and supplied one of the abbey's two mills (*see* p 75). It was partially diverted to function also as a main drain **E**, to serve the latrines of the east range and, probably, also those of the lay brothers. The precinct would have contained kitchen and fruit gardens, as well as one mill; and it is known that there was an orchard, with a lockable postern door, although whether this was within the precinct is unclear (these may have been sited in Area 2 *see* pp 72–80). A charter in the Melrose Regality Records defines clearly typical burgage plots in the town in the sixteenth century, but, more importantly, indicates that the monastery also had garden lands to the east of the main south entrance gate **S**. In 1556, John Clennan and his wife Agnes Watsoun were infeoffed of 'a tenement with pertinents before the front door of the monastery of Melrose, between the tenement of the deceased John Watson on the south and the tenement of John Lorimer on the north, having the High Street on the west and the garden of the monastery called the 'Prenteyse yairdis' **T** on the east'.

which have effectively sealed and preserved medieval levels. A metalled surface was exposed, probably a pathway within the precinct.

Water was essential to a great abbey, and the monks were experts in water management. At Melrose, the Abbey Lade **F** drew water from a sluice system known as The Cauld (**area 2**), which can still be seen today, upstream of the Tweed. This transferred a supply of fresh water over 450 m to the main abbey complex, powering at least one mill before doing so. A number of footbridges must have crossed the lade, of which only one survives today **d**. A network of subsidiary drains would have supplied water to a range of ancillary buildings, gardens and orchards, as well as other drains which would have returned water into the lade downstream of the main abbey complex. Where the water was used for washing and cooking, lead pipes were used; sections of these have been found during excavations at Melrose. Sometimes ceramic, interlocking pipes were used, as at Glenluce (Dumfries and Galloway).

The Great Drain **E** flowed through the main claustral buildings, interconnecting the latrines of the lay brethren and monks. For the most part it was roughly constructed, but where it serves the reredorter it was better constructed to avoid waste accumulating. Drains are frequently found within monastic precincts and are a valuable source of information for the archaeologist. They often provide the richest source of finds, as objects were thrown in to be flushed away, and soils that accumulated in the base of the drains also preserve environmental data—plants, seeds, insects, foodstuffs, and the bones of small mammals such as rats and mice. The living conditions, diet and economy of the abbey can be reconstructed from analysis of these microscopic remains. Fine examples of monastic drains have been found at St Andrews and Dunfermline, but perhaps the finest of all was recently discovered at Paisley Abbey. Here, both the floors and walls of the

The whole complex was surrounded by a stone wall, some of which has been located by excavation, and there are remnants in cellars in Area 2 (*see* pp 72–80). The precise line of the wall in Area 1 is unknown, but its possible siting is indicated with a dotted line on **figures 20** *&* **22**. There was possibly an east gate, as well as a north, a west and a south gate **S**. The location of the east and north gates is unknown, although presumably the north gate stood on the main route north through the precinct to the ford. Dr Curle believed he had found the sites of both the east **U** and north **V** gates; but this has not been confirmed more recently. The west gate was in Area 2. Nineteenth-century comments that Melrose occupies the site of an ancient lake and that the Tweed had moved northwards by nearly one hundred yards in places would suggest that the area around the north gate might have been marshy. In 1576, the tenants and farmers of Gattonside and Mosshouses defaulted on the payment of rentals, the excuse being that they had lost some sixteen score of acres by the rising of the Tweed. Clearly, the river was still shifting its banks. The south gate **S** was the most important and stood astride the modern Abbey Street, a little back from where it now joins the Market Place (*see* **figure 8**). It had a chapel built at the gatehouse, or above it, as at Beaulieu in Hampshire.

Melrose Abbey was greatly favoured by royalty. William I, for example, was some considerable time at Melrose between May and July 1209. It was here, in the chapter house, that the Yorkshire barons swore fealty to Alexander II in 1216. Alexander III chose Melrose as a strategic place to await his army in September 1258; and David II was at Melrose in 1369/70. It was to Melrose that James I returned from exile in 1424. It was from Melrose also that James II checked the power of Archibald, fifth earl of Douglas, whose predecessor and brother-in-law, the fourth earl had been 'defender and protector' of Melrose Abbey. Successive kings resided at the monastery. James IV, for example, based himself at Melrose for his attack on Northumbria in 1496; spent Christmas there in 1497, for which a copious supply of geese and 'birds of the forest' was required; and, two years later, received the archbishop of Canterbury at Melrose, an occasion necessitating elaborate provisions. Alexander II also chose Melrose as his burial place, to which his remains were brought from Kerrera after his death on 8 July 1249. His body reputedly

history

---

archaeology

drain were of polished ashlar, with curved arches supporting the roof. Archaeological excavation of the Paisley drain produced one of the finest assemblages of medieval finds from any site in Scotland: pottery including one whole pot; lead seals; dice and gaming pieces; and slates inscribed with musical notation and lyrics. The environmental evidence included wood, bone, shells, seeds, textile and plant remains. The bone assemblage showed that the monks ate beef, pork and lamb, as well as fish; while the plant remains indicated that they grew specific plants for medicinal purposes, collected mosses for wound dressings and as toilet paper, and that wheat was grown for bread and barley for brewing beer. Of the more exotic items, spices had been imported, probably to disguise badly preserved meat, and Mediterranean figs were also found. These are often found in medieval cess pits and were used as purgatives.

The Abbey Lade **F** would have powered the mill, which was sited within the precinct, and subsidiary drains would have supplied or served some of the ancillary buildings. Few examples of the agricultural buildings that once stood within monastic precincts have been identified; one exception is the known site of a barn at St Andrews. The numerous other buildings of which we know nothing, but which may lie within Area 1 include the brewhouse, smithy, kiln house, stables, barns, well house, possibly a fulling mill and guest houses.

Tanning is the only semi-industrial activity for which there is any physical evidence at Melrose (although the corn mill in Area 2 may have been built over an earlier medieval structure). The three rectangular, stone-lined tanning pits **R** were housed within a building abutting the north end of the lay brothers' range, which also contained the latrines. The main drain **E** ran below the floor. The tanks would have contained batches of hides soaking in various solutions. Lime was used to strip the hides of flesh and hair;

rests beside the High Altar (although others have argued that the slab marks the grave of St Waltheof; *see* p 24); and his wife, Joanna, was buried in the south aisle. The heart of Robert I reputedly rests in the abbey, after having been taken on crusade (*see* pp 59, 66).

Melrose Abbey suffered in the on-going struggle between England and Scotland for control of the Borders. It is noteworthy that a successful appeal was made to Edward I not only to confirm all their charters of infeftment, but also to grant them timber in Selkirk forest (Ettrick Forest), since their buildings had been burned and destroyed while at his peace and protection. This destruction may have been accidental, since there would have been little point in Edward granting the wherewithal to repair damage deliberately effected by his policies. By May 1316, however, Bruce was using Melrose as a base to harry the English in Berwick; and in 1322 the abbey complex was burnt by Edward II. The granting by Robert I, in 1326, of £2,000 for the rebuilding of the policies suggests that Melrose was by now firmly in the Scottish king's camp; as does the grants of ferms and customs to be applied to the abbey fabric and daily sustenance of the monks. The regular visits of the king and his decision in 1329 that his heart should be buried there would support this. Melrose, however, remained in a vulnerable geographical position; but, in 1328, with the arrival of temporary peace, Edward III's regents restored to the abbey the pensions and lands seized by his father. Six years later, Edward III granted his protection to Melrose and the other Border abbeys. Relations were sufficiently warm that, in 1341, Edward III visited while spending Christmas at Newcastle; and in 1348 he granted further lands to Melrose.

In 1385, Richard II spent the night at the abbey and—it was said—was so 'exasperated' that he burned it on leaving. The recent Scottish invasion of England, in support of France, however, was probably the real explanation for the concerted devastation of the eastern Borders. As it was chronicled, the English destroyed everything

history

---

archaeology

and then animal dung (dog dung in particular) and vegetable extracts were used to de-lime the skins. Finally, they were soaked in a solution of water and bark for up to eighteen months to preserve the leather and inhibit fungal decay. A recent excavation in St Andrews revealed the remains of a fourteenth-century tannery, on the site of the present visitors' centre at St Andrews Castle. The excavation uncovered a series of wood-lined pits housed within an open barn and demonstrated that the techniques employed in tanning remained more or less unchanged until the advent of chemicals in relatively modern times.

Beyond the north wall of the abbey complex lay the water meadows, which slope gently down to the Tweed; these were known as The Annay, meaning river island, no doubt a reference to their continual flooding. Along the bank of the river, set slightly back from the water's edge, are a series of earthen banks faced with stone, which act as flood defences. These are known locally as The Battery **H**. Their date of construction is uncertain, but the stone facing may be a later addition to what could be a medieval feature.

Crops, vegetables and fruit were grown in abundance to supply the monks and visitors, but exactly where is unclear. Fruit trees thrive naturally alongside the path by the river and perhaps this was one of the orchards. A series of raised beds **e** can be seen in the field to the north of Prior's Walk, and to the west of the abbey graveyard, and are also visible on aerial photographs **figure 5**. There are no documentary records of these but they could be medieval in date.

All the buildings within the former precinct, from large Victorian villas such as Priorwood, to the smaller cottages and farm buildings, may have used stone robbed from the abbey. Equally, they may have been constructed over, or have incorporated, fragments of the ruinous outbuildings and ancillary buildings, elements of which may be preserved within or beneath the floor levels of the present standing buildings.

Archaeological monitoring of any future ground disturbance or development within the precinct is essential, if the inner workings of this important monastic settlement are to

'saving nothing and burning down with the fiery flames God's temples and holy places, to wit the monasteries of Melrose, Dryburgh and Newbattle'.

The work of rebuilding the abbey began within a few years of its destruction, probably with the active support of Richard II. Architectural evidence supports the theory that English masons were participating in the reconstruction work. Financial provision was also made in 1389; and a grant of two shillings for every 1,000 sacks of wool exported by the Cistercian monks via Berwick was instituted. The architecture of the abbey indicates that the responsibility for building work passed to masons influenced by the European tradition; part of the south transept was the responsibility of the French master-mason, John Morow. The reconstruction was to last throughout the fifteenth and into the sixteenth century; and Melrose Abbey was to re-emerge as one of the most magnificent complexes in Scotland, even though work petered out inconclusively as it approached the west end (*see* p 97) **figure 10**.

The use, from at least 1443, of the erstwhile lay brothers' choir as the parish church **W** brought closer contact between the lay settlement at the south gate and the abbey. The gradual decline in the numbers of lay brothers would, in its turn, mean that the abbey would have had to look to lay settlement nearby for assistance, not only in running their granges, but also for the more mundane services of cleaning, washing, gardening and supplying food. On-going reconstruction of the abbey complex would also have created a demand for a labouring workforce. The continued use of the abbey complex as a temporary resting place for the monarchy throughout the fifteenth century would have brought a further demand for services (*see* pp 32, 63); and it may be guessed that in this century there was a growth in settlement (*see* **area 3**).

The work of reconstruction of the abbey continued until sometime after 1505, King James IV giving drink silver to the masons working there, for example, in November 1502

history

---

archaeology

be understood. Remains of the precinct boundary, outbuildings and other features here are likely to be preserved not only in the fields and open areas, but also beneath the houses that have gradually infilled the precinct since the Reformation. The streets themselves are also likely to preserve archaeological deposits beneath them. Although Abbey Street probably marks the line of the main thoroughfare within the precinct, others such as Cloisters Road are later additions. Medieval features more than likely survive beneath both, as the lay brothers' range **Q** extends out into Abbey Street, and Cloisters Road overlies the main north range of the abbey **O**.

It is also important to trace how settlement developed here in the post-Reformation period. Evidence for this may also be contained both beneath and within the fabric of existing standing buildings, along Abbey Street in particular. Here, earlier floor levels may be preserved below present floors, and perhaps earlier buildings too. For all these reasons, the scheduled area at Melrose Abbey has recently been extended *see* **figure 25**.

summary of previous archaeological work and chance finds

Melrose Abbey, NT 549 343

abbey complex
   1920s excavations The ruins now visible were largely exposed in excavations in the 1920s by the then Ministry of Works. Few records of this work were kept, unfortunately, although a fascinating assemblage of finds was retrieved **figure 9**, now on display in the Commendator's House **D**. Tabraham, C, *Melrose Abbey* (1995).
   geophysical surveys, NT 5485 3425 **a** Geophysical surveys were carried out at Melrose Abbey in 1996. An area of approximately 1.4 hectares was surveyed in the abbey grounds, and an additional 0.26 hectares in Melrose Abbey Gardens. Three techniques were employed—geomagnetic, resistivity and ground penetrating radar—the aim being to construct a three-dimensional plan of the archaeological features in the abbey grounds.

and just before Christmas 1504. The *Treasurer's Accounts* at the turn of the century indicate that James IV was resident at Melrose on several occasions, for example in 1502 when he received the French ambassador (*see* p 32). James IV, with nine earls and many others, died at the disastrous Battle of Flodden in 1513. In September 1516, the Lords of Council decided that the Lord Governor (John, duke of Albany, nephew of the deceased king) should 'pas with ane honest company to Melros, and fra thin to Jedburgh and forthir as it sall be thocht necessar for gud reule to be maid apon the bourdoris and for the expulsioun of thevis and putting of the kingis lieges to rest and quiet'.

In 1536, there were still at least thirty-two monks at Melrose; although as witness to the decline of the order, the last abbot, Andrew Durie, was forced to resign, to be replaced by a commendator (and his administrator) in 1541. The nominal commendator was James V's eldest illegitimate son, James Stewart—then an infant.

Henry VIII of England was determined to unite the crown of Scotland with that of England by the marriage of his son Edward with the young Queen Mary (1542–67). When negotiations failed, he moved to beat Scotland into submission. There followed seven years of devastation, much of its main toll falling on the Border region. Melrose suffered greatly in this war of attrition. In 1544, the abbey was burnt by the English under Sir Ralph Eure (Evers). Considerable damage was done to the abbey fabric, including the desecration of the Douglas tombs (*see* p 33) **figure 11**. The following year, in 1545, it was 'raced' by the forces of the earl of Hertford, numbering, it was claimed, 15,000. Little seems to have been done to repair the devastation to the abbey; perhaps there was little point. English troops were not ousted from the Borders. In 1549, for example, they were in Jedburgh, backed by a fifth column of 'assured Scots' who were bribed or bullied into taking an oath of allegiance to the king of England.

Not surprisingly, in 1549 the abbey was stated to be in great and urgent need of money. By 1556, the monks were still warning that 'without the kirk be repairit this instant sommer God service will ceise this winter'. The following year, sixteen monks received an assignation for their living, the rents amounting to £63 'for repartion and bigging of the place being ruinous' and £200 from teinds to the 'bursour' or master of works for application 'quhair maist neid is'. In 1555–6, James Stewart, the commendator of

history

---

archaeology

The results (especially resistivity and geomagnetic anomalies) showed good evidence for the survival of features of archaeological interest in the subsoil. The most significant results comprised the recovery of the ground plan of the western end of the chapter house, hitherto undiscovered buildings to the west and south of the Abbot's Hall and between the chapter house and the presbytery, the inner wall of the cloisters walkway and fragmentary footings of the refectory, warming room and kitchen. Geoquest Associates (1996, unpublished report).

1996/7 excavations, NT 5486 3417 **N** A programme of excavations, sponsored by Historic Scotland, was undertaken within the scheduled area in 1996 and 1997. Its aims were both to test the results of the geophysical surveys and to complement our understanding of the structural chronology of the abbey. The excavation revealed details of the construction sequence of the chapter house, one of the most important buildings on the cloister. A sequence of three successive chapter houses was determined: the initial twelfth-century example, through a thirteenth-century rebuilding and culminating in the fourteenth-century building. The latter two saw extension of the chapter house eastwards, whereas the initial chapter house probably sat within the east range. In the latter two phases the chapter house had an elaborate tiled floor. A number of graves were also discovered, most of which had been previously disturbed. In 1996, the excavators unearthed a lead casket, originally uncovered in 1921, believed to contain the mummified heart of King Robert I. This has since been re-buried, and the site marked by a commemorative plaque. 'Melrose Abbey: Excavations on the Chapter House', 1996 (Kirkdale, unpublished interim report); 'Melrose Abbey: Excavations 1997' (Kirkdale, unpublished interim report); DES (1996), 89; DES (1997), 67.

Melrose and Kelso, granted a feu charter in return for funds 'towards the repair and rebuilding of the abbey of Melrose destroyed by the English'. This was signed by the commendator, the sub-prior and eleven monks. There is charter evidence of many such instances, which would suggest that there was at the very least intent to effect repairs; as would a precept of sasine by the commendator to infeft one John Hunter in a husbandland of land, which specifically excluded the fishings on the Tweed and 'stone quarries and stone necessary for the ... monastery of Melrose'. A complaint by the monks in 1556, however, reveals that some of these monies were diverted to other uses; and lead from the roof of the abbey was being sold off.

Political and religious events were to bring profound changes to Melrose after 1560, with the establishment of a Protestant church. The old order, however, did not change overnight. In 1536, twenty-nine monks, including the abbot and sub-prior, had subscribed a charter, although a further three, at least, were identifiable at the time. Their numbers appear to have fallen after the 1545 destruction and probably at the Reformation there were seventeen monks left, although it has been argued that there may have been as few as twelve by 1556. The surviving members of convent became pensioners, a number of them continuing to live in Melrose and perhaps functioning as Protestant ministers. The community of monks may have become extinct shortly after 1590, with the death of Jo (John) Watsoun, pensioner of Melrose; although possibly one monk lived until 1609, when he was functioning as the bailie of Melrose regality.

In 1581, the newly organised Melrose parish was created, with parishioners still worshipping in the outer church or choir. And it is known that on 25 April 1573 the regality court of Melrose was held within the abbey kirk. Clearly parts of the church were still able to function, in spite of the damage it had suffered over the decades. The English, however, were not the sole desecrators. James Douglas, the commendator, with Alexander Colville, commendator of Culross as coadjutor and adminstrator (during his minority) took action against Sir Walter Scott of Branxholm in February 1570 for committing a 'spuilze at the place of Melrose'. In the June of that year he was recalled to court for the removal of lead from 'the place and kirk of Melrose'. He had dismantled the 'inner queir, uter kirk, the stepile, an croce kirk of the same'. His defence was that he was merely

history

---

archaeology

Cloisters Road NT 3486 3417 **f**
monastic features
A watching brief, carried out during the laying of electricity cables at the east end of Cloisters Road in 1995, revealed extensive and important archaeological evidence in the small area affected. Features observed possibly include the main abbey drain and a post-monastic building. All features were sealed by a series of road deposits, the earliest relating to access to the brewery **j**. *DES* (1996), 89.

Priorwood Gardens NT 548 430 **g**
medieval abbey environs
The extension of visitor facilities required a watching brief. The ground was found to have been artificially raised, probably in the nineteenth century, and no archaeologically sensitive deposits were disturbed. *DES* (1994), 6.

Priorwood Gardens NT 549 340 **i**
medieval abbey environs
Exploratory trenching was carried out to assess the depth of overburden and the extent and nature of the underlying archaeological material in the south-east corner of the flower garden. A metalled road, aligned north–south and possibly associated with the adjacent abbey, was partly exposed at the extreme south end of the site, 1.1 m below the present ground surface. Numerous fragments of medieval roof tiles overlay the road, although no associated structure was located. *DES* (1992), 7.

removing them to save them from the English! He was not the sole culprit. In June of the same year, letters of arrestment were raised by the commendator and 'convent of our said abbey of Melrose' against those who had violently taken the 'haill leid of the kirk and place of' Melrose, with the intention of, amongst other things, taking it to the port of Leith to export out of the realm. The majority of the perpretators were local, such as Thomas Scot, tailor in Jedburgh, but not from Melrose. James Douglas was himself happy to pillage the abbey ruins to build the Commendator's House in 1590.

the developing townscape

As a result of these upheavals, the late sixteenth century saw significant developments in the townscape. In April 1589, for example, a tack was issued by James, commendator of Melrose, to John Scott, the town's notary public, and John Scott, his son and heir, that they were to be infeoffed of a 'yard within the abbey walls sometime pertaining to the deceased dean Thomas Mein, monk'. There were adjacent occupied properties to the north, the south-east and the west. The bakehouse yard, which stood within the precinct or 'mantill wall' near to the mill, and the mill itself were set to tack (*see* **area 2**). John Knox, the minister from 1584, was given tack of a dwelling and garden in the north-east of the precinct, close to where Dene John Watson had his 'roume', with 'the auld ruinus wallis one the east syd of the closter on the vest'. The commendator, significantly, retained the stones for his own use. The colonisation of the erstwhile abbey precincts had already begun.

By 1618, a decision had been made to form a parish church from the partial ruins of the old abbey. Architectural evidence suggests that the western archway of the crossing had already been blocked; it was in the original abbatial aisle, or nave, (as opposed to the lay brothers' aisle where the parish church originally functioned) that the new, barrel-vaulted, parish church **X** was constructed. According to the *Old Statistical Account*, it was only around 1649 that the statues in the abbey were demolished. The interior of the church was modified on a number of occasions, in order to house the parishioners. On 12 March 1643, one Robert Pringall applied to build the first loft in the church. These were

history

---

archaeology

St Helen's, The Eddy Pool NT 536 347—NT 562 346 **H**
medieval riverside works
A spate in the River Tweed in the winter of 1990, and again in 1994, followed by unusually low water in June 1995, exposed a number of features along the south bank of the River Tweed which may be evidence of riverside works built by the monks of Melrose Abbey. A detailed survey of these features, which extend from St Helen's in the west to The Eddy Pool in the east, was undertaken by the Royal Commission of the Ancient and Historical Monuments of Scotland. The main features comprised a timber and stone box, revetment walls (some supported by timber piles), artificial water-courses and a cobbled surface.

The stone and timber box is a part of a sluice system, known locally as The Cauld (NT 543 345), which transferred fresh water over 450 m to the abbey complex *via* the Abbey (or Mill) Lade. Further east (downstream) at The Eddy Pool (NT 562 346), three courses of ashlar masonry retaining the south bank of the River Tweed were exposed. This section of the riverside wall is known as The Battery, and stone and timber foundations have now been traced intermittently over a 300 m stretch of the river edge (from NT 5546 3466 to NT 5578 3494).

A similar revetment wall was also identified to the west of The Cauld at St Helen's (NT 536 347). Here, the wall was also found to have been supported by timber piles, and a cobbled surface had been laid in a gap in the wall. An artificial channel of well-laid masonry was also identified at St Helen's, at the point where the Huntly Burn flows into the River Tweed. *DES* (1994), 5–6; *DES* (1995), 8.

raised seats for the use of particular families or craftsmen. From this time, a number of lofts were built in the church. On 30 October 1669, the weavers were given permission to build a loft 'providing they go no further then the north end of Thomas Lythgows loaft that no person be wronged yrby'. On 7 January 1683, 'the masons in Neusted desyred the priviledge of building a loft in the east end of the church'. Permission was granted.

Houses soon lined the street which was once the main entrance into the precinct. It later became called The Bow and then Abbey Street. Two buildings, both in Abbey Street (*see* p 98)—Abbey House, still standing, and *no* 12, the town's first post office, standing until recently, were indicative of the new and improved middle-class housing of the later eighteenth century and of a growing prosperity, albeit modest.

The township also benefited from the consolidation and enclosure of erstwhile run-rig lands, which included the Annay. This initiative of three Melrose lawyers, along with other agricultural improvements, such as the draining of land and the introduction of new farming techniques and crops were all part of the gradual increase in Melrose's prosperity.

The overall impression, however, is of a small town, dominated by the ruins of the abbey; although sections of the old abbey were still useable, in particular the parish church. The local school stood across the road (*see* **area 2**). By 1763, the school was in need of repair, so a collection was made to repair the session house and convert it into a school. Soon after this a chapel in the south aisle was converted into a public school. Although this appears to have been only a temporary measure, clearly parts of the abbey were relatively wind and water tight. When Daniel Defoe visited in 1724, his main interest was in 'the ruins of the once famous abbey of Melrose'. Heron, in 1799, noted merely 'the magnificent remains of Melrose abbey, the finest of any in Scotland'. Robert Burns, visiting in 1787, commented on 'that far-famed glorious ruin'. It is also clear that even for local people, there was an increasing awareness of the need to maintain their parish church and provide for adequate light. The building of lofts was blocking light; and agreements were made that extra windows should be broken into the church walls. It seems, however, that good intentions did not materialise fully into actions. In 1776, a

history visitor to Melrose wrote of his impressions on entering the parish church:

---

archaeology *Priorwood Gardens NT 549 341* **h**
garden feature
Investigation of a low-lying oval mound before re-landscaping of the southern garden area showed that it consisted of a dump of twentieth-century waste material. The line of a path, shown running to the south wall on the 1859 Ordnance Suvey map, was also revealed. *DES* (1996), 90.

The Annay NT 548 344 **c**
military prisoner of war camp
A long (*c* 75 m) machine cut trench in this field to the north of the abbey revealed nothing of the huts known to have stood here during World War II. More importantly, it failed to expose the northern stretch of the precinct wall of the abbey, thought to have passed east–west through this field. (Borders Regional Council, 1991).

Brewery NT 549 342 **j**
nineteenth-century brewery and medieval vault

The brewery marked on Wood's 1826 map of Melrose **figure 17** lay to the east of the abbey church and adjacent to the manse. Its early history is unclear as the 'Abbey Brewery' is recorded as having been founded in 1839 by James Simson, who also opened St Mary's Brewery in Canongate, Edinburgh, in 1864. Simson & Co merged with the brewing, whisky and blending operation of John E McPherson of Newcastle in 1896; and, when the new company was taken over by Robert Deuchar Ltd in 1900, the Abbey

70

On opening the doors it is not to be expressed the disagreeable scene which presented itself; this place is filled with lofts in the disposition of which irregularity alone seems to have been studied; some are raised on upright beams as scaffolds, tier above tier, others supported against the walls and pillars, no two are alike in form, height or magnitude; the same confusion of little and great, high and low, covers the floor with pews; the lights are so obstructed that the place is as dark as a vault; the floor is nothing but the damp earth; nastiness and irregularity possess the whole scene. The fine workmanship of the pillars whose capitals for flowers and foliage exceed all the rest of the building; the ribs of the arches and ornament of their intersections are scarce to be seen in the horrid gloom which possesses the place. What idea concomitant to religion can dictate filthiness and confusion in a house of worship, I know not…Many of the old churches of Scotland I have seen filthy and foul…but for uncleanliness this place exceeds them all.

The concern for the state of the abbey and parish church was one of the first signs that growing prosperity was to encourage a new approach to the townscape. A report on the 'sufficiency or insufficiency' of the fabric of the parish church highlighted its dilapidated state. Numerous repairs were essential; but it was suggested that 'if instead of … repairs the heritors think proper to build a new church we are of the opinion that the whole of the modern church in filling up arched windows, the pillars in the inside supporting the arch over the church, the arch itself and the buttresses placed against the pillars of the east end (all modern) may be taken away with perfect safety and thereby the old ruin will be restored to its former elegance and grandeur'. The heritors adopted this last option and in 1810 the congregation transferred to the new parish church on Weirhill (*see* **area 2**).

Equally important for the town was the restoration work on the abbey, begun in 1822 under the supervision of Sir Walter Scott, with the advice of his builder, John Smith. It

history

archaeology

Brewery ceased brewing the following year. It had initially been retained to brew stouts and porter before being converted to a store, and part of the building was leased to a local joiner, William Brown.

Today, the little that survives of the brewery lies within Historic Scotland's works yard. It is clear, however, that the brewery had been built over, or incorporated, part of the outlying abbey buildings. As the foundations of the infirmary are thought to have been

figure 21
Abbey Hotel
before its demolition
in 1948

history

was this same man who was responsible for the building of the manse **Y** in 1815. The manse and the nearby Prior Bank **K** were merely two of a number of elegant houses built in the nineteenth century in the erstwhile monastery precinct. Not all the colonising property was gracious, however. When Dorothy Wordsworth visited in 1803 she commented that the abbey ruins were 'unfortunately ... surrounded by insignificant houses'. These were the remnants of the dwellings that had begun to line Abbey Street from the sixteenth century. The Abbey Hotel **Z** also stood within the precincts, to the right of the entrance to the abbey **figure 21**. Most of these were cleared by the twentieth century, enhancing the setting of the abbey ruins.

archaeology

revealed during the building of the manse in 1815 (now called *The Cloisters*), the infirmary may equally have extended further eastwards under the brewery. More interestingly, however, a fragment of a medieval vault incorporated into the brewery still survives, and the style of the vault suggests that this could indeed have been a cellar of the original medieval brewery. (Information supplied by Archivist, Scottish Brewing Archives, University of Glasgow).

GD0303ZG/1997

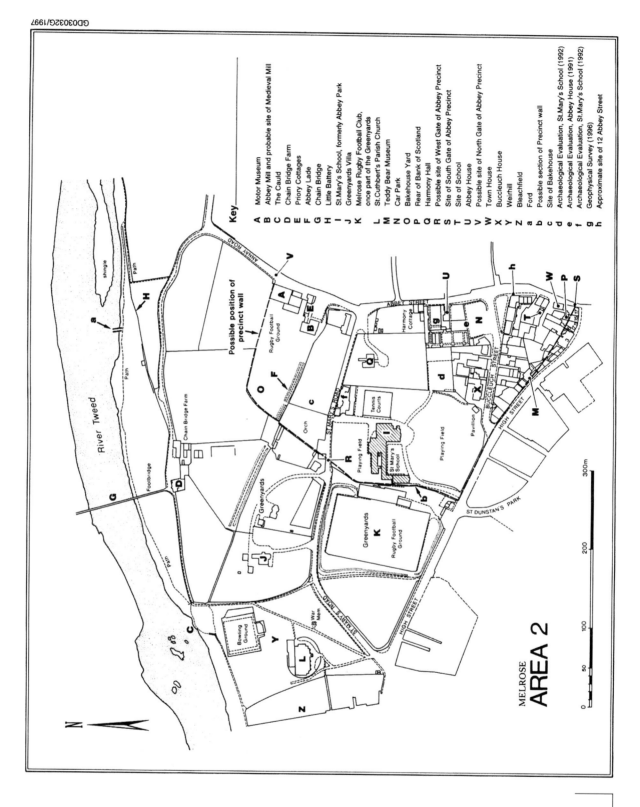

Key

A Motor Museum
B Abbey Mill and probable site of Medieval Mill
C The Cauld
D Chain Bridge Farm
E Priory Cottages
F Abbey Lade
G Chain Bridge
H Little Battery
I St.Mary's School, formerly Abbey Park
J Greenyards Villa
K Melrose Rugby Football Club,
   once part of the Greenyards
L St.Cuthbert's Parish Church
M Teddy Bear Museum
N Car Park
O Bakehouse Yard
P Rear of Bank of Scotland
Q Harmony Hall
R Possible site of West Gate of Abbey Precinct
S Site of South Gate of Abbey Precinct
T Site of School
U Abbey House
V Possible site of North Gate of Abbey Precinct
W Town House
X Buccleuch House
Y Weirhill
Z Bleachfield
a Ford
b Possible section of Precinct wall
c Site of Bakehouse
d Archaeological Evaluation, St.Mary's School (1992)
e Archaeological Evaluation, Abbey House (1991)
f Archaeological Evaluation, St.Mary's School (1992)
g Geophysical Survey (1996)
h Approximate site of 12 Abbey Street

MELROSE
AREA 2

figure 22

Area 2

area 2

Abbey Street / River Tweed / Weirhill / High Street (north side) / High Street (rear of properties)
figure 22

description

This area, like Area 1, represents the gradual infill of the medieval abbey precinct, but remains largely undeveloped **figure 5**. The western half of the precinct is contained within this area, although there are few clues as to its former tenants. One such clue, however, is the Mill Lade **F** which continues under Abbey Street (and the Abbey Mill, **B**) and cuts across the fields to its source, the system of sluices known as The Cauld **C**. The green fields to the north of the lade are owned by the adjacent Chain Bridge Farm **D**. On the opposite side of Abbey Street from Priory Farm are Priory Cottages **E** and the Motor Museum **A**, and behind them a rugby football ground. The suspension bridge **G** is a notable landmark in this largely open area. It was opened in 1826 **figure 14**, and the adjacent Chain Bridge Farm **D** was built as the toll house. Along the south bank of the Tweed, long stretches of stone walling, known as the Little Battery **H** and further east as The Battery (**area 1**), lie at varying distances back from the river's edge, and represent former flood defences. Plum trees grow wild along the inner edge of the bank.

The wooded slopes to the south of the lade, which extend up to St Mary's Road, are partly used as playing fields by St Mary's School **I**. Greenyards **J**, a substantial Victorian villa, possesses extensive grounds at the western end of St Mary's Road, which are gradually being broken up for development. Several other Victorian villas are dotted around this area, including Abbey House, on Abbey Street, Buccleuch House and Braidwood on the north side of Buccleuch Street, and Harmony Hall on the south side of St Mary's Road. All have large walled gardens. Perhaps the largest of these villas, however, was Abbey Park, now St Mary's Preparatory School **I**. To the west of the school, in an area known as Greenyards, is the home of Melrose Rugby Football Club **K**. A grassy triangle separates the club ground from Weirhill, on top of which, in amongst the trees, stands the parish church of St Cuthbert **L**. Between the church and the river is the bowling club.

The only developed part of this area is the triangular block defined by Buccleuch Street, Abbey Street and High Street, through which the boundary for this area runs. Properties extend back from all three frontages creating a maze of unnamed closes and back alleys. Tucked in here is the Teddy Bear Museum **M**. At the east end of Buccleuch Street (south frontage) is a block of post-war housing, which continues around into Abbey Street. The west end is more commercial, with cafes, businesses and shops. On the north side of Buccleuch Street is a large car park **N**, used by visitors to the town, and in particular the abbey and Priorwood Gardens.

historical background

the westerly part of the abbey complex

The history of the abbey is fully described in Area 1 (*see* pp 57–71). Running through this westerly part of the abbey complex was the Mill Lade **F** that fed one of the abbey's two mills (*see* p 75). Fed from a dam on the Tweed 460 m west of the abbey, the lade was

archaeological potential

the abbey precinct

Much of Area 2 lies within the precinct of the abbey and so the archaeological potential is considerable. The exact boundaries of the precinct are still unclear, but late sixteenth-

partially diverted also to function as a main drain to serve the latrines of the east range and, probably, those of the lay brothers (*see* **area 1**). The precinct contained kitchen and fruit gardens, as well as the mill **B**, and it is known that there was an orchard, which may have been within this westerly part of the precinct, although there were also gardens in the eastern section (*see* **area 1**). According to local tradition, the monks also had orchards on the other side of the Tweed, on the 'sunny banks' of Gattonside. The abbey bakehouse **O** also stood in the north-west corner of the precinct, conveniently near the corn mill.

The abbey precinct was surrounded by a stone wall, sometimes called the 'mantill wall' in contemporary sources. The line of the precinct wall may be located on the south side by its presence in cellars, for example at the Teddy Bear Museum **M** and to the rear of other properties, for example the Bank of Scotland **P**. Immediately to the west of the bank, a property consisting of a house and garden had previously been two properties. The more northerly part was within the old precinct, but the southerly part was not. The remaining part of the wall that falls within this area has not been the subject of recent archaeological work; but Dr Curle conducted some excavations, the results of which have not been confirmed. Based on his research, the possible line of the wall is marked with dotted lines on **figures 20** & **22**. The wall was broken by gates in probably four places: the east, west, north and south gates. The south gate **S** was the most important and stood astride the modern Abbey Street, a little back from where it now joins the Market Place (**figure 8**). It had a chapel built at the gatehouse, or above it, as at Beaulieu. Although the north and west gates **R** & **V** cannot be precisely located, Dr Curle believed that he had discovered them by excavation. This has not been confirmed more recently, but their possible sites are marked on **figures 20** & **22**. Nineteenth-century comments that Melrose occupied the site of an ancient lake and that the Tweed had moved northwards by nearly one hundred yards in places would suggest that the north gate might have been marshy. This might also have been the case at the west gate, as the area of the Greenyards was not totally satisfactorily drained until the middle of the nineteenth century.

Political and religious events brought profound changes to Melrose after 1560, with the official transference to Protestantism from the old faith. In consequence, there were soon significant developments in the townscape; the dismantling and colonisation of the abbey buildings and precincts began (*see* pp 69,98), and houses soon lined the street which was

history

archaeology

century documentary sources—which record properties as being within or outwith the mantle wall—have enabled its course, and therefore the limits of the abbey grounds, to be traced. There has been relatively little modern development within this western part of the former precinct **figure 5**. Any house or garden here, therefore, may contain within its fabric, or may have been built over, the remains of earlier medieval buildings or features associated with the abbey.

The building of a wall enclosing the abbey grounds was a considerable undertaking and must have taken some time to complete. It is likely, therefore, that the wall replaced an earlier boundary. This was the case at Dunfermline, where archaeological excavations revealed the stone wall to have replaced an earlier ditch some time in the late thirteenth or fourteenth century. Precinct walls rarely survive in an urban setting, as they provided a useful quarry for the townsfolk; but imposing sections can still be seen at St Andrews and Arbroath. A short section may also survive at Melrose. Between St Mary's School and Melrose Rugby Football Ground, a low, largely ruinous wall of grey whinstone still stands **b**. Elsewhere, the wall may have been incorporated into the fabric of those properties that front onto High Street; and in the north of Area 2, it may lie buried beneath the grass fields.

There are thought to have been four gateways into the abbey precinct, and three of these lie within Area 2: the main south gateway at the south end of Abbey Street **S**, around which the town developed **figure 8**; the western gateway, which stood near the western end of St Mary's Road **R**; and the northern gateway **V**, which lay somewhere to the north of Priory Farm Cottages on Abbey Street. Nothing remains of any of these

once the main entrance into the precinct. It later became called The Bow and then Abbey Street. Public buildings also began to occupy the ertwhile abbey precinct.

the schools of the burgh

The town's original school probably stood on the site of the present Station Hotel (**area 3**) before being transferred to Little Fordell, on the west side of Abbey Street **T**. There was a schoolmaster by at least 1608, William Coke, who had 'bluid drawin' in an incident with one John Rogear. In 1617, Alexander Wishart was the master; and in 1623, Robert Brown. It is clear that the public school, supported by the church and heritors, was to be the only school. Some time before February 1669, an unnamed woman had attempted to set up a school, but the kirk session ruled that 'no woman school be for reading in the town of Melrose'. Later in the year, in a further attempt to prevent rival schools, it was enacted that 'no schules be kept in Melrose, Daneltione, Darnick and Newstead besides the publick schuile under pain of ten marks'. A year later, a new school building was erected, with monies bequeathed by the Bishop of Lismore and Argyll, David Fletcher, once minister at Melrose. This needed regular upkeep; and in 1672, for example, 'ane sneck to the school door and oyr things needfull' were bought. The session seems to have been relatively diligent in its maintenance of the school and helping to support poor scholars. Some instances suggest, however, that funds were occasionally not readily forthcoming. In 1657, Mr James Strang, the schoolmaster, took out a decreet against all 162 elders of the parish of Melrose for their failure to collect the stent from their regions of the parish. Some pupils boarded with the schoolmaster, and seem to have shared a bed. In March 1668, one Patrick Lukup was paid for 'putting of a bed bottome to the common bed of the school'. How many children boarded and how many walked to school is unclear. The school certainly had a large catchment area, extending over Newton, Eildon, Newstead, Darnick, Bridgend, Gattonside, Westhouses, Appletreeleaves, Longhaugh, Threepwood, Newhouses, Blainslie and Danzeltoun, as well as over other properties in private hands, such as Old Melrose.

By 1704, the schoolhouse was in need of repair and 'like to fall'. The following year, on learning that the costs would be £364 Scots, plans to add a new upstairs and a chimney

history

---

archaeology

structures but they may survive below street level. Structural elements of the south gate may also survive within the properties on either side of Abbey Street, or towards the rear of those that front on to The Square. Fine examples of monastic gatehouses can be seen at St Andrews, Arbroath and Dunfermline.

The layout within monastic precincts in Scotland is little understood, and Melrose is no exception. A range of ancillary buildings would have been sited here, such as infirmaries, almshouses, at least one mill, storehouses, barns, stables, brewhouses and kilns. Water meadows, pasture fields, orchards and gardens would have provided food for the table and for the many visitors to the abbey, and an elaborate network of drains and paths would have linked the various parts of the precinct.

Water was essential to a great abbey, and the monks were experts in water management. At Melrose the Abbey Lade **F** drew water from a sluice system known as The Cauld **C**, which can still be seen today, upstream of the Tweed. This transferred a supply of fresh water over 450 m to the main abbey complex, powering at least one mill along the way. A number of footbridges must have crossed the lade, but only one survives today (**area 1**). A network of subsidiary drains would have supplied water to a range of ancillary buildings, gardens and orchards, and other drains would have returned water into the lade downstream of the main abbey complex. Where the water was used for washing and cooking, lead pipes were used, and sections have been found during excavations at Melrose. Drains are frequently found within monastic precincts and are a valuable source of information for the archaeologist. They often provide the richest source of finds, as objects were thrown in to be flushed away, and soils that accumulated in the

were dropped. Repairs were still needed in 1710 and two years later the heritors decided 'to set up the roof and to cover it sufficiently with thatch and divots. By 1713, further measures had to be taken to make the school habitable; and a collection was made throughout the parish the following year. By 1723, a decision was made to finance major refurbishment of the school; and, a year later, it was agreed to supply 'two sufficient floors, put in windows, timber and glass, two stairs within the house and partitions needful with doors, to make up the chimney, to convert the door designed for a stair without to a window, lay hearthstones, cast the house within and without with lime and to playster the windows of the said schoolhouse, to cleanse the grounds of it, to lath and thatch the roof'. In spite of these efforts, by 1763 the school was again in need of repair, so a collection was made to repair the session house and convert it into a school. Soon after this, a chapel in the south aisle was converted into a public school; but by the end of the eighteenth century, there were eighty scholars at the school and the master had a house and garden at its old site.

There was some upset in the town in 1785, when the minister, Frederick MacLagan, was charged with debts to the kirk session and, more alarmingly, adultery. Three years later, perhaps in consequence, it was the schoolmaster, not the minister, who was asked to give some thought to a Sabbath school, which was, indeed, opened. There had also been a suggestion that there should be a 'school of industry for young indigent girls by spinning'. Whether this was ever opened is unclear; as is how long either of these two schools functioned and where their sites were.

eighteenth- and nineteenth-century prosperity

Two buildings (*see* pp 69, 98), both in Abbey Street—Abbey House **U** and *no* 12 Abbey **h**—the latter being the town's first post office, were both standing until recently, although now only Abbey House remains. They were indicative of the new, improved middle-class housing of the later eighteenth century and of a growing modest prosperity in the town. On a much grander scale, Harmony Hall **Q**, a Regency dwelling of three storeys, was one of many comfortable villas erected to accommodate the growing number of substantial families in the town. Built in 1807, it was named after the Jamaican plantation of the

history

---

archaeology

base of the drains also preserve environmental data, such as plants, seeds, insects, foodstuffs, and the bones of small mammals such as rats and mice. The living conditions, diet and economy of the abbey can be reconstructed from the analysis of these microscopic remains.

Few examples of the agricultural buildings that once stood within monastic precincts are known. A possible barn is known at Balmerino (Fife), and the site of a barn is known at St Andrews. The corn mill **B** at Melrose is one of only two sites known with any certainty in Scotland, the other being at St Andrews. The surviving corn mill at Melrose is not itself medieval in date, but was probably built over or incorporated an earlier mill. It lies adjacent to the Abbey Lade, on the north side, where an off-shoot drew water from the lade to power the wheel before returning the water slightly further downstream to the east.

Only one other outbuilding is known from Melrose. The bakehouse **c**, ruinous as early as 1584, stood to the south of the Abbey Lade and to the north of St Mary's Road, and is said to have comprised several storeys of ovens stacked as high as the church steeple. The bakehouse yard **O** lay on the north side of the lade, a small footbridge no doubt connecting the two. There are no excavated examples of bakehouses from Scotland, but there are three English examples: Thornholme Priory, Bradwell Abbey and Grove Priory. The first had been converted from an earlier building, a common feature of semi-industrial, monastic buildings. Only the very foundations and perhaps the ground floor are likely to survive at Melrose. A heavy stone floor with ovens ranged against the inner walls and chimneys could be expected, with a stair tower providing access to the upper

owner, Robert Waugh. Abbey Park **I**, constructed *c* 1820, with its classical stable block, and Prior Bank (in Area 1) were, along with Harmony Hall, all sited within the old abbey precinct.

In 1822, the superior of the town and parish, the duke of Buccleuch, whose family had acquired the barony from the earls of Haddington, contracted John Smith to build a new Town House in Abbey Street **W**. This still remains, largely in its original state, with later nineteenth-century additions, although it has been reglazed. A sixteenth-century armorial panel from the abbey is built between the centre windows at first floor level above the inserted memorial panel.

Another development in the nineteenth century resulted from pressure for dwelling houses. The old precinct was not highly developed west of Little Fordell and Abbey Street, and so a decision was taken to cut a new road across Captain Stedman's land. This is now called Buccleuch Street, and is still lined with the original, quality dwellings erected in the mid nineteenth century. Buccleuch House **X**, for example, retains much of its period grace, in spite of the unfortunate flat-roofed addition to its west.

markets and trade

During the seventeenth, eighteenth and nineteenth centuries, Melrose struggled to emerge as a modest market town; the records indicate that the Melrose market had some difficulty in attracting all within its hinterland to attend. Markets were mainly held in the small market place, by the market cross (*for fuller discussion see* **area 3**); but, on occasion, markets were held at the Weirhill **Y**. Whether this was because there was congestion at times at the market place is unclear. In 1616, when the market was known to have been held at Weirhill, victuals ('viveris') were being sold. Perhaps there is here indication that the food market needed more space than the small market place could offer; or possibly this was the traditional, medieval site of the market. Certainly, John Sandilands, an indweller from Kelso, had been accustomed to sell food at the Weirhill market for the previous twenty years. On 1 August 1616, however, a group of men, including some from Melrose, 'insolently destroyed tua barrellis full of aill, with quheit breid and uther viveris ... they strak and dang him doun undir their feit ... and brusit him with thair handis and

history

---

archaeology

floors. If the ground floor ovens do survive, they may still contain the wood ash left by continuous firings. The numerous other ancillary buildings, of which we know nothing but which may lie within Area 2, include a brewhouse, smithy, kiln house, stables, barns, well house, perhaps a fulling mill and guest houses.

Beyond the north wall of the precinct lay the water meadows, which slope gently down to the Tweed. Along the bank of the river, set slightly back from the water's edge are a series of earthen banks, faced with stone, which act as flood defences. These are known locally as The Little Battery **H**, and further east as The Battery (**area 1**). Their date of construction is uncertain, but the stone facing may be a later addition to what could be a medieval feature. Crops, vegetables and fruit were grown in abundance to supply the monks and visitors, but exactly where is unclear. Fruit trees thrive naturally alongside the path by the river, and perhaps this was one of the orchards.

Villas such as Harmony Hall **Q** and Abbey Park **I**, and the smaller cottages along Abbey Street and St Mary's Road, were all built within the former precinct and may have used stone robbed from the abbey. Equally, they may have been constructed over, or incorporated, fragments of the ruinous outbuildings and ancillary buildings, elements of which may be preserved within or beneath the floor levels of the present standing buildings.

The Town House **W** lies just within the abbey precinct and very close to the site of the main south gateway **S** *&* **figure 8**. Whether it was built at least partially over it is uncertain, but as with many other buildings in the town, it was probably built using stone from the ruined abbey.

feit', even though he was a cripple. Failure of proof, however, meant the case was dropped.

Melrose also had the right to three fairs by 1660, at least. In 1695, a formal ratification of a fair on the second Tuesday of May, to last for two days was approved by parliament. Fairs are known to have been held on the Greenyards **K**, the town's common lands, where the people grazed their animals (*see* pp 36, 80); but the traditional site of the Lammas, or Scare Thursday Fair, was at the foot of the Eildon Hills, on the site of the present golf course.

Melrose moved into the eighteenth century as a small market town. It still held its Saturday market, although it was said in 1743 that it 'was not much frequented'. There were also, by then, four fairs: at Martinmas, Lammas, on the last Wednesday in May and on the Thursday before Easter.

The records also indicate that a number of trades were being pursued by the townspeople. The weavers were the most highly organised, receiving their seal of cause from the earl of Haddington in 1668. As an incorporated body, they were then entitled to control quality within their craft, lay down rules over training of apprentices, appoint their own officers and raise funds for their own welfare. For a while, they brought considerable renown to the town, exporting linen as far afield as London and abroad. In 1755, 33,282.5 yards were manufactured, at a revenue of £2,575 10s 11.25d. Ten years later, however, only 32,300.625 yards were produced, for £2,495 14s 9.25d. In 1774, the output had dropped further to 20,789.75 yards, at an income of £2,051 16s 7.25d; and in 1784 a mere 17,792 yards was woven, bringing in only £1,845 12s 4d. There were fears that the town would lose 'its name and business'; and the decline was blamed on the promotion of woollen manufacturing, at the expense of linen. Nearby Galashiels had invested a considerable sum in plant and machinery for wool manufacture, which was drawing away customers from Melrose; and women were paid more highly in the woollen industry. The linen manufacturers could not compete, and the workforce was therefore declining as well. Once work was undertaken in the woollen industry, it was claimed, hands were spoiled for linen. Added to this, the price of Dutch flax had risen beyond the means of the Melrose manufacturers.

history

archaeology

Of the 1815 parish church **L**, which lies outwith the precinct, only the steeple remains. In the early twentieth century, most of it was destroyed by fire. The new church appears to be slightly larger than the 1815 church, which comprised a square building with four porches, one midway along each side. The modern church may, therefore, preserve elements of the old church within its fabric or preserve its ground plan beneath floor level.

Archaeological monitoring of any future ground disturbance or development within the abbey precinct is a priority, if we are to understand the inner workings of this important monastic settlement. Remains of the precinct boundary, outbuildings and other features here are likely to be preserved not only in the fields and open areas, but also beneath the houses that have gradually infilled the precinct since the Reformation. Alhough St Mary's Road and Abbey Street probably mark the line of internal roads within the precinct, others such as Buccleuch Street are later additions. Medieval features may also be preserved here, sealed beneath the modern road surface.

It is also important to trace how settlement developed here in the post-Reformation period. Evidence for this may be contained both beneath and within the fabric of existing standing buildings, along Abbey Street in particular. Here, earlier floor levels may be preserved below present floors, and perhaps earlier buildings too.

summary of previous archaeological work and chance finds

St Helen's, The Eddy Pool NT 536 347–NT 562 346 **H**
medieval riverside works
A spate in the River Tweed in the winter of 1990, and again in 1994, followed by

In spite of the competition from Galashiels, Melrose was initially able to hold its own in the woollen industry. By 1776, there were 140 looms in Melrose, compared with forty at Galashiels. It has been argued that all of Melrose's looms were for woollen goods. It seems, however, that an interest in linen must have continued to some extent—in 1778, Selkirk was refused a linen stamper as linen was sold only at two fairs and both of these were attended by the Melrose stamper.

The bleachfield **Z** was an essential for the linen industry. Sited on the west side of Weirhill, it had been established in 1748 by the minister, James Brown, who had done much to encourage the linen industry. It was soon said to be decaying through lack of water in the dry seasons and its ancillary buildings were in a state of disrepair. In the latter years of the century, however, the bleachfield once more came into its own. In 1787, for example, 715 pieces of cloth were bleached; in 1789, 917; and in 1791, 1,232. This was further boosted by the introduction of cotton looms into the town; and Melrose was to witness a rapid conversion to the cotton industry, as did many other towns. How far child labour was utilised in Melrose's mills is unclear. In 1797, after an inspection of the Lanark cotton mills, the minister offered this 'humane information', that children of nine years and over might profitably be employed in the mills. It seems that three years later, parents were put under some pressure to 'get some children put up, in particular those of nine years or older'; but the records do not indicate the success of this project.

St Cuthbert's parish church

Concern for the state of the abbey and seventeenth-century parish church (*see* **area 1.X**) was one of the first signs, at the turn of the eighteenth and nineteenth centuries, that growing prosperity was to encourage a new approach to the townscape. A report on the 'sufficiency or insufficiency' of the fabric of the parish church highlighted its dilapidated state. Numerous repairs were essential; but it was suggested that 'if instead of ... repairs the heritors think proper to build a new church we are of the opinion that the whole of the modern church in filling up arched windows, the pillars in the inside supporting the arch over the church, the arch itself and the buttresses placed against the pillars of the

history

---

archaeology

unusually low water in June 1995, exposed a number of features along the south bank of the River Tweed which may be evidence of riverside works built by the monks of Melrose Abbey. A detailed survey of these features, which extend from St Helen's in the west to The Eddy Pool in the east, was undertaken by the Royal Commission of the Ancient and Historical Monuments of Scotland. The main features comprised a timber and stone box, revetment walls (some supported by timber piles), artificial water-courses and a cobbled surface.

The stone and timber box is a part of a sluice system, known locally as The Cauld (NT 543 345), which transferred fresh water over 450 m to the abbey complex *via* the Abbey (or Mill) Lade. Further east (downstream) at The Eddy Pool (NT 562 346), three courses of ashlar masonry retaining the south bank of the River Tweed were exposed. This section of the riverside wall is known as The Battery, and stone and timber foundations have now been traced intermittently over a 300 m stretch of the river edge (from NT 5546 3466 to NT 5578 3494).

A similar revetment wall was also identified to the west of The Cauld at St Helen's (NT 536 347). Here, the wall was also found to have been supported by timber piles, and a cobbled surface had been laid in a gap in the wall. An artificial channel of well-laid masonry was also identified at St Helen's, at the point where the Huntly Burn flows into the River Tweed. *DES* (1994), 5–6; *DES* (1995), 8.

St Mary's School NT 5475 3425 **d**
garden features
Geophysical survey and trial trenching was undertaken before a proposed housing

east end (all modern) may be taken away with perfect safety and thereby the old ruin will be restored to its former elegance and grandeur'. The heritors adopted this last option and in 1810 the congregation transferred to the new parish church, dedicated to St Cuthbert, on Weirhill **L**. All that now remains of this new parish church is the tower that abuts the south side of the twentieth-century church, the rest being destroyed by fire early in the twentieth century.

crossing the Tweed

A little to the north-east of the new nineteenth-century parish church, the Chain Bridge was built in 1826 **G figure 14**. Tolls had to be paid to cross this new bridge over the Tweed, which joined the communities of Melrose and Gattonside. Chain Bridge Farm, at the south end of the bridge, is the former toll house **D**. A single storcycd building, with an attic, its central door, which is now masked by a timber porch, was aligned with the bridge; and it was here that payment was made. In the circumstances, it is not surprising that the old ford **a** (*see* p 22) remained the main crossing point of the Tweed for most people, with a box of stilts at each side of the river, to assist pedestrians. Even until about 1929, the refuse cart trundled over it through the water. At some point, the Turf Ford had been paved. This paving was not broken until the twentieth century, when Gattonside sewage pipes were inserted.

new use for the town's common lands

Perhaps one of the most important innovations for the Melrose townspeople was the introduction of rugby and the birth of seven-a-sides in the town itself. The Greenyards *see* **figure 17,** once the common land of the town, where inhabitants grazed their stock and held their fairs, was to become famous as the home of Melrose rugby.

history

---

archaeology

development within a walled garden in the grounds of the school. A simple sequence of garden soils with few archaeological features was found in the six trenches opened. The location of a linear spread of stones corresponded to one of several garden paths which appear on both the 1859 and 1964 Ordnance Suvey maps. *DES* (1992), 7.

Melrose Abbey NT 547 342 **e**
multi-period road
A small geophysical survey employing impulse radar was carried out in 1990, after which two trial trenches were opened to the west of the abbey: one at the back of Abbey House (Trench 1); and the other in the adjacent car park (Trench 2). Trench 1 revealed areas of metalling, comprising rounded and sub-angular pebbles, representing a road or courtyard. Trench 2 revealed levelling material and metalling. The results seem to reflect a genuine absence of substantial archaeological features (such as the foundations of buildings), within the area surveyed. *DES* (1991), 7.

St Mary's School NT 546 343 **f**
garden features
A machine-cut trench, prior to development, revealed nothing of archaeological interest. *DES* (1992), 7.

Melrose Abbey, NT 5485 3425 **g**
abbey complex
Geophysical surveys were carried out at Melrose Abbey in 1996, concentrating on the abbey grounds (*see also* pp 65–6). Three small garden areas were surveyed in Area 2, but the results were disappointing: the brick walls, flower beds, paths and greenhouses within the gardens obscured the readings. Geoquest Associates (1996, unpublished report).

area 3

High Street (north side) / High Street (rear of properties) / High Road (north side) / Gallows Brae / Douglas Road / Quarry Hill / Huntly Road **figure 23**

description

The historic (medieval) core of the town is contained within this area. It centres on the large triangular market place upon which all the main streets converge **figure 5**. Shops and banks predominate on the north and east sides, hotels line the south side. Both Abbey Street and East Port narrow markedly as they enter onto the market place, causing severe traffic problems at times. The Cross **figure 18**, much altered over the centuries, stands at the east end of the market place **A**. The central area has been set aside for short-term parking. The south side of High Street retains some of the typical characteristics of a medieval town, with long, narrow plots to the rear of the hotels, and vennels between the properties.

The miniature Toytown Fire Station at the north-west corner of Gibson Park is a gem **B**. Built in the nineteenth century, it housed, by all accounts, an extremely small fire engine. Next door is the Police Station and behind that Melrose Grammar School **C**.

There has been some new housing development in this area, with access provided by St Dunstan's Park. Also off St Dunstan's Park is a new health centre **D**. To the south of Gibson Park **E** is St Dunstan's Well **F**, situated in a grassy area adjacent to a footpath.

The recently opened Melrose Bypass was constructed approximately on the line of the old railway line **figure 15**, closed down in the 1960s. The former railway station **G**, off Palma Place, now faces onto a busy road giving it a rather surreal quality. The main part has since been converted into a restaurant and offices.

The bypass, opened in 1987, has had a dramatic impact on the eastern approach to the town. Here, a massive stone revetment has been built into the bank on the south side of East Port/High Road and is a useful reminder of the natural topography of the town.

Dingleton Road climbs the steep slope up the western flanks of the Eildons. Rosebank **H**, a large Victorian villa, on the west side of the road, is now the head office of Eildon Housing Association. A row of cottages lines the east side of the road; and behind them flows the Malthouse Burn. Most of the housing here is on the west side, centred around Newlyn Road and Douglas Road.

historical background

the lay settlement by the abbey

The same factors that drew the Cistercians to Melrose some time before 1136—the fertility of the land, its location at a geographical 'cross roads', and the close presence of a ford across the Tweed—would also have tended to attract lay settlement, as would the existence of the monastery itself. Whether there were already settlers at Melrose in 1136, however, is unclear. Since the focus of the Cistercian Rule was one of prayer, the monks would have been unlikely perhaps to adopt a heavily populated site; but it is likely that the area was lightly populated with a few native landowners, tillers and foresters of the king.

archaeological potential and future development

This area contains the core of the medieval town, and the archaeological potential is, therefore, considerable. Contained within Area 3 are a wide range of sites and features, including the market place, the main street frontage and associated burgage plots, and a number of wells. Given the lack of any archaeological work in the town to date, and the absence of any chance finds, only general comments can be made about the archaeological potential of this area.

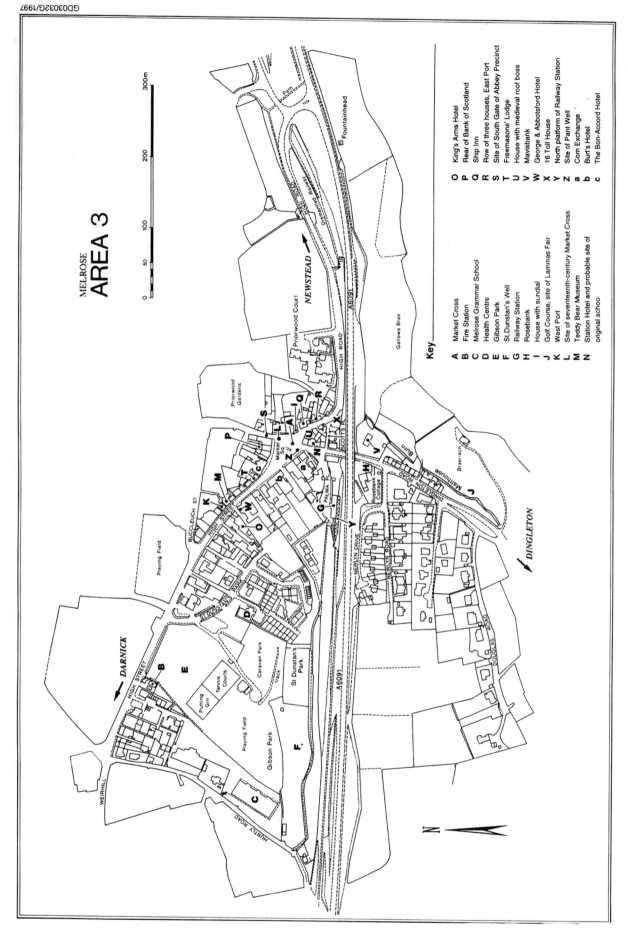

MELROSE
AREA 3

Key

A	Market Cross
B	Fire Station
C	Melrose Grammar School
D	Health Centre
E	Gibson Park
F	St.Dunstan's Well
G	Railway Station
H	Rosebank
I	House with sundial
J	Golf Course, site of Lammas Fair
K	West Port
L	Site of seventeenth-century Market Cross
M	Teddy Bear Museum
N	Station Hotel and probable site of original school

O	King's Arms Hotel
P	Rear of Bank of Scotland
Q	Ship Inn
R	Row of three houses, East Port
S	Site of South Gate of Abbey Precinct
T	Freemasons' Lodge
U	House with medieval roof boss
V	Mavisbank
W	George & Abbotsford Hotel
X	16 Toll House
Y	North platform of Railway Station
Z	Site of Pant Well
a	Corn Exchange
b	Burt's Hotel
c	The Bon-Accord Hotel

figure 23
Area 3

From early days, the abbey became the resort of kings, abbots and papal legates; and, even though there were lay brothers attached to the abbey, the services and supplies of local people were probably required to host these visitors. It would be expected that there would have been a small clustering of people near one of the precinct gates, as there was at the gate of the Cistercian abbey of Coupar Angus. One of the first firm pieces of evidence that there was early settlement here comes in 1303. During his invasion of Scotland, Edward I encamped at Dryburgh. One of his aides, Hugh de Audley, took a small detachment of sixty men to seek accommodation at Melrose. Hearing of his presence, John Comyn, Guardian of Scotland, forced an entry into the abbey precincts. In an attempt to save his life, one English knight, Thomas Gray, fled out of the gate, 'a la maner', which might be interpreted as 'village' or 'small township', and there seized the house outside the gate, where he took refuge until it was burned down around his head and he, too, was taken prisoner. It seems, then, that the first settlement was clustered at the south gate to the abbey **S figure 8**, as it was in later centuries. It may also be presumed that the dwellings were simple structures of wood, if it was possible to force Gray out so easily by burning.

As time went by, with the abbey remaining a resting place for important personages and the fame of Melrose as a place of pilgrimage becoming more widespread, support from an ancillary lay settlement would have been even more essential, particularly as the original ruling of isolation for the monastery became more relaxed. Pilgrims travelling to Melrose would have required the facilities of hostelries and provisions, as would those tenants who came to pay their dues to the abbey overlord.

Whatever small settlement there was, it could not but be affected by the troubled times that resulted from the succession crisis—the Great Cause, the War of Independence and, after an uneasy peace, the effects of the Auld Alliance. Melrose's geographical location ensured that the abbey remained vulnerable as political events unravelled in the fourteenth century. The abbey and some of the ancillary buildings, for example, were destroyed by fire in the early years of the fourteenth century. A successful appeal to King Edward I to grant timber in Selkirk forest (Ettrick Forest), since they had been burned while at his peace and protection, would suggest that the burning was not on his instructions. It seems unlikely that the conflagration would not also catch the small wooden dwellings at the abbey gate.

By May 1316, King Robert I was using Melrose as a base to harry the English in Berwick; and in 1322 the abbey complex was burned by Edward II. The granting of £2,000 for the rebuilding of the policies by Robert I, in 1326, suggests that Melrose was by now firmly in the Scottish king's camp; as did the grants of ferms and customs to be applied to the abbey fabric and daily sustenance of the monks. The regular visits of the king and his decision in 1329 that his heart should be buried there would support this. Melrose remained in a vulnerable geographical position, but with the arrival of temporary peace, it may be assumed that the lay settlement, as well as the monastery complex, had some respite.

the medieval settlement

Medieval Melrose was almost certainly a small settlement. The northern limit of the town was the precinct boundary of the abbey, which ran behind, and possibly under, the properties on the north side of High Street. East Port **figure 13** is a good indicator of its eastern limit, but the western and southern limits are a little more difficult to identify. There was a property known as West Port **figure 12** on the north side of High Street **K**, at the edge of the built-up area shown on Wood's 1826 plan of the town **figure 17**. The southern limit would have been the end of the burgage plots which ran behind the south frontage of High Street, unfortunately not marked on Wood's plan. Scott's Place probably marks the southern limit of the plots that extended back from the market place or East Port, the steep slope here forming a natural barrier to growth.

In 1385, Richard II of England overnighted at the abbey and then burned it on leaving—as part of a concerted devastation of the eastern Border region. As it was chronicled, the English destroyed everything 'saving nothing and burning down with the fiery flames God's temples and holy places, to wit the monasteries of Melrose, Dryburgh and Newbattle'.

Little or nothing is known of the effects of such long term harrying and destruction on the small settlement that clustered at the south gate of the abbey; but it must have suffered along with the Cistercian complex. In such circumstances, it seems unlikely that it would have expanded greatly from the early decades of the century. As a free regality, the abbey would have a measure of impact, through its regality court, on the peoples within its lands; but it is possible that the abbatical court, which dealt with the temporal affairs of the abbey, had greater powers in pre-Reformation days. The use from at least 1443 of the erstwhile lay brothers' choir in the parish church would also have brought closer contact between settlement and abbey (*see* **area 1**). And the gradual decline in the numbers of lay brothers would, in its turn, mean that the abbey would have had to look to lay settlement nearby for assistance, not only in running their granges, but also for the more mundane services of cleaning, washing, gardening and supplying food. On-going reconstruction of the abbey complex would also have created a demand for a labouring workforce. The continued use of the abbey complex as a temporary resting place for the monarchy throughout the fifteenth century would have brought a further demand for services (*see* p 32); and it may be guessed that in this century there was a growth in settlement.

Documentary evidence from the primary sources and observation give a relatively clear picture of how and where this small settlement developed. The line of the precinct wall may be located on the south side by its presence in cellars, for example at the Teddy Bear Museum **M** and to the rear of other properties, for example the Bank of Scotland **P**. Immediately to the west of the bank, a property consisting of a house and garden had previously been two properties. The more northerly part was within the old precinct, but the southerly part was not. Documentary evidence shows that, in the sixteenth century, part of the small township hugged the wall, facing southwards to the open market place and across to other properties lining the east–west routeway. It is safe to assume that this was also the morphology of the settlement in the fifteenth century.

In 1422, when pronouncing a decree of excommunication, the abbot, David Binning, had canonical admonitions proclaimed three times—once in the chapter house, once in the chapel at the gate and, interestingly, at the cross before the gate. Here is clear evidence that a cross had already been set up in the market square of Melrose. Other crosses, or possibly markers, stood near the township. The High Cross, for example, to the west of Melrose centre and another marker on the present golf course, the 'Haly Sing of St Waltheof', were religious spots, offering first views of the abbey to pilgrims. The presence of a cross, if it was secular, in the market square is clear indication not only of trading activities at the gate of the monastery; but also of an established trading settlement, which although still perhaps more of the nature and size of a village was probably already displaying certain urban characteristics.

The reconstruction of the abbey continued until sometime after 1505, using masons probably from Newstead. Contemporary documentation gives some small detail of other

history

archaeology

Buildings situated in the core of the medieval burgh were almost certainly constructed on the site of, or directly over, earlier buildings, a sequence possibly going back to the medieval period and continuing up to the present day. In other Scottish towns, archaeological excavations have revealed street frontages as promising for the preservation of archaeological deposits, in spite of the fact that cellarage may also have destroyed evidence. Although there has been no opportunity so far to examine archaeologically any of the street frontages in Melrose, evidence of earlier, possibly medieval, structures may be expected to survive, sealed beneath eighteenth- or nineteenth-century standing buildings—particularly those that front onto the main market place. Generally, modern

types of occupation of the local people. Tree fellers, wheel wrights, coal quarriers, metal workers, fishers and masons were all at work, as well as the expected farmers and food producers. In a letter to Pope Julius II in April 1507, however, King James IV noted that 'the lands of Melrose are on the border and so exposed to war and to banished Scots during peace that resources formerly ample will not meet bare necessities'. To the Cardinal of St Mark, he wrote that the abbey of Melrose was 'occupied by banished men and outlaws in time of peace'. Life in the small township was still disturbed.

This view was confirmed some nine years later. The disastrous Battle of Flodden had been fought in 1513 and James IV, with nine earls and many others, was dead. In September 1516, the Lords of Council decided that the Lord Governor (John, duke of Albany, nephew of the deceased king) should 'pas with ane honest company to Melros, and fra thin to Jedburgh and forthir as it sall be thocht necessar for gud reule to be maid apon the bourdoris and for the expulsioun of thevis and putting of the kingis lieges to rest and quiet'. The next years were ones of continued strife for the Borders. One of the closest skirmishes to home for the town was the Battle of Melrose in 1526. This was fought in the presence of the young king James V, when Archibald Douglas, sixth earl of Angus, who had been married to the Queen Mother, defeated Walter Scott of Branxholm and Buccleuch who was reported to be attempting to free the teenage king from Angus. The king was not to gain his freedom for another two years.

Even in the following reign, the townspeople were pulled into the maelstrom of political events. Henry VIII of England was determined to unite the crown of Scotland with that of England by the marriage of his son Edward with the young Queen Mary. When negotiations failed he decided to beat Scotland into submission. There followed seven years of devastation, much of its main toll falling on the Border region. Melrose was to suffer greatly in this war of attrition. In 1544, the abbey was burnt by the English under Sir Ralph Eure (Evers). The following year, in 1545, it was 'raced' by the forces of the earl of Hertford, numbering, it was claimed, some 15,000 men.

The town must have suffered as much as the abbey during the years of battering; although there is little or no evidence in the records of the effects on the townspeople. Little seems to have been done to repair the devastation to the abbey; and there was perhaps little point. English troops were not ousted from the Borders; in 1549, for example, they were in Jedburgh, backed by a fifth column of 'assured Scots' who were bribed or bullied into taking an oath of allegience to the king of England.

The cessation of the Rough Wooing and marriages of Queen Mary did not see the end of warfare and troops. The militia was instructed, for example, in September 1566, to convene in Melrose to meet 'thair majesteis' (Mary and Henry, king of Scots, Lord Darnley) on 8 October and pass from there to Jedburgh. A similar order went out in May 1567 to meet with Queen Mary on 15 June. On the date set, however, Mary and her husband, James Hepburn, fourth earl of Bothwell, were not in the vicinity of Melrose as both were involved in the fateful Battle of Carberry. The ongoing presence of troops and constant warfare must have affected the townscape; but of this the records tell us little.

In the early years of the seventeenth century, the little township was elevated to a burgh. There is mention of it being a burgh of barony in 1605, but no firm evidence that this was so. In 1609, Melrose was erected into a burgh of barony for John Ramsay, first

history

archaeology

construction techniques involve building from a solid base, usually the natural sub-soil, effectively removing all potential archaeological deposits in the process. The older a building is, therefore, the more likely it is to have preserved earlier, possibly medieval, features below it, or to have incorporated them into their fabric.

Given the number of quarries nearby, the use of stone as foundations could be expected. More typically, however, the early houses would have been of timber and thatched, or possibly even turf-walled—a local tradition. At the front of properties would have been small, temporary stalls, or booths, erected on market days, selling locally made produce as well as providing services such as repairs to shoes, clothes and tools. Evidence

Viscount Haddington. This was, in effect, a gift from King James VI to Viscount Haddington, who was one of his favourites; and thus the lands and barony of Melrose, together with the abbey, were constituted a free lordship and barony in his favour. By 1618, he had resigned his lordship to his relative, Sir George Ramsay of Dalhousie, at which time the latter was granted the barony with the title of Lord Ramsay of Melrose. Within a few weeks, he, in turn, resigned the barony to Thomas Hamilton, Lord Binning, who in 1619 became the earl of Melrose and eight years later opted, as a greater honour from the crown, to use the title of Earl of Haddington. As the earl of Melrose, he received a new grant, in 1621, which raised the burgh to the status of a burgh of regality. He had now, as burgh superior, full powers to create a provost, bailies and councillors, and to hold markets and levy customs from those using it.

markets, fairs and the tolbooth

The town had had a market cross from at least the sixteenth century; and, even though the town did not then enjoy burghal status, it is clear that the regality court had tried to enforce a monopoloy at the Melrose market. One John Hastie, in 1608, for example, was 'condempnit' for selling food outside the town and not presenting it at Melrose market. Soon after this, the Haddington coat of arms, perhaps replacing an earlier abbatial one, was placed on the seventeenth-century market cross **L**—although whether this was done immediately after Viscount Haddington became burgh superior is unclear. One tradition has it that the old cross was destroyed in 1604 and replaced in 1642. The date 1645 on the capital may be an indication of replacement or, perhaps, the date of alteration and, possibly, repair work at the same time. The market cross, as well as being the site of the market, also functioned as the place for public proclamations, as did the kirk door at times (*see* **area 1**).

The records indicate that Melrose market had some difficulty in attracting all within its hinterland to attend. In October 1660, the Saturday weekly market was 'almost altogether decayed ... be reason of the haile inhabitants of [the] paroch who aucht and sould bring their cornes to [Melrose] market doth carrie them to other mercats in the cuntrie'. All those within the lordship of Melrose who lived in the parish, or the sheriffdom of Roxburgh and Berwick, or who were vassals of the earl of Haddington were, therefore, obliged to bring any goods for sale to the Melrose market on 20 October and, thereafter, for three consecutive Saturday markets. Only if goods failed to sell at this point were they to be sold elsewhere. James Mertoun, tailor in Melrose, feued the custom of the market from October 1661 to October 1662; and James Elleis did likewise the following year. Payments respectively of £5 8s and £4 13s 4d for this right are clear indication that the annual profits on the market tolls were slight. On occasion, markets were also held at the Weirhill. Whether this was because there was congestion at times at the small market place of Melrose, is unclear. In 1616, when the market was known to have been held at Weirhill, victuals ('viveris') were being sold (*see* **area 2**), which perhaps indicates that the food market needed more space than the small market place could offer.

history

archaeology

for these often flimsy structures has been found during excavations in Perth, for example at 80–86 High Street in 1992.

streets and street frontages

Recent excavations in Perth, Dunfermline and Arbroath have also shown that the width and alignment of the main streets in historic burghs could change over the centuries. There are many reasons why street frontages shift. The stalls or booths encroached onto streets in an effort to lure potential buyers; and the stairs providing access to the upper floor of a tenement often stood 'tacked on' to the front of the building. With modifications over time, the building line moved forward. Good examples of this occurrence in

Melrose also had the right to three fairs by 1660, at least. In 1695, a formal ratification of a fair on the second Tuesday of May, to last for two days, was approved by parliament. Fairs are known to have been held on the Greenyards; but the traditional site of the Lammas, or Scare Thursday Fair, was at the foot of the Eildon Hills, on the site of the present golf course **J**. If the fragment of the last will and testament of Gibbie Hatley of Gattonside, dated 1547, is to believed, the Scare Thursday Fair was already in existence in his time. It has, certainly, traditionally, been accepted as an 'ancient' fair, sometimes called the Keir or Scarce Thursday Fair.

The weights used at the market and fair were held in the tolbooth, which also functioned as the town gaol and as a meeting place for courts. When, for example, thieves and 'lymmars' [villains] called 'Egyptians' [often meaning gypsies] arrived at Gattonside, a justice court to deal with the problem was held in Melrose tolbooth. The tolbooth, which had a forestair, stood in the High Street—but precisely where in the High Street the records do not say. Without doubt, it would be very close to the market square. In 1682, there was some concern over security. On 4 March of that year, it was decided that the keys to the tolbooth should not be taken out of the town 'but left in some honest mans hands'. Nine days later, a new padlock was put on the door, although all knowledge of the taking away of the old lock was denied. Two years later, however, there is evidence of a John Aitken being 'apprehended on suspicion of breaking Melrose tolbooth', which suggests that the security problem had not been solved.

the seventeenth-century townscape

Apart from development into the erstwhile abbey precincts (*see* **areas 1** *&* **2**), the street pattern changed little in the seventeenth century. Major settlement was around the market place, stretching only short distances westwards along the road to Darnick, eastwards towards Newstead and southwards to Danzeltoun. One well-known house, with a date stone of 1635 was perhaps the most westerly building at this time. It stood, with gable projecting into the street opposite the King's Arms Hotel **O**. Sometimes called the West Port **K**, it was a two-storeyed thatched house, built of rubble and harled on top. It was here that General Leslie stayed in 1645, the night before the Battle of Philiphaugh. The town's original school probably stood on the site of the present Station Hotel **N** before being transfered to Little Fordell, on the west side of Abbey Street (*see* **area 2**), although how early it was founded is not clear.

Two charters, contained in the Melrose Regality Records, define clearly typical burgage plots in the town. In 1556, John Clennan and his wife Agnes Watsoun were infeoffed of 'a tenement with pertinents before the front door of the monastery of Melrose **S**, between the tenement of the deceased John Watson on the south and the tenement of John Lorimer on the north, having the High Street on the west and the garden of the monastery called the Prenteyse yairdis on the east, the said tenement containing twenty ells and twenty inches in length and seven ells seven inches in breadth'. A Scots ell was approximately one fifth smaller than the English ell, which was a variable measurement,

history

---

archaeology

medieval towns can be seen in St Andrews, at 19–21 North Street and 13–15 South Castle Street. Here, some properties have moved forward to enclose the stair-towers (often referred to as forestairs) within their fabric; while others have not, leaving the stair-tower standing forward of the main building line.

As a result, earlier cobbled street surfaces and contemporary buildings may be preserved up to three or four metres behind the line of the modern street frontage. This was certainly the case at 80–86 High Street, Perth, where the medieval street lay some four metres further back from the present High Street. At the Abbot House, in Dunfermline, recent excavations uncovered a whole section of the medieval street itself, within and sealed below the floor of the standing building. Up to six phases of street surfaces were revealed, each separated by thick dumps of midden, containing broken

being the length of an arm. In tailoring terms it became accepted as one and a quarter yards. This ell used in Melrose was probably about a yard; so the plot was very approximately 61 feet 8 inches in length and 21 feet 7 inches in breadth.

A plot of this size was needed because life in Melrose town was still essentially rural, the backland of the plots being used for growing produce and rearing animals. It also housed the midden or cess-pit and, sometimes, also a well. This rural nature was reinforced by the grant, along with the tenement, of 'an acre and half a rood of arable land lying in Quarelhill [*sic*] at the west side thereof and a garden outwith the walls of [the] monastery, with pasturage for two cows in the commonty of Danzeltoun and a horse in the green yaird and Weirhill'. When George Hall inherited on the death of his uncle in 1573, a tenement 'before the front gate of the monastery' and on the south side of the High Street between the land of the deceased John Noitman on the west and the land of the deceased James Turnbull on the east and the lands of Quarrelhill on the south and the said High Street on the north, a further grant of agricultural land was also made. He received 'an acre of arable land of the Quarrelhill and pasture for two cows in the commonty of Danzeltoun and of a horse or heifer in the Green Yaird and Veirhill from 1st April yearly till harvest, and for the remainder of the year where the animals of the monastery were in use to pasture, with rights of peat etc'. Such grants continued into the seventeenth century. The Quarrel Hill was the Quarry Hill, still extant, south of the by-pass. Gallows Hill is also often mentioned in primary sources. It is assumed that this was where capital punishment took place in the days of the Regality; but no evidence of gallows, as such, has come to light.

Melrose was described in 1618 as 'tour fortalice and manor place containing and comprehending thainn the abbay place and monasterie of Melrose with the hous biggingis yairdis orcheardis doucawis and utheris lyand within the precinct and boundis thairof'. When King Charles I (1625–49) *de novo* granted the lands, lordship and barony of Melrose to Thomas, earl of Haddington, Lord Binning and Byres, Melrose town was detailed as 'the monastery and precinct of Melrose' and 'thirty-one tenements and portions of land'. These thirty-one tenements were not all necessarily occupied and are an indication of the smallness of the town. Using a multiplier of 4.5 per household, this would imply about 140 townspeople. The fact that proclamations from the market cross could be heard by all inhabitants is further evidence of the small size of the town.

A number or trades were being pursued in the town by the end of the seventeenth century. The weavers were the most highly organised, receiving their seal of cause from the earl of Haddington in 1668. As an incorporated body, they were then entitled to control quality within their craft, lay down rules over training of apprentices, appoint their own officers and raise funds for their own welfare. Those who were involved in the supply of food included millers, fleshers, fishermen, brewers, vintners, bee keepers and inn

history

keepers. Masons, wrights, carpenters, boxmakers, tailors, cordiners [shoemakers] and

archaeology

pottery, leather and oyster shells. Here, archaeology clearly demonstrated how dramatically street frontages can shift over time, and the potential for archaeological deposits to be buried beneath later buildings.

The old market cross of Melrose **A**, albeit considerably altered, provides a useful reminder that High Street itself was the centre of activity. This should not be forgotten when considering, for example, environmental improvements or the insertion of new services **figure 18**. Archaeological monitoring of any ground disturbance or developments in this area should be undertaken as a matter of routine. Evidence of medieval street levels could be preserved either as metalled surfaces, or as accumulated midden deposits (as was the case at Abbot House, Dunfermline). The remains of other important features of the medieval townscape may also be sealed beneath the present road surface, such as the tolbooth; the site of the earliest market cross (it was moved to its present position from a point nearer the abbey gate **L**); possible toll-barriers at East Port **X** and West Port **K**; earlier street surfaces and wells—for none of which has any archaeological evidence yet

calsay men [pavement makers] are referred to in the contemporary records, as were tailors. Merchants and notaries were an important element in society, as was the town herd, the town clerk, the schoolmaster, the town piper and the town jailor. A number of the inhabitants worked as servants to the larger houses; and Melrose had its ubiquitous quota of prostitutes.

Melrose in the eighteenth and nineteenth centuries

Melrose moved into the eighteenth century as a small market town, supporting a level of manufacturing. It still held its Saturday market, although it was said in 1743 that it 'was not much frequented'. There were also four fairs, at Martinmas, Lammas, on the last Wednesday in May and on the Thursday before Easter (the Scare Fair).

   Although there were a few writers to the signet in the town and a few merchants by the end of the eighteenth century, the majority of the occupants still pursued humbler occupations, as in the previous century. Candle-making was also under way in the town, and Melrose was one of the four centres engaged in the industry in Roxburghshire. In the 1790s, the town was paying an annual excise in the region of £12 to £13. When this is compared with Hawick's £32, Jedburgh's £58 and Kelso's £186, it is obvious that this was not a thriving industry. By the middle of the century, there had been some immigration of workers from Galashiels, bringing their manufacturing skills. The town's weavers brought considerable renown to the town for a while, exporting linen as far afield as London and abroad (*see* p 41). The small prosperity that the product of the trades brought prompted the assessment at the end of the eighteenth century that the townspeople were better fed and clothed than ever before; and that, although consumption and rheumatism were prevalent in the 'lower classes', due to the coldness of the winters, most people were healthier due to the introduction of innoculations and improvements to drains. To alleviate their condition further, in 1790 the townspeople established a Friendly Society, to which an annual subscription was made as insurance against ill fortune resulting from sickness and death.

   There was no change in the town plan in this century. The main thoroughfare passed from east to west, with cottages near to the East Port, by at least the middle of the century. The West Port **K** (*see* p 38) still defined the western limit of the town. Houses remained small, usually of only one or two storeys high, with thatched roofs. There is evidence of some improvements in the townscape during this century. There was a certain dilapidation of some properties in the early decades. In 1720, for example, the elders of the town met to discuss the weavers' houses which were 'fallen down'. These were of the smaller type of houses in the town, being single storeyed of harled rubble and thatched. There were two rooms, one each side of the central entrance, and one of these housed the loom. Loft accommodation above provided extra sleeping accommodation and storage space.

history

archaeology

been found. Similarly, the smaller wynds between properties should also be monitored routinely.

backlands and burgage plots

Behind the High Street frontage were the backlands of the burgage plots. Over time, these were gradually built over as pressure for space within the town increased and the frontages were filled up (a process known as repletion). Evidence of burgage plots, however, does survive buried beneath modern buildings and car parks. Burgage plots are an extremely valuable source of information to the urban historian and archaeologist, as they often document the activities and conditions of everyday life in a medieval and later town; for this reason, all development in them should be monitored. Excavations in other medieval towns in Scotland, such as Perth, Aberdeen and St Andrews, have revealed middens, rubbish pits, cess pits and vegetable plots to be common features of medieval

90

The Ship Inn **Q** at East Port, although much altered in both the nineteenth and twentieth centuries, retains some of its original late eighteenth-century character **figure 24**. Built as two dwellings, they were converted into an inn in the mid nineteenth century. Next door **R**, the row of three terraced houses, all two-storeyed, harled and slate roofed, hugs the original curve of the road. The sundial built in 1762 onto the window sill of a house near the East Port, which could be viewed only by those inside, is evidence of a level of sophistication in some dwellings **I**. In 1791, the joint oldest lodge of Freemasons moved from Newstead to Melrose **T**; a feature of the lodge building, common in the town, is the reuse of stones from the abbey, as may be seen in the frontage wall.

Across the road, on the south side of Market Square, shop premises with flats above, which originally, in the eighteenth century, formed at least two separate properties, also reveal cannibalisation from the abbey. A medieval roof boss has been inserted above the central lintel **U**. Mavisbank **V**, in Dingleton Road, a two-storeyed dwelling with a central door with pilastered doorpiece and fanlight and a slated roof is also indicative of the new, improved middle-class housing of the later eighteenth century and of a growing prosperity.

The writings of Scott in the early nineteenth century added to the interest of the town, as did the renovations initiated amidst the abbey ruins (*see* **area 1**); and Melrose soon became a major tourist attraction in the Borders. Visitors were assisted by the new turnpike road system and the fact that Melrose was on the main stage coach route between Edinburgh and Jedburgh. A daily stage left in each direction from the George Inn (now the George and Abbotsford Hotel) **W**, departing for Edinburgh at 9.30 am and for Jedburgh at 2 pm. In 1826, the toll house was built at the East Port **X**, for the collection of dues. A nineteenth-century painting shows the roadway barred by a gate, which would be opened on payment of toll for the use of the road.

backlands, alongside craft workshops and kilns. A series of three excavations at Canal Street, in Perth, for example, showed that the boundaries of these plots were not at all rigid—in fact the very opposite. They appear to have shifted regularly, revealing a fascinating sequence of continually changing plot boundaries and properties being amalgamated and sub-divided throughout the medieval period.

The ends of the burgage plots were sometimes marked by small walls, wooden fences or ditches, beyond which may have been a back lane. The topography in this part of Melrose suggests that this would not be true to the north of High Street, as these properties backed directly onto the boundary of the abbey precinct in whatever form it took—ditch or wall. There was no such impediment on the opposite side of the High Street, where the plots may have been considerably longer. The potential for the preservation of medieval backlands is, therefore, highest here. As in most of Scotland's medieval towns, the

The town was to become even more accessible in 1849, with the arrival of the railway. The station, the north platform **Y** of which is still to be seen lining the newly constructed by-pass road, had been constructed over the previous two years. According to an account of 1861, 'a considerable street known as Dingleton Wynd occupied the situation ... covered by the railway station'. Its clearance, along with that of the east side of Abbey Street, 'compelled many inhabitants to resort to the neighbouring villages'. In spite of this, the town was growing. John Mason, visiting in 1826, noted that the town had about 500 inhabitants and that the houses were 'in general good ... and more ... have lately risen or are now rising'. By 1845, there was a population of 689; by 1851, 964 and by 1861, 1141. An assessment in this last year was that 'the town [had] witnessed an influx of the middle and higher classes, with a diminution of the poorer and industrious ones'.

Melrose became a favoured residential area; with a number of elegant dwellings gracing the townscape (*see* pp 99–100). Smaller residences, such as Rosebank **H**, built for James Curle, the Baron Bailie Depute, in Dingleton Road, to a design of John Smith in 1814 also appeared; and the many detached and semi-detached villas that spread westwards up High Cross Street are standing reminders of the popularity of the town as a place of residence.

There were other tangible signs of increasing comfort. Early in the century, there was an improvement to the water supply to the town. A private venture, it fed water from the south of Gallows Hill to the Pant Well **Z** in the market square. Although this well was replaced in the mid nineteenth century, it is a familiar sight in a number of contemporary illustrations. It stood close to the market cross, which according to these same illustrations and from John Wood's map of 1826 **figure 17**, had probably been moved from its original site right outside the abbey gates some time before this. The market cross then stood on an octagonal stepped base supporting an octagonal shaft **A**.

The century would see the arrival of banks, an enlarged school with seventy to eighty scholars and a subscription library. By 1886, there were six hotels and about thirty inns, which catered not only for the sight-seeing visitors, but also for those who came to the town's three fairs and, by 1861, its 'capital weekly market' held on Mondays for the sale of stock and grain at its corn exchange **a**.

Burt's Hotel **b**, which stands in The Square, played an important part in town life from its first building, in 1722. It was to hostelries such as this that those attending the town's market would resort. By the nineteenth century, it was known as Anderson's Temperance Hotel and catered also for the increasing number of visitors that came to Melrose. The western end of the present hotel now incorporates a one-time baker's shop, built in the mid eighteenth century. Although much altered, particularly on the ground floor, this two storeyed building with attic retains much of the original character of an important hostelry in a prime site at the market centre. The George and Abbotsford Hotel **W**, once called the George Inn, was built in the nineteenth century. Later additions, such as a second floor, an attic and an extension on the west, are clear indications of the growing demand for accommodation in Melrose. Nearby stands the King's Arms Hotel **O**; a three-

backlands of the burgage plots have gradually been built over, but any further development should be monitored archaeologically, because remnants of the burgage plots and their boundaries may be preserved below ground.

the potential for prehistoric sites

Not discussed in this section is the potential for the discovery of medieval or earlier chance finds, and for the remains of prehistoric sites and features to have survived within the confines of the historic burgh. It needs to be emphasised here that the Melrose area was intensively used by early peoples (*see* pp 13–20), and there is every likelihood that undiscovered prehistoric sites lie within the area under survey here.

storeyed building with attic, it retains much of its original character. The long, single-storeyed range to the rear was once the stable block, a reminder of the days of horse-drawn carriages. The Bon-Accord Hotel **c** on the north side of the Market Square and, at the foot of Dingleton Road, the Station Hotel **N** are further examples of the growth of Melrose as a tourist centre.

Melrose had established itself in the role that it fulfils to this day—as a town that attracts visitors to its abbey, its rugby and its splendid setting at the foot of the Eildon Hills.

history

archaeology

summary of previous archaeological work and chance finds

No archaeological work has previously taken place in Area 3 and no chance finds have been reported.

an overview

On present evidence, there is considerable potential for the survival of important archaeological deposits within the abbey precinct (a Scheduled Ancient Monument); but within the medieval core of Melrose town the potential is more difficult to predict. Nevertheless, routine monitoring and excavations in many other Scottish towns, especially Perth and Aberdeen but also in some smaller burghs, have demonstrated that medieval and later archaeological remains often survive beneath the modern town. Therefore, the site of any proposed ground disturbance or development along the main street frontages in the historic section of Melrose must be accorded a high archaeological priority, and arrangements made for the site to be assessed, monitored and, if necessary, excavated in advance of the development scheme. Similarly, any proposed ground disturbance of the surviving streets and wynds themselves (for instance, for essential repairs, access to services, or environmental improvements) should also be monitored routinely, because the remains of important features of the medieval townscape—the market cross, tolbooth, tron, ports and wells, of which no archaeological evidence has yet been found—may be sealed beneath them.

To date, all of the archaeological work undertaken within Melrose has been within the abbey precinct. Of necessity, therefore, this assessment of the archaeological potential has been made without evidence from archaeological work in the town. Thus, the conclusions and recommendations expressed here should be regarded as provisional; this survey will require periodic review in the light of results from any future campaigns of archaeological fieldwork (assessment, monitoring and excavation), and from other sub-surface investigations.

It is important also to stress that the survey was limited to the core of historic (medieval) Melrose, the abbey and its immediate environs. There is a recognised, though unquantifiable, potential for the discovery of prehistoric and early historic archaeological remains, both within and outwith the confines of the historic burgh (this is *not* assessed or shown in **figure 25**).

Finally, the potential for archaeological features and deposits to be preserved both beneath the floors and within the structures of historic standing buildings in Melrose (*see* pp 97–101) must not be forgotten. The archaeological potential of Melrose's standing buildings is *not* shown on **figure 25**, but the potential of individual buildings is considered in the next section.

Turning to the specific areas of Melrose (as identified in this survey), previous archaeological work and documentary and cartographic evidence have demonstrated the archaeological potential of all three areas, with Areas 1 and 2 comprising the abbey and precinct, and Area 3, the core of the medieval town. It should be borne in mind, however, that the limits of both the medieval burgh and the boundaries of the abbey precinct remain uncertain.

figure 25 distinguishes between areas of known potential (shaded green) and unknown potential (shaded lighter green). *All green areas should be treated as potentially archaeologically sensitive. Areas designated red are Scheduled Ancient Monuments and are protected under law.* Effectively redeveloped areas (shaded blue) are probably archaeologically sterile.

area 1 (*see also* **figure 20**)

Clearly the most archaeologically sensitive of the three areas, **area 1** comprises the eastern half of the abbey precinct, within which lies the abbey church and cloisters. A scheduled ancient monument, the abbey complex is coloured red on **figure 25**. There has been little modern development within the former precinct, and any earlier house or garden here may have been built over, or contain within its fabric, the remains of earlier medieval buildings or features associated with the abbey.

The ruins of the abbey are clearly laid out for the purposes of visitors but, as the 1996/7 geophysical surveys and excavations have shown, the remains of previously unknown buildings still lie below the present ground surface. Abbey Street, which divides Areas 1 and 2, itself partly overlies the western end of the lay brothers' range, the main drain and the Abbey Lade.

Away from the main claustral buildings, other features associated with the abbey in this area include the boundary wall of the precinct, and the Abbey Lade. No trace survives of the former or the eastern gateway through it, although its course has been plotted using documentary sources. The southern gateway, around which the burgh grew, stood near where Abbey Street opens out onto the market place. The Abbey Lade is still a notable landmark, but nothing remains of the many small bridges that must have crossed it.

Little is known of the outer areas of the precinct at Melrose, but a range of ancillary buildings would have been sited here, such as infirmaries, almshouses, mills, storehouses, barns, stables, brewhouses and kilns. Water meadows, pasture fields, orchards and gardens would have provided the food for the table and for the many visitors to the abbey. A network of drains and paths would have linked the various parts of the precinct.

Even today, the former precinct is relatively undeveloped, with infill largely confined to Abbey Street, Cloisters Road and some large Victorian villas in the south-eastern corner. Recent archaeological work has demonstrated the archaeological potential of the outer precinct, notably at Priorwood Gardens. Here, the deep deposits of garden soil which have accumulated have effectively sealed and preserved earlier medieval features associated with the abbey.

At the north end of this area, outwith the precinct, the Little Battery and The Battery may originally have been constructed as earthen banks, before they were faced with stone, and so could be medieval in date.

area 2 (*see also* **figure 22**)

The western half of the abbey precinct is contained within this area. In contrast to Area 1, there is little physical evidence of the abbey other than the Abbey Lade and The Cauld and, as such, the overall potential is more difficult to predict. There has been, however, little modern development within the former precinct, and therefore any earlier house or garden here may have been built over, or contain within its fabric, the remains of earlier medieval buildings or features associated with the abbey.

The course of the precinct wall has been traced, a short stretch of which may still survive between St Mary's School and Greenyards. The western gateway into the precinct stood at the western end of St Mary's Road. The southern gateway, around which the burgh grew, stood near where Abbey Street opens out onto the market place.

Little is known of the outer areas of the precinct at Melrose, but a range of ancillary buildings would have been sited here, such as infirmaries, almshouses, one and possibly two mills, storehouses, barns, stables, brewhouses and kilns. Water meadows, pasture fields, orchards and gardens would have provided the food for the table and for the many visitors to the abbey. A network of drains and paths would have linked the various parts of the precinct. A little more is known about the outlying area of the western precinct (**area 2**) than the eastern precinct (**area 1**). The bakehouse, ruinous as early as 1584, stood to the south of the Abbey Lade and to the north of St Mary's Road, and is said to have comprised several storeys of ovens stacked as high as the church steeple. The bakehouse yard lay on the north side of the lade. The corn mill, nearby, may have been built over an earlier medieval mill.

Infill within this part of the precinct is mostly limited to Abbey Street and Buccleuch Street. Elsewhere, the gardens of the many Victorian villas and cottages, and indeed the buildings themselves, may preserve features associated with the abbey.

At the north end of this area, outwith the precinct, the Little Battery may originally have been constructed as an earthen bank, before it was faced with stone, and so could be medieval in date.

area 3 (*see also* **figure 23**)

This area comprises the core of the medieval town. The street frontages and associated backlands offer the most archaeological potential, with deposits likely to be concentrated in a band along either side of High Street. This band is likely to be much narrower on the north side, as the properties here backed onto the precinct wall. On the south side, it may be much wider as more land was available, stretching back behind the frontages. The street frontages of High Street, East Port and the south end of Abbey Street offer the most archaeological potential. Here, the remains of earlier buildings may survive beneath present floor levels, or, indeed, within the fabric of the standing buildings. Behind the street frontages, the gardens and car parks may seal evidence of the former burgage plots. These narrow strips of land once contained the workshops and outbuildings which served the frontage buildings, as well as the rubbish pits and cess pits, middens and vegetable patches.

Nineteenth-century Ordnance Survey maps record a patchwork of fields on the south-west fringes of the town, in existence until development pressures subsumed them. Traces of these, in the form of boundary walls, may still survive below ground within more recent housing developments.

historic buildings

pp 97–101

Melrose is dominated by the buildings of its historic past—*the Cistercian abbey and complex* **figures 5** *&* **10** (*see also* **area 1**). Although partially destroyed by time and human wilfulness, restoration work in the nineteenth and twentieth centuries has not only highlighted the beauty of the ruins, but also brought a clearer understanding of the original functions of the various parts of this fine medieval monastery.

A section of the west wall **figure 20.L** is all that remains of the first church built by Abbot Richard and his twelve monks, dedicated in 1146. In 1385, Richard II destroyed the twelfth-century church, 'saving nothing and burning down with the fiery flames God's temples and holy places, to wit the monasteries of Melrose, Dryburgh and Newbattle'.

The work of rebuilding the abbey began within a few years of its destruction— probably with the active support of Richard II. Architectural evidence suggests that English masons were participating in this work, but that responsibility for the building work later passed to masons influenced by the European tradition. The tracery in the south transept window and in the south aisle chapels, for example, suggests that the original English masons had been replaced by others influenced by French fashion. Part of the south transept was the responsibility of the French master mason, John Morow. An inscription on the west wall of the south transept, now removed to the Commendator's house for safe-keeping, and another, still *in situ*, refer to this master-mason. The first reads: 'John Morow sometimes called was I and born in Paris certainly and had in keeping all the mason work of St Andrews, the high kirk of Glasgow, Melrose and Paisley, of Nithsdale and Galloway. I pray to God and Mary both and sweet St John to keep this holy church from harm'; and the second: 'As the compass goes evenly about, so truth and loyalty shall do without doubt. Look to the end quoth John Morow.'

The work of reconstruction continued throughout the fifteenth and into the sixteenth century; and Melrose Abbey re-emerged as one of the most magnificent in Scotland **figure 10**, even though work petered out inconclusively as it approached the west end, the existing front not being entirely demolished. The western part of the nave was for the use of the lay brothers, who appear to have disappeared from the order some time in the fifteenth century. It was perhaps for this reason that the necessity to complete the western section had become less urgent.

The other conventual buildings stood to the north of the church, an unusual location for a Cistercian establishment, perhaps determined by the water supply, the River Tweed, to the north. Ruins of these buildings also attest to the splendour of the complex. These consisted of the cloister **figure 20.B**, which was an open garth, probably laid out as a garden, surrounded by covered walkways. Near the east processional door to the church the surviving walls indicate that they were elaborately arcaded and had stone benches. An east range **20.M**, which partially survives, contained the sacristy, immediately to the north of the church. This was where vestments, altar frontals and other pertinents of church service were kept. Next to this was the chapter house **20.N**, where the monks met every morning to listen to a chapter of the Rule, discuss monastic business and confess to failings and misdemeanours. It was here, also, that important burials took place **figure 9**, perhaps the most noted being that of St Waltheof. Other offices abutted, probably the inner parlour, where there was limited conversation, perhaps a novices' day room and a latrine block, all of which were under the monks' dormitory, which ran along the full length of the east range, on the first floor. There is now no evidence of this last.

To the north, was a range that housed the domestic buildings **figure 20.O**; such as a warming room, the only room heated for monks in the complex; and a refectory, where meals were taken in silence. The refectory ran parallel to the north walk in the twelfth century, but was realigned to be sited at right angles in the thirteenth century, perhaps to accommodate more monks. Opposite the refectory was the wash room or lavatorium **20.P**. Water was fed to this large circular basin, still visible in the ground, in lead pipes from a well sunk to the south of the conventual buildings, at Danzeltoun (Dingleton). To the west of the refectory was the kitchen.

The lay brothers, who did many of the more menial tasks for the monastery, lived apart from the monks, in the west range **figure 20.Q**. It was two storeys high, extending some 108 m from the west porch of the church and was formed of two blocks. Parts of the ground floor level are still clearly visible. The southern end of the northern block was the lay brothers' refectory; and a tiled fireplace in the west wall indicates the site of their warming room. At right angles at the northern end was a further block **20.R**, which housed their latrines and three pits which may have been used for tanning.

To the north-east of the cloister and ranges are the foundations of the Abbot's Hall **figure 20.C**, which date from the thirteenth century. It was probably a two-storeyed building, accommodating storage on the ground floor and the abbot's private chambers on the upper. Little of this now remains. A little further west stands the Commendator's House **20.D**, first built in the fifteenth century, but largely converted in 1590 by James Douglas, the last commendator of the abbey. Originally consisting of at least three rooms on the ground floor, each with a hooded fireplace, the upper floor was reached by an outside staircase to the north and a timber gallery on the eastern façade. The Douglas reconstruction removed the gallery, added a square stair-tower in the south-east corner, inserted vaulted cellars and a kitchen on the ground floor and reorganised the upper rooms.

To the north ran the Mill Lade, or Abbey Lade, **figure 20.F** that fed at least one of the abbey's mills; and was partially diverted also to function as a main drain to serve the latrines of the east range and, probably, also those of the lay brothers. Both of these are clearly visible, as are the tanning pits in the lay brothers' range, all a reminder that monastic life was not simply one of prayer.

There is little or nothing standing to recall the secular medieval past of the town. But occasional glimpses give some insight into the everyday life of Melrose from the seventeenth century. The focal point of town life was the *market cross* **figure 18** & **23.L**. According to early illustrations and maps, the original site of the cross was closer to the top of Abbey Street; and this is confirmed by the fact that it is known from documentary evidence that it stood in front of the main entrance to the abbey **figure 8**. Very little of the original cross now remains. An engraving of about 1814 shows the cross with a stepped base. This base was replaced some time in the nineteenth century. The original shaft was so worn that it, too, had to be replaced as recently as 1988, although the staple that held the jougs was fitted to the new shaft. The jougs were an iron neck ring on a chain where offenders were held for punishment and public ridicule. The finial, a unicorn, holding between its front feet a shield bearing the royal arms, was mounted on a square capital, which bore the date 1645 and the initials of the contemporary burgh superior, John, earl of Haddington. It is believed, however, that this date commemorated restoration work to the cross, rather than its construction date. A mallet and rose, a pun on the name 'Melrose' was also represented. Both the finial and the capital were so weather-worn that they, too, were renewed in 1990.

Early illustrations also show that the majority of housing was small, often wooden and thatched. It is not surprising, therefore, that little has survived. A number of eighteenth- and nineteenth-century properties, many partially built of stone from the monastery complex, however, remain standing and give some clues to old Melrose. *Abbey House* **figure 22.U**, in Abbey Street, now used as the tourist information office, is an attractive two-storeyed block of three bays, with a two bayed extension to the west. With slated roof and Tuscan pilastered entrance doorway, it is probably typical of other late eighteenth-century properties which once clustered down the west side of Abbey Street. A little further down and across the road, the rubble *enclosure wall*, with flagged cope and stepped up hill, is also of eighteenth-century origin. The wrought-iron work in the circular scallops is twentieth-century work. Also within the erstwhile abbey precincts is an early eighteenth-century *doocot*. Of the lean-to type, it is built of rubble with ashlar dressings and has crowstepped flanks with moulded skewputts. The slated roof has a central gabled dormer which contains tiered flight holes. It is a clear indication of quality building in eighteenth-century Melrose.

The *Ship Inn* at East Port **figure 23.Q** & **24**, although much altered in both the nineteenth and twentieth centuries retains some of its original late eighteenth-century character. Built as two dwellings, they were converted into an inn in the mid nineteenth century. The skew putts on the east and west flank walls and the massive rectangular chimneys at the wall-head are indications of the original wall-head gable that was removed in the mid nineteenth century. Next door, the row of three *terraced houses, East Port* **figure 23.R** all two-storeyed, harled and slate roofed, hugs the original curve of the road. The *sundial* built in 1762, onto the window sill of another house in East Port **figure 23.I**, which could be viewed only by those inside, is evidence of a level of sophistication in some dwellings by this time. Another feature, common in the town, is the *reuse of stones* from the abbey, as may be seen in the frontage wall of a property in this street.

Across the road, on the *south side of Market Square*, shop premises with flats above, which originally, in the eighteenth century, formed at least two separate properties, also reveal the reuse of stones from the abbey **figure 23.U**. A medieval roof boss has been inserted above the central lintel. *Mavisbank*, in Dingleton Road **figure 23.V**, a two-storeyed dwelling with a central door with pilastered doorpiece and fanlight and a slated roof, is also indicative of the new, improved middle-class housing of the later eighteenth century and of a growing prosperity.

Burt's Hotel, which stands in The Square **figure 23.b**, played an important part in town life from its first building, in 1722. It was to hostelries such as this that those attending the town's market would resort. By the nineteenth century, it was known as 'Anderson's Temperance Hotel' and catered also for the increasing number of visitors that came to Melrose. The western end of the present hotel now incorporates a one time baker's shop, built in the mid eighteenth century. Although much altered, particularly on the ground floor, this two-storeyed building with attic retains much of the original character of an important hostelry in a prime site at the market centre.

The growing attraction of Melrose as a tourist centre was reflected in the increase in the numbers of hotels, inns and hostelries. By 1886, there were six hotels and about thirty inns, which catered not only for sight-seeing visitors, but also for those who came to the town's three fairs and, by 1861, its 'capital weekly market' held on Mondays for the sale of stock and grain at its corn exchange. *The George and Abbotsford Hotel*, once called the 'George Inn' **figure 23.W**, was one of these. An early nineteenth-century building, it was originally a two-storeyed block of six bays, with a pilastered doorcase containing the door and side lights. The ground floor windows have moulded architraves and cornices, as do the upper floor windows, with a tripartite window over the door. Later additions, such as a second floor, an attic and an extension on the west, are clear indications of the growing demand for accommodation in Melrose. Nearby stands the *King's Arms Hotel* **figure 23.O**, a three-storeyed building with attic. With its painted Tuscan columned doorpiece and moulded cornice and blocking course and some original glazing (although not at ground floor and attic levels), it retains much of its original character. The long, single storeyed range to the rear was once the stable block, a reminder of the days of horse-drawn carriages.

The *Bon-Accord Hotel* on the north side of the Market Square **figure 23.c** was originally two properties, the west part being of the early nineteenth century and the east part later. The west section is two storeyed and two bayed, rendered and lined as ashlar. With a pilastered doorcase, it has a segmental bowed projection with a tripartite window on each floor. The east side has been more radically altered, with a modern shop front inserted. At the foot of Dingleton Road, the *Station Hotel* **figure 23.N** is another example of the growth of Melrose as a tourist centre. A mid nineteenth century building, it is two storeyed with gabled dormers in the attic. The centre door has a cornice and blocking course and the roof is slated.

Melrose, however, was proving to be not merely a resort for temporary visitors. *Harmony Hall*, a Regency dwelling of three storeys **figure 22.Q**, is one of the many comfortable villas erected in the town to accommodate the growing number of substantial families in the town. Built in 1807, it was named after the Jamaican plantation of the owner, Robert Waugh. A three bay residence, fronting to the south, the centre bay has an advanced and pedimented entrance with steps and a projecting Ionic columned porch. The south front is of coursed squared whinstone with freestone dressings, while the flanks and rear are of course squared rubble. There are two more modern wings to the rear. The property is surrounded by tall, rubble walls with a flagged cope, broken by a gate with corniced piers to the east. Nicknamed 'Melancholy Jaques', Robert Waugh rarely emerged from behind his protective walls.

The manse, called *The Cloisters* **figure 20.Y**, was built in 1815 to a design of John Smith of Darnick. A two-storeyed dwelling house with three bays, it has a piended slated roof. The centre door has a corniced architrave and fanlight. *Abbey Park* **figure 22.I**, constructed *c* 1820, now St Mary's Preparatory School, is a two-storeyed, three bay classical villa with a Tuscan pilastered doorpiece. It is built of coursed squared rubble with polished ashlar dressings and has a piended slated roof. Its classical stable block of a similar date is yet another remnant of the times of horse drawn transport.

Smaller residences, such as *Rosebank* **figure 23.H**, built for James Curle, the Baron Bailie Depute, in Dingleton Road, to a design of John Smith in 1814 also appeared. A two-storeyed house with slated roof, it is a three bayed building with an advanced pedimented centre bay. Soon the pressure for dwelling houses was such that a new road was cut across Captain Stedman's land, now called Buccleuch Street. This street is still ligned with the original, quality dwellings erected in the mid nineteenth century. *Buccleuch House* **figure 22.X**, for example, retains much of its period grace, in spite of the unfortunate flat-roofed addition to its west. The many properties along the High Street and the detached and semi-detached villas that spread westwards up High Cross Street, which developed also in the nineteenth century, are standing reminders of the popularity of the town as a place of residence.

Nearby, on the Weirhill, stands St Cuthbert's, the parish church of Melrose **figure 22.L**. Prior to 1815, the parish church was housed in the western part of the nave of the abbey church. By 1618, a decision had been made to form a parish church from the partial ruins of the old abbey. Architectural evidence suggests that the western archway of the crossing had already been blocked; and it was in the original abbatial aisle or nave that the new *barrel-vaulted parish church* **figure 20.X** was constructed. The interior of the church was modified on a number of occasions, in order to house the parishioners (*see* pp 67, 69). Little remains of this seventeenth-century church, but traces of it may still be seen in, for example, part of the barrel-vaulted roof and supporting wall to the north in the ruined nave of Melrose Abbey.

Of the 1815 parish church only the *steeple* remains as a testament to the initiative of the Melrose people. The old parish church, housed in the abbey, had fallen into neglect and disrepair; and, rather than attempting to effect necessary changes, the decision was taken to build a totally new parish church. In the early twentieth century, most of this was destroyed by fire.

In 1822, the superior of the town and parish, the duke of Buccleuch, whose family had acquired the barony from the earls of Haddington, contracted John Smith to build a new *Town House* in Abbey Street **figure 22.W**. This still remains, largely in its original state, with later nineteenth-century additions, although it has been reglazed. A sixteenth-century armorial panel from the abbey is built between the centre windows at first floor level above the inserted memorial panel.

Soon after this, in *c* 1830, the *East Port* was constructed as a station for the collection of tolls **figure 13**. Whether there was ever a toll gate barrier here is uncertain; but a nineteenth-century painting suggests that one did exist, even if only for a very short while. The building underwent extensive renovation in 1980, but it retains much of its nineteenth-century character.

Tolls had also to be paid to cross the new bridge over the Tweed, which joined the communities of Melrose and Gattonside. Constructed in 1826, it is a footbridge with iron-link suspension chains, iron rods as vertical suspenders and a wooden deck. The *Chain Bridge* **figures 14 & 22.G** no longer charges tolls, which was one of the factors in the abandoning of the use of the ford, a little further east. Chain Bridge Farm, at the south end of the bridge, is the former *toll house* **figure 22.D**. A single storeyed building, with an attic, its central door, which is now masked by a timber porch, was aligned with the bridge; and it was here that payment was made.

Although toll, or turnpike, roads and bridges meant greater accessibiltity for Melrose, it was the opening of the *railway* that transformed the town **figure 15**. One of the few remaining original railway buildings in Scotland, Melrose north platform is still standing and retaining much of its former dignity, although now fronting onto the by-pass instead of the Waverley line. Opened in 1849, the town was now to become a major visitor attraction and a home for people who worked as far afield as the capital. This upsurge in the town's prosperity is reflected not only in the expanded townscape, but also in the later nineteenth-century buildings that sit with their older counterparts in the historic core of Melrose.

suggested avenues for further work

pp 103–5

Melrose is fortunate in both the breadth and depth of its regality and monastic documentary sources. These tell a great deal about the functioning of the Cistercian abbey and its regality; but only occasionally, and inadvertently, do they inform about the small settlement that grew up at its south gate. Although the *Chronicle of Melrose* and Melrose Regality Records have been used extensively in this Survey, time did not permit a full, in-depth study of these sources. These records merit such a study; not only to give a fuller understanding of the monastery and regality but, more importantly, to assess whether there exists more information on the nature of the medieval secular settlement, about which we know so little, and its relationship with the abbey.

From the seventeenth century, it is possible to gain a clearer picture of the functioning of the town, even though there are no extant burgh court records. The lack of these records may signify that Melrose never had a burgh court; and, indeed, that it may not

archaeological objectives for the future

Preparation of the Melrose Burgh Survey has highlighted a number of directions for future archaeological work. These can be broadly divided into management objectives, priorities for future fieldwork, and other areas which merit further research. Any such list cannot be exhaustive but it should cover the main areas of concern in the foreseeable future.

management objectives

1   Wherever possible, it is important to monitor the impact of any development (in its broadest sense) on the potential archaeological resource (the **green** areas on **figure 25**). This will require the routine provision of site-specific desk-based assessments, through to watching briefs, trial excavations and, where necessary, controlled excavation, post-excavation analysis and publication. Over time, the cumulative results will 'calibrate' this assessment of the archaeological potential of the burgh, providing evidence about the burgh's origins, and its physical, economic and social development through the centuries.

2   Developments should similarly be monitored to shed more light on the prehistory of the Melrose area, a period for which there is a growing body of evidence.

3   The degree and nature of cellarage along the main streets, notably High Street and East Port, were not systematically examined during the preparation of this report. More accurate information would be most useful to managers/curators of the archaeological resource in assessing the archaeological potential of these and the other main street frontages in the burgh.

4   Engineers' boreholes offer a convenient glimpse of the depth and nature of sub-surface deposits, man-made or not, ancient and modern. It would be useful if the results obtained from engineers' boreholes in and around the core of the historic burgh could be gradually collected and collated. Borehole results, especially those in the hands of private contractors, have proved difficult to access, and it might be worth considering mechanisms by which such information could more easily (and preferably routinely) be made available to managers/curators of the archaeological resource.

5   Opportunities should continue to be taken to increase public awareness of the potential archaeological interest of Melrose—both generally, and within and beneath historic standing buildings.

have functioned as a burgh in the constitutional sense, with its own bailies, provost and other burghal officers. The relationship of the town with its burgh superior might, therefore, merit further research.

The Buccleuch Muniments were assessed for this Survey, as they are a crucial source for our understanding of eighteenth-century Melrose; and may, indeed, contain further information than so far gained, on such matters, for example, as the precise line of the erstwhile abbey precinct walls. These deserve much greater analysis than was possible in this study. Likewise, the Melrose Parish Registers of baptisms, marriages and

history

---

archaeology

6   Periodic review and updating of this Survey would be desirable to take account of the results of any future archaeological work, and of the comprehensive collection and collation of other types of sub-surface investigations, such as engineers' boreholes, and the systematic survey of cellarage on the main street frontages. In particular, the colour-coded map **figure 25** should be revised and re-issued at regular intervals.

priorities for future fieldwork

Essentially, Melrose comprises three parts: the medieval abbey and precinct, the medieval settlement and the post-Reformation settlement. The archaeological work that has been undertaken in Melrose has all taken place within the abbey precinct. The priorities for future archaeological fieldwork within the burgh are, therefore, fairly rudimentary. However, the following priorities should be borne in mind during preparations of future project designs:

1   Recover any evidence for the earliest monastic settlement at Melrose. A range of timber buildings might have housed the community during the construction of the church and claustral range.

2   Confirm that the boundaries of the abbey precinct are those which Curle identified in the 1920s. A stretch of this wall 'may still survive above ground as the western boundary of St Mary's School'. The stone wall may also have replaced an earlier ditch.

3   Develop a fuller understanding of the layout and workings of the abbey precinct. Here were sited most of the mills, bakehouses, brewhouses, stables, gardens and orchards necessary to support the abbey and its numerous guests.

4   Confirm that the original secular settlement focused upon the main south gate into the abbey precinct.

5   Define the limits of the medieval town or settlement, and the character and date of any urban boundaries.

proclamations of marriages provide interesting insights into the lives of the townspeople; as might the mortuary rolls from the seventeenth to nineteenth centuries. All deserve greater attention than it was possible to give them.

There was no attempt to analyse the extent of the records of the surrounding settlements, with which Melrose had such close links. Newstead, Darnick and Gattonside all played a crucial role in the life of Melrose. A study of these settlements could provide a fuller understanding not only of their inter-relationship, but also a greater insight into the functioning of Melrose itself.

history

---

archaeology

6   Locate important features of the medieval townscape—the earliest tolbooth, market cross, tron, ports and wells, for example—of which no archaeological evidence has yet been found.

7   Recover any evidence for medieval industry, both within the township and within the abbey precinct. The only surviving industrial feature, the abbey mill, may have been built directly over, or incorporated the remains of, an earlier medieval mill.

8   Identify any sequence of planning in the layout and expansion of the burgh, particularly building infill within the precinct; and determine any changes in street alignment and width.

9   Assess the nature of the burgage plots: the topography of the burgh suggests that those on the north side of High Street must have been much shorter than those on the south side.

10   Ascertain the nature and date of the river works along the Tweed.

areas for further archaeological research

1   A reconstruction of the layout, extent and physical setting of the lay settlement and abbey precinct would be invaluable for our understanding of the development of the burgh. This would be particularly useful when assessing the impact of future development and in presenting the current state of knowledge.

2   Much of the abbey precinct remains open and largely undeveloped. A detailed review of the aerial photographic evidence, together with further geophysical and other field survey work, might yield evidence of outlying features, networks of drains and possibly the precinct boundaries themselves.

street names

pp 107–8

street names

Abbey Street

Areas 1 & 2
The main gateway into the medieval abbey stood at the south end of Abbey Street, where it opens out onto the market place. The line of Abbey Street probably marks the line of the main route through the abbey precinct. It was still known as 'The Bow' or 'Bow Street' in 1826, 'Bow' often meaning 'archway' in Scottish towns.

Annay Road

Areas 1 & 2
In Roxburgh dialect, *ana* means a river island. The name 'The Annay' has been given collectively to the fields to the north of the abbey, and probably reflects the periodic flooding of this area. The Battery and Little Battery, former flood defences constructed along the south bank of the Tweed, also highlight this historic problem.

Buccleuch Street

Area 2
The connection between the Buccleuchs and the abbey date back centuries. After the erection of the abbey into a heritable jurisdiction by David II (1329–71), the abbots delegated the duties to a layman, and the appointment became hereditary in the hands of the Scotts of Branxholm, who became dukes of Buccleuch. The first holder seems to have been Sir Walter Scott, also known as Wicked Watt, appointed bailie of the abbey in 1519, by Robert, abbot of Melrose. 'The Priory', now the Commendator's House, was their residence when in Melrose. The abbey was handed over to the nation by the duke of Buccleuch in 1919.

Cloisters Road

Area 1
This lane was named after the great cloister of the abbey that lies immediately to the south. Laid out directly over the lay brothers' range, the refectory, the novices' day room and the Great Drain, it more recently provided access from Abbey Street to the manse and the brewery situated at the eastern end of the lane.

Dingleton Road

Area 3
Dingleton derived from Danzeltoun, to which this road leads.

Douglas Road

Area 3
This modern street was probably named after the last commendator of the abbey, James Douglas. He was second son of Sir William Douglas of Lochleven, later James, earl of Morton, regent during the latter part of the minority of James VI. He was also responsible for the Commendator's House, a fifteenth-century building which he converted in the late sixteenth century into a private residence.

East Port

Area 3
The East Port, or gate, was the official entrance into the town. The East Port itself was built to collect tolls. It is not clear whether a toll barrier across the street ever existed here, although a nineteenth-century painting portrays a gate.

Greenyards

Area 2
Greenyards now refers to the area bounded by St Mary's Road, High Street and Weirhill, although originally probably referring to a larger area to the west of the abbey precinct. The name has also been given to both the Victorian villa on the north side of St Mary's

108

Road, and, more recently, to the ground of Melrose Rugby
Football Club. Wood's 1826 map of the town shows Greenyards as
a roughly square meadow edged by trees and as being the property
of Captain Steedman for whom Abbey Park was built. In the
south-western corner was a pond, since filled in.

High Road

Area 3

High Road approaches the town from the east, originally carrying
traffic south to Jedburgh. The line of High Road, as it approaches
East Port, marks the approximate line of the abbey precinct wall.
Like High Street, High Road means the main or principal
thoroughfare.

High Street

Area 3

Like most Scottish towns, the main thoroughfare in Melrose was,
and still is, High Street (High Street meaning the main or principal
road). From the junction with Buccleuch Street westwards to the
entrance into St Mary's School, High Street also marks the
precinct boundary of the abbey.

Palma Place

Area 3

Given that Palma is the island capital of Majorca, the origin of
this street name is uncertain. The road itself dates from the arrival
of the railway to Melrose in 1849.

Prior's Walk

Area 1

The prior in an abbey was second in office to the abbot. The
continuation of Prior's Walk was essentially the back road to the
neighbouring village of Newstead.

Scott's Place

Area 3

This narrow lane which runs off East Port has created an island of
buildings in the south-eastern corner of the market place. Scott
may refer either to the poet and novelist Sir Walter Scott (1771–
1832) who resided at Abbotsford from 1812, or the Scotts of
Buccleuch, whose association with the abbey dates from the early
sixteenth century.

St Dunstan's Park

Area 3

St Dunstan was born around AD 909 near Glastonbury, of a noble
family. He was archbishop of Canterbury, appointed in 959, until
his death in 988. As a friend and advisor of successive kings, he
was an important figure in the English reform movement of the
tenth century. One of the many wells in and around Melrose was
dedicated to him, from which this road derives its name.

St Mary's Road

Area 2

The abbey church was dedicated to the Virgin Mary. Within the
precinct, St Mary's Road probably led to the west gate of the
abbey.

Weirhill

Area 3

This slight eminence to the north-west of the abbey, slopes down
to the Tweed. It may have derived its name from the weir, known
locally as 'The Cauld', which diverted water into the mill lade.

glossary

Antonine	A period of Roman history, named after the Emperor Antoninus Pius (AD 138–160).
assemblage	A group of finds.
backlands	The area to the rear of the burgage plot behind the dwelling house on the frontage. Originally intended for growing produce and keeping animals; site of wells and midden heaps. Eventually housed working premises of craftsmen and poorer members of burgh society.
bailies	Burgh officers who performed routine administration.
barrow	A distinctive type of Bronze Age pottery.
boundaries	*see* burgage plot
burgage plot	A division of land, often of regular size, having been measured out by liners, allocated to a burgess. Once built on, it contained the burgage house on the frontage (*see* frontage) and a backland (*see* backlands). In time, with pressure for space, the plots were often subdivided—repletion. Plots were bounded by ditches, wattle fences or stone walls.
burgher	Person who enjoyed the privileges and responsibilities of the freedom of the burgh., as opposed to an indweller, the unprivileged, non-burgher dwellers in a town.
cairn	Mound of stones, often covering Bronze Age burials.
chert	A flint-like stone, which can be 'struck' to make tools.
cinerary urns, cremation urns	Pottery vessels in which cremated remains were placed, in a form of burial dating to the Bronze Age.
Cistercian Order	A monastic movement established at Cistercium (Cîteaux), near Dijon, in 1098.
cists	Stone lined graves.
craft	Trade.
cropmark	Crops which grow over buried archaeological sites ripen at differing rates and show up as shadows or colour-changes on aerial photographs.
cross slab	Sculptured stone bearing a cross in relief.
documentary sources	Written evidence, primary sources being the original documents.
Flavian	A period in Roman history, dating to the late first century AD (AD 69–81).
fluvioglacial	Combined action of water and ice.

frontage	Front part of burgage plot nearest the street, on which the dwelling was usually built.
geophysical	Non-intrusive techniques to detect buried remains.
grange	Much of the wealth of medieval abbeys and priories derived from the many outlying farms they owned, known as granges.
hinterland	Rural area around a burgh, to which the burgh looked for economic and agricultural support; hinterland likewise dependent on burgh market.
henge	A Bronze Age ritual enclosure.
hoard	A collection of material deposited in the ground, often buried for safe-keeping but never recovered.
igneous rock	Rock produced by volcanic agency.
improvement period	Beginning in the eighteenth century when land was improved and enclosed.
indwellers	Unprivileged, non-burgess dwellers in a town.
infilled	Open area that has later been developed.
inhumation	A burial.
in situ	An archaeological term describing layers of soil or features undisturbed by later activity.
lay brothers	Men who took the monastic vows and lived the life of a monk but who undertook a greater part of the manual labour at the expense of the religious life, for which they received longer sleep and more food for their pains.
microburin	A distinctive type of stone tool, usually of flint or chert.
microliths	Small stone tools, usually of flint or chert.
midden	Rubbish heap consisting of mainly food debris and other waste products, often found in the backlands of medieval properties.
mortaria	Large Roman bowls used in the preparation of food.
natural	A term used by archaeologists to describe the undisturbed sub-soil.
nave	Main body of a church.
palstaves	A distinctive type of Bronze Age axe.
precinct	Area enclosed within the boundaries of the abbey.
prehistory	Period of human history before the advent of writing.

pulpitum	A screen which separated the monks' choir from the lay brothers.	111
radar	A technique used to detect buried remains using sound waves.	
radiocarbon	A technique used in archaeology to date organic materials.	
rampart	An artificial earthen or stone bank.	
refectory	Eating room in monastery.	
repletion	*see* burgage plot	
resistivity	Detects buried remains by measuring the differences in the resistance to an electrical current passed through the ground.	
rig	*see* burgage plot	
Severan	A period of Roman history, named after the Emperor Septimius Severus (AD 193–195).	
souterrain	Stone-built underground passage dating from between the late first millennium BC and the early first millennium AD.	
tectonic movements	Displacements in the earth's crust.	
temporary camp	Often called marching camps, these were constructed each night by the Roman army on military campaigns.	
tolbooth	The most important secular building; meeting place of burgh council; collection post for market tolls; often housed town gaol.	
tolls	Payments for use of burgh market; or turnpike roads.	
townhouse	Principal modern civic building.	
transepts	The cross-arms of a cruciform plan church.	
tron	Public weigh-beam.	
tumulus	An artificial mound.	
vallum	A ditch.	
vennel	Alley; narrow lane.	
£	£ Scots.	

bibliography

pp 113–118

Borders Regional Archive, Selkirk
R/CS/1/4 Valuation Roll of the shire of Roxburgh, 1643.
R/CS/1/15 Valuation Book.
R/CS/1/16 Valuation Book.
R/LR/1/1 Lieutenancy Records for Roxburghshire.

Scottish Record Office
CH2/386 Kirk Session Records, Melrose.
E69/21 Melrose Hearth Tax Records.
GD1 Miscellaneous Accessions.
GD32 Elibank Papers.
GD45 Dalhousie Muniments.
GD111 James Curle Writs.
GD150 Morton Papers.
GD224 Buccleuch Muniments.

printed primary sources

Accounts of the Lord High Treasurer of Scotland, 13 vols, edd T Dickson *et al* (Edinburgh, 1877–).
Accounts of the Masters of Works for Building and Repairing Royal Palaces and Castles, 2 vols, edd H M Paton *et al* (Edinburgh, 1957–82).
Acts of the Lords Auditors of Causes and Complaints, ed unknown (London, 1839).
Acts of the Lords of Council in Civil Causes, 3 vols, edd G Neilson *et al* (London and Edinburgh 1839–1994).
Acts of the Lords of Council in Public Affairs, 1501–54, ed R K Hannay (Edinburgh, 1932).
Acts of the Parliaments of Scotland, 12 vols, edd T Thomson *et al* (Edinburgh, 1814–75).
Anderson, A O (ed), *Early Sources of Scottish History, 500–1286*, 2 vols (Edinburgh, 1922).
Annals of the Free Church of Scotland, 2 vols, ed W Ewing (Edinburgh, 1914).
Balfour Paul, J (ed), *The Scots Peerage*, 9 vols (Edinburgh, 1904–14).
Bede's Ecclesiastical History of the English People, edd B Colgrave & R A B Mynors (Oxford, 1969).
Calderwood, D, *History of the Kirk of Scotland*, 8 vols (Woodrow Society, 1842–9).
Calendar of Documents relating to Scotland, 5 vols, ed J Bain *et al* (Edinburgh, 1881–1986).
Calendar of the State Papers relating to Scotland, 13 vols, edd J Bain *et al* (Edinburgh 1898–1969).
Cartularium Abbathiae de Rievalle, ed J C Atkinson (Surtees Society, 1889).
Chronicle of Melrose, ed J Stephenson (Felinfach, 1988).
Cowan, I B & Easson, D E, *Medieval Religious Houses: Scotland* (London, 1976).
Dawson, J H, *An Abridged Statistical History of Scotland* (Edinburgh, 1855).
Defoe, D, *A Tour Through the Whole Island of Great Britain*, edd P N Furbank & W R Owens (New Haven, 1991).
Donaldson, G (ed), *The Thirds of Benefices, 1561–72* (SHS, 1949).
Dunbar, A H, *Scottish Kings, 1005–1625* (Edinburgh, 1906).
Extracts from the Records of the Burgh of Edinburgh, 1626–41, ed M Wood (Edinburgh, 1936).
Extracts from the Records of the Burgh of Edinburgh, 1689–1701, ed H Armet (Edinburgh, 1962).
Fasti Ecclesiae Scoticanae, ed H Scott, 10 vols (Edinburgh, 1915–1981).
Firth, C H (ed), *Scotland and the Commonwealth* (SHS, 1895).
Firth, C H (ed), *Scotland and the Protectorate* (SHS, 1899).
Groome, F H, *Ordnance Gazetteer of Scotland: A Survey of Scottish Topography*, 6 vols (Edinburgh, 1886).
Hamilton Papers, 2 vols, ed J Bain (Edinburgh, 1890).
Heron, R, *Scotland Delineated* (Edinburgh, 1799: Edinburgh facsimile 1975).

Hume Brown, P (ed), *Early Travellers in Scotland* (Edinburgh, 1891).

Inventory of Ancient and Historical Monuments of Roxburghshire (RCAHMS, 1956).

Kirk, J (ed), *The Books of Assumption of the Thirds of Benefices. Scottish Ecclesiastical Rentals at the Reformation* (Oxford, 1995).

Kyd, J G (ed), *Scottish Population Statistics, including Webster's Analysis of Population, 1755* (SHS, 1952).

Laing Charters 854–1837, ed J Anderson (Edinburgh, 1899).

Lawrie, A (ed), *Early Scottish Charters, Prior to 1153* (Glasgow, 1905).

Lewis, S, *A Topographical Dictionary of Scotland*, 2 vols (London, 1843–6).

Liber Sancte Marie de Melros, 2 vols, ed C Innes (Bannatyne Club, 1837).

MacFarlane, W, *Geographical Collections Relating to Scotland*, 3 vols, ed A Mitchell (SHS, 1906–08).

Mackie, R L (ed), *The Letters of James IV* (SHS, 1953).

Marwick, J (ed), *Extracts from the Records of the Convention of Royal Burghs of Scotland*, 7 vols (Edinburgh, 1870–1918).

Marwick, J (ed), *Miscellany of the Scottish Burgh Records Society* (Scottish Burgh Records Society, 1881).

Mason, J, *Border Tour 1826* (Edinburgh, 1826).

Milne, A, *A Description of the Parish of Melrose* (Edinburgh, 1743).

New Statistical Account of Scotland, 14 vols (Edinburgh, 1845), vol iii, *Roxburgh-Peebles-Selkirk*, ed Committee of the Society for the Benefit of the Sons and Daughters of the Clergy.

Origines Parochiales Scotiae, 2 vols, ed C Innes *et al* (Bannatyne Club, 1850–5).

Pococke, R, *Tours in Scotland: 1747, 1750, 1760*, ed D W Kemp (SHS, 1887).

Pryde, G S (ed), *The Burghs of Scotland: A Critical List* (Oxford, 1965).

Ptolemy's Geography, edd C Müller & C T Fisher (Paris, 1883–1901).

Regesta Regum Scottorum:

vol i *The Acts of Malcolm IV, King of Scots, 1153–1165*, ed G W S Barrow (Edinburgh, 1960).

vol ii *The Acts of William I, King of Scots, 1165–1214*, ed G W S Barrow & W W Scott (Edinburgh, 1971).

vol v *The Acts of Robert I, King of Scots, 1306–1329*, ed A A M Duncan (Edinburgh, 1988).

vol vi *The Acts of David II, King of Scots, 1329–1371*, ed B Webster (Edinburgh, 1982).

Register of the Great Seal of Scotland, 11 vols, edd J M Thomson *et al* (Edinburgh, 1882–1914).

Register of the Privy Council of Scotland, ed J H Burton *et al*
First Series, 14 vols (Edinburgh, 1877–98).
Second Series, 8 vols (Edinburgh, 1899–1908).
Third Series, 16 vols (Edinburgh, 1908–).

Register of the Privy Seal of Scotland (Registrum Secreti Sigilli Regum Scotorum), 8 vols, edd M Livingstone *et al* (Edinburgh, 1908–).

Romanes, C S (ed), *Selections from the Records of the Regality of Melrose*, 3 vols (SHS, 1914–17).

Scalacronica of Thomas Gray, trans H Maxwell (Glasgow, 1907).

Scottish Population Statistics, ed J Gray (SHS, 1952).

Spottiswoode, J, *History of the Church of Scotland*, 3 vols (Edinburgh, 1845–51).

Statistical Account of Scotland 1791–9, vol iii, *The Eastern Borders*, ed J Sinclair. New Edition, edd D J Withrington & I R Grant (Wakefield, 1978).

Third Statistical Account, vol xiii, ed J Herdman (Edinburgh, 1992).

Watt, D E R (ed), *Fasti Ecclesiae Scoticanae Medii Aevi ad Annum 1638* (SRS, 1969).

Wilson, J M (ed), *The Imperial Gazetteer of Scotland* (Edinburgh, n.d.).

secondary sources

Allen, J R & Anderson, J, *The Early Christian Monuments of Scotland* (Edinburgh, 1903).

Baldwin, J R, *Exploring Scotland's Heritage: Lothian and the Borders* (Edinburgh, 1997).

Barrow, G W S, *Robert Bruce and the Community of the Realm of Scotland* (Edinburgh, 1976).

Barrow, G W S, *Scotland and its Neighbours in the Middle Ages* (London, 1992).
Brown, C J & Shipley, B M, *Soil Survey of Scotland: South East Scotland. Soil and Land Capability for Agriculture* (The Macaulay Institute for Soil Research, Aberdeen, 1982).
Brown, M, *James I* (Edinburgh, 1994).
Burl, A, *The Stone Circles of the British Isles* (London, 1976).
Campbell, R H, *Scotland since 1707* (Oxford, 1971).
Chalmers, G, *Caledonia: or a Historical and Topographical Account of North Britain*, 8 vols (Paisley, 1887–94).
Coppack, G, *Abbeys and Priories* (London, 1990).
Croft Dickinson, W, *Scotland from Earliest Times to 1603*, 3rd edn, ed A A M Duncan (London, 1977).
Cruden, S, *The Scottish Castle* (Edinburgh, 1981).
Cruden, S, *Scottish Medieval Churches* (Edinburgh, 1986).
Curle, J, *A Roman Frontier Post and its People: the Fort of Newstead in the Parish of Melrose* (Glasgow, 1911).
Curle, J, *A Little Book about Melrose* (Edinburgh, 1936).
Darvill, T, *Prehistoric Britain* (London, 1987).
Dennison, E P & Coleman, R, *Historic Coupar Angus* (SBS, 1997).
Dilworth, M, *Scottish Monasteries in the Late Middle Ages* (Edinburgh, 1995).
Discovery and Excavation in Scotland (Edinburgh, 1966, 1967, 1974, 1976, 1977, 1982, 1986, 1987, 1988, 1991, 1992, 1993, 1994, 1995, 1996, 1997).
Donaldson, G, *Scotland: James V to James VII* (Edinburgh, 1987).
Dunbar, J G, *The Historic Architecture of Scotland* (London, 1966).
Duncan, A A M, *Scotland: the Making of the Kingdom* (Edinburgh, 1989).
Edmonds, E, *The Geological Map: an Anatomy of the Landscape* (HMSO, London, 1983).
Fawcett, R, *Scottish Abbeys and Priories* (London, 1994).
Fawcett, R, *The Architectural History of Scotland* (Edinburgh, 1994).
Feachem, R, *Guide to Prehistoric Scotland* (London, 1977).
Ferguson, W, *Scotland: 1689 to the Present* (Edinburgh, 1987).
Gilbert, J, *Hunting and Hunting Reserves in Scotland* (Edinburgh, 1979).
Gilbert, J, *Melrose. Its Kirk and People, 1608–1810* (Melrose, 1991).
Gilbert, J M (ed), *Flower of the Forest: Selkirk: A New History* (Galashiels, 1985).
Gore-Brown, R, *Lord Bothwell* (London, 1937).
Grant, A, *Independence and Nationhood: Scotland 1306–1469* (London, 1984).
Greene, J P, *Medieval Monasteries* (Leicester, 1992).
Hanson, W S, *Agricola and the Conquest of the North* (London, 1987).
Hanson, W S & Maxwell, G, *The Antonine Wall: Rome's North West Frontier* (Edinburgh, 1983).
Hanson, W S & Slater, E A (edd), *Scottish Archaeology: New Perspectives* (Aberdeen, 1991).
Hardie, R P, *The Roads of Medieval Lauderdale* (Edinburgh, 1942).
Henshall, A S, *Prehistoric Chambered Tombs of Scotland*, 2 vols (Edinburgh, 1963–72).
Hill, P, *Whithorn and St Ninian: the excavation of a monastic town* (Stroud, 1997).
Hood, M *et al*, *Melrose. 1826* (Melrose, 1978).
Jeffrey, A, *Guide to the Antiquities and Picturesque Scenery of the Border, including Abbotsford, the Abbeys of Melrose, Dryburgh, Kelso, Jedburgh and Spots of Classic and Romantic Interest in the Neighbourhood* (Edinburgh, 1838).
Jeffrey, A, *The History and Antiquities of Roxburghshire and Adjacent Districts from the Most Remote Period to the Present Time*, 4 vols (London, Edinburgh, 1855–64).
Keay, J & Keay, J (edd), *Collins Encyclopaedia of Scotland* (London, 1994).
Kapelle, W E, *The Norman Conquest of the North: the Region and its Transformation, 1000–1135* (London, 1979).
Keppie, L J F, *Scotland's Roman Remains: An Introduction and Handbook* (Edinburgh, 1986).
Lacaille, A D, *The Stone Age in Scotland* (London, 1954).
Lindsay, J, *View of Coinage of Scotland* (Cork, 1845).
Lynch, M, *Scotland: a New History* (London, 1992).
Lynch, M, Spearman, M & Stell, G (edd), *The Scottish Medieval Town* (Edinburgh, 1988).

MacGibbon, D, & Ross, T, *The Castellated and Domestic Architecture of Scotland from the Twelfth to the Eighteenth Century*, 5 vols (Edinburgh, 1887–92).

Mackie, E W, *Scotland: an Archaeological Guide from the Earliest Times to the Twelfth Century* (London, 1975).

Macleod, I, Cairns, P, Macafee, C & Martin, R, (edd) *The Scots Thesaurus* (Aberdeen, 1990).

Maxwell, G S, *The Romans in Scotland* (Edinburgh, 1989).

Nicholson, R, *Scotland: the Later Middle Ages* (Edinburgh, 1989).

Nicolaisen, W H F, *Scottish Place-Names: Their Study and Significance* (London, 1976).

Murray, N (ed), *The Scottish Hand-Loom Weavers, 1790–1850* (Edinburgh, 1978), 2.

Omand, D (ed), *The Borders Book* (Edinburgh, 1995).

RCAHMS, *National Sites and Monuments Record* NT 53 SE, SW, NW & NE.

Richardson, J S & Wood, M, *Dryburgh Abbey, Berwickshire* (Edinburgh, 1948).

Richardson, J S & Wood, M, *Melrose Abbey, Roxburghshire* 3rd edn, (Edinburgh, 1995).

Richmond, H & Turton, A (edd), *The Brewing Industry: A Guide to Historical Records* (Manchester, 1990).

Rideout, J S, Owen, O A & Halpin, E, *Hillforts of Southern Scotland* (Edinburgh, 1992).

Ritchie, G & Ritchie, A, *Scotland: Archaeology and Early History* (Edinburgh, 1991).

Ritchie, R L G, *The Normans in Scotland* (Edinburgh, 1954).

Rivet, A L F & Smith, C, *The Place-Names of Roman Britain* (London, 1979).

Sanderson, M H B, *Mary Stewart's People* (Edinburgh, 1987).

Sissons, J B, *The Geomorphology of the British Isles: Scotland* (London, 1976).

Skene, W F, *Celtic Scotland*, 3 vols (Edinburgh, 1886).

Small, J W, *Scottish Market Crosses* (Stirling, 1900).

Smout, T C, *A Century of the Scottish People* (London, 1969).

Smout, T C, *A History of the Scottish People* (London, 1987).

Smyth, A P, *Warlords and Holy Men: Scotland AD 80–1000* (London, 1984).

Spence, A, *Discovering the Borders* (Edinburgh, 1992).

Strang, C A, *The Borders and Berwick: An Illustrated Architectural Guide to the Scottish Borders and Tweed Valley* (RIAS, 1994).

Tabraham, C, *Melrose Abbey* (Historic Scotland, 1995).

Thomas, C, *Celtic Britain* (London, 1986).

Thomas, C, *The Early Christian Archaeology of North Britain* (Oxford, 1971).

Wade, J A, *History of St Mary's Abbey, Melrose, the Monastery of Old Melrose and the Town and Parish of Melrose* (Edinburgh, 1861).

Wainwright, F T, *The Souterrains of Southern Pictland* (London, 1963).

Watson, W J, *History of the Celtic Place-names of Scotland* (Edinburgh, 1926).

Whittrow, J, *Geology and Scenery in Britain* (London, 1992).

Wickham-Jones, C, *Scotland's First Settlers* (London, 1994).

Williams, A, Smyth, A P & Kirby, D P, *A Biographical Dictionary of Dark Age Britain: England, Scotland and Wales, c 500–c 1050* (London, 1991).

Yeoman, P, *Medieval Scotland* (London, 1995).

articles, journals, book chapters and unpublished theses

Border Advertiser, 24/06/1859

Border Advertiser, 15/07/1859

Border Advertiser, 07/10/1859

Anderson J & Black, G F, 'Reports on local museums in Scotland, obtained through Dr R H Gunning's jubilee gift to the Society', *PSAS*, xxii (1887–8).

Black, G F, 'Descriptive catalogue of loan collections of pre-historic antiquities from the shires of Berwick, Roxburgh, and Selkirk', *PSAS*, xxviii (1893–4).

Bremner, D, 'The industries of Scotland, their rise, progress and present condition', in *The Scottish Hand-Loom Weavers, 1790–1850*, ed N Murray (Edinburgh, 1989).

Callander, J G, 'Scottish Bronze Age hoards', *PSAS*, lvii (1922–3).

Callander, J G, 'A collection of Tardenoisian implements from Berwickshire', *PSAS*, lxi (1926–7).

Christison, D, 'The forts of Selkirk, the Gala Water, the southern slopes of the Lammer-
    moors, and the north of Roxburgh', *PSAS*, xxix (1894–5).

Coles, J M, 'Scottish Late Bronze Age metalwork: typology, distribution and chronology',
    PSAS, xciii (1959–60).

Coles, J M, 'Scottish Early Bronze Age metalwork', *PSAS*, ci (1968–9).

Corrie, J M, 'Notes on some stone and flint implements found near Dryburgh, in the Parish
    of Mertoun, Berwickshire', *PSAS*, l (1915–16).

Corrie, J M, 'Notes on a group of chipped stone implements from Roxburghshire and
    Berwickshire', *PSAS*, lix (1924–5).

Cruden, S, 'Scottish medieval pottery: The Melrose Abbey collection', *PSAS*, lxxxvii (1952–3).

Cruden, S, 'Melrose abbey', *Archaeological Journal*, cxxi (1965).

Curle, J, 'Melrose: the precinct wall of the monastery and the town', *Hist Berwickshire Natur
    Club*, xxix, i (1935).

Curle, J, 'Some notes upon the abbey of Melrose', *Hist Berwickshire Natur Club*, xxix, i (1935).

Dodgshon, R A, 'The removal of runrig in Roxburghshire and Berwickshire, 1680–1766',
    Scottish Studies, xvi (Edinburgh, 1972).

Duncan, A A M, 'The *Acta* of Robert I', *SHR*, xxxii (1953).

Elliot, J W, 'Dryburgh Mains Farm near St Boswell's, flint implements', *DES* (1967).

Elliot, W, 'The age of reason? 1690–1780', in *Flower of the Forest: Selkirk: a New History*, ed
    J M Gilbert (Galashiels, 1985).

Gilbert, J, 'The monastic record of a border landscape, 1136–1236', *Scottish Geographical
    Magazine*, ix (1983).

Gillen, C, 'Landscape', in D Omand (ed), *The Borders Book* (Edinburgh, 1995).

Gillen, C, 'Rocks', in D Omand (ed), *The Borders Book* (Edinburgh, 1995).

Halliday, S, 'The Borders in prehistory', in D Omand (ed), *The Borders Book* (Edinburgh,
    1995).

Hanson, W S & Breeze, D J, 'The future of Roman Scotland', in W S Hanson & E A Slater
    (edd), *Scottish Archaeology: New Perspectives* (Aberdeen, 1991).

Henderson, W, 'Scottish late Bronze Age axes and swords', *PSAS*, lxxii (1937–8).

Jones, R F J, 'The Newstead project: the archaeological search for acculturation' *Scottish
    Archaeol Review*, vii (1990), 104–113.

Jones, R F J *et al*, 'The Newstead Project', University of Bradford, Archaeological Sciences
    5th Annual Report (1990–91).

Keppie, L, 'The Romans', in D Omand (ed), *The Borders Book* (Edinburgh, 1995).

Lacaille, A D, 'Some Scottish core-tools and ground-flaked implements of stone', *PSAS*, lxxiv
    (1939–40).

Laing, D, 'A contemporary account of the earl of Hertford's second expedition to Scotland
    and of the ravages committed by the English forces in September 1545', *PSAS*, i (1854).

MacKinlay, J M, 'The patron of St William's Well at Melrose', *Transactions of the Hawick
    Archaeological Society*, (1908).

McLachlan, J E, 'The Story of Fastern's E'en', *Border Magazine*, viii (1908).

Mann, J C & Breeze, D J, 'Ptolemy, Tacitus and the tribes of north Britain', *PSAS*, cxvii
    (1987).

Maxwell G S & Wilson, D R, 'Air reconnaisance in Roman Britain 1977–84', *Britannia*,
    xviii (1987).

Mulholland, H, 'The microlithic industries of the Tweed Valley', *Transactions of the Dumfries
    and Galloway Natural History and Antiquarian Society*, 3rd series, xlvii (1969–70).

O'Connor, B & Cowie, T, 'A group of bronze socketed axes from Eildon Mid Hill, near
    Melrose, Roxburghshire', *PSAS*, cxv (1985).

Owen, O A, 'Eildon Hill North, Roxburgh, Borders', in J S Rideout *et al*, *Hillforts of Southern
    Scotland* (Edinburgh, 1992).

Richmond, I A, 'Excavations at the Roman fort of Newstead, 1947', *PSAS*, lxxxiv (1949–50).

Rivet, A L F, 'Eildon hill-fort', *Archaeological Journal*, cxxi (1964).

Robertson, A S, 'Roman coins found in Scotland, 1951–60', *PSAS*, xciv (1960–1).

Sanderson, M H B, 'The farmers of Melrose', in M H B Sanderson, *Mary Stewart's People*
    (Edinburgh, 1987).

118

Scott, T, 'Collection of flint arrowheads, spearheads, knives, scrapers, borers, flakes—about 600 in all—from Craigsfordmains mostly', *Hist Berwickshire Natur Club*, xv (1894).

Smith, A, 'Neolithic, Bronze Age and Early Historic Features near Ratho, Edinburgh', *PSAS* 125 (1995), 69–138.

Smith, I A, 'The archaeological background to the emergent kingdoms of the Tweed basin in the Early Historic period' (unpublished PhD thesis, University of Durham, Department of Archaeology, 1990).

Stell, G, 'Urban Buildings', in M Lynch, M Spearman & G Stell (edd), *The Scottish Medieval Town* (Edinburgh, 1988).

Steer, K A & Feachem, R W, 'A Roman signal-station on Eildon Hill North, Roxburghshire', *PSAS*, lxxxvi (1951–2).

Stevenson, W B, 'The monastic presence: Berwick in the twelfth and thirteenth centuries', in M Lynch, M Spearman & G Stell (edd), *The Scottish Medieval Town* (Edinburgh, 1988).

Tait, J, 'On the Black Dyke and some British camps in the west of Berwickshire', *Hist Berwickshire Natur Club*, x (1882–4).

Talbot, E, 'A possible medieval tile-kiln near Melrose', *Glasgow Archaeological Society Bulletin*, ii (1976).

Walker, J R, '"Holy Wells" in Scotland', *PSAS*, xvii (1882–3).

unpublished archaeological and technical reports

'Excavations at Castle Park, Dunbar: 1988–90', Perry, D *et al*, SUAT (forthcoming).

'Melrose Abbey: car park assessment', AOC-HBM, 1990.

'Melrose Abbey: report of trial excavation', Scotia Archaeology Ltd, 1991.

'Priorwood Garden, Melrose: report of trial excavation', Scotia Archaeology Ltd, 1992.

'Geophysical surveys at Melrose Abbey 1996', Geoquest Associates for Historic Scotland 1996.

'Melrose Abbey: Excavations on the Chapter House, 1996', Kirkdale Archaeology, 1997 (Interim Report).

'Melrose Abbey: Excavations 1997', Kirkdale Archaeology, 1997 (Interim Report).

'The Annay NT 548 344: Military Prisoner of War Camp', Borders Regional Council, 1991.

cartographic sources

McNeill, P & Nicolson, R, *An Historical Atlas of Scotland c 400–c 1600* (Conference of Scottish Medievalists, 1975).

Moir, D G (ed), *Early Maps of Scotland*, 2 vols, (Edinburgh, 1973).

'Lauderdalia', in John Blaeu, *Atlas Novus*, (Amsterdam, 1654).

'Plan of the Property-Lands and part of the Feus in the Lordship and Barony of Melrose belonging to His Grace the Duke of Buccleuch and Queensberry, *c* 1815.

'Ptolemy's map of Britain' in Mercator, *Orbis Antiqui Fabulae Geographicae*, first published Amsterdam 1578 (Amsterdam 1730). As described (Me 8) in Dr Ir C Koeman, *Atlantes Neerlandici*, (Amsterdam, 1969).

SRO RHP 93534 'Plan of the Property Lands in the Lordship of Melrose belonging to his Grace the Duke of Buccleuch and Queensberry'.

SRO RHP 93533 'Contents of the Dukes Property'.

SRO RHP 9635 'A Rood Draught of Melros Land Town by a scale of two chains in the inch' 1764.

Roy, W, 'Military Survey of Scotland' [1747–55] Sheet 8.

Ainslie, J, 'Berwickshire', 1821.

Thomson, J, 'Roxburghshire', 1822.

Wood, J, 'Sketch of Melrose and Gattonside', 1826.

'Roxburghshire', Ordnance Survey, 6" County Survey, 1859.

'Melrose', Ordnance Survey 1:2,500, 1992.

'Melrose', Ordnance Survey 1:10,000, 1994.

abbatial court 31
Abbey Brewery 69–70
Abbey Hotel 43, 71 **figure 21**
Abbey House 42, 69, 73, 76, 80, 98
Abbey Lade, Mill Lade 24, 59, 62–3, 68, 73, 76, 79, 94, 98
Abbey Mill 73
Abbey Park 45, 73, 77, 100
Abbey Place 59, 61
Abbey Street 10–11, 31, 37, 38, 42, 43, 45, 48, 57, 59, 61, 63, 65, 69, 71, 73, 74, 75, 76, 77, 78, 87, 94, 98
abbeys
    siting 9
Abbot's Hall 24, 59, 60, 62, 66
Abbotsford 8, 45
Abercorn 20
Aberdeen 89, 93
Aberdeenshire 25
Adam,
    bishop of Caithness 24
Adam of Lennox 22
aerial photography 13, 19, 20, 64
aerial survey technique 18
Agricola 15, 17
agricultural equipment
    Roman 18
agricultural improvements 42, 69
Albany, duke of *see* Stewart, John, Duke of Albany
Aldwin of Jarrow 22
Alexander II,
    king of Scotland 22, 26, 27, 29, 63
Alexander III,
    king of Scotland 24, 26, 29, 63
almshouses 61, 75
amphitheatre 17
Anabaptists 41
Ancrum 40
Anderson's
    Temperance Hotel 91, 99
Angles 19
Anglo-Saxons 19
Annals of Ulster 19
Annay, the 42, 57, 64, 69
Annay Road 59, 107
antiburghers 41
Antonine Wall 17, 18
Antoninus Pius,
    Emperor of Rome 17

Appletreeleaves 37
Arbroath 61, 86
Arbroath abbey
    gatehouses 75
    precinct walls 74
Archibald,
    fifth earl of Douglas 26
Ardwall 20
Argyll 18
arrowheads 14
    flint 14
Audley, Hugh de,
    Guardian of Scotland 27, 83
Avenel, Robert 25
axes
    Early Bronze Age flat 14
    polished stone 14
    socketed 14
Ayrshire 25, 34

b
backlands 38, 88, 89–91
Bagimond,
    Italian merchant 26
bailie of Melrose regality 34
bailies 35, 36
bakehouse 35, 74, 76
bakehouse yard 68
Balliol, John,
    king of Scotland 29
Balmerino 76
Bank of Scotland 31, 74, 84
banks 48
barley 63
barns 61, 63
barrows, wood and turf 13
bathhouse 18
Battery, The 59, 64, 68, 77, 79, 94
Battle of Carberry 35, 85
Battle of Flodden 32, 66, 85
Battle of Melrose 32
Battle of Philiphaugh 38, 87
Battle of Solway Moss 33
Beaulieu 31
Bede 20
bee keepers 40
Bemersyde Hill 8
Benedictine abbey
    at Coldingham 26
Benedictine Order 22
benefices 34
Berwick 5, 7, 8, 17, 25, 30, 64, 65, 83
    wool export 30

Berwickshire 5, 7
Biggar Gap 8
Binning, David,
abbot of Kelso 32
Binning and Byres, Lord *see* Hamilton, Thomas,
first earl of
Haddington

Black Bull Inn 35
Black Hill 8
blades 13
   flint 14
Blaeu, J, *Lauderdalia* 21 **figure 7**
Blainslie 37
bleachfield 41, 79
Bogly Burn 36
Bon-Accord Hotel 92, 99
Bo'ness 17
booths 85, 86
Border Advertiser 48
Borders Region 5
Boston, Linolnshire 26
Bothwell, earls of *see* Hepburn, Stewart
Bow, The 38, 69, 75
Bowden 20, 38
Bowhill 7
bowling club 73
boxmakers 40
Bradford University 17
Bradwell Abbey
   bakehouse 76
Braidwood 73
brewers 40
brewery 69–70
brewhouses 61, 75
brewing 63
Bridgend 37, 42
bridges 5
   aerial view **7 figure 4**
   suspension 73
Briggate 25
Britons 18, 19
Bronze Age
   metalwork 14
   settlement 14
bronze jugs
   Roman 18
Brown
   James, minister 41, 79
   Robert, schoolmaster 37, 75
   William, joiner 70
Bruce, Robert 30, 64
Brus, Robert de *see* Bruce
Buccleuch 48, 55, 77
   dukes of 33
   laird of 73, 77, 100

Buccleuch Muniments 104
Buccleuch Street 10–11, 73, 77, 78,
94, 107
burgage plots 38, 62, 81, 83, 87,
89, 91, 95
burgh of barony 25, 35, 85
Burgh Hill 14
burgh of regality 35
burghers 41
burghs 25, 35, 39
   royal 7
burials 13–14
   Bronze Age 14
   cremation 13
   in Melrose Abbey 66
   monumental 14
   single grave 14
Burns, Robert 42, 69
Burt's Hotel 91, 99

c
cairns 14
   chambered 13
Caledonian
   mountain chain 8
Caledonians 15, 17
Calgacus 15
Calsay men 40
calves, income from 26
candle-making 41, 89
Canterbury,
   Archbishop of 27, 63
Cardinal of St Mark 32, 85
Carham 19
carpenters 40
carriages 92
Carrick 34
Cartimandua,
   Brigantian queen 15
Cartleyhole 45
carved stones 18, 19
Cauld, The 62, 68, 73, 75, 79,
94
Cauldshiels Hill 14
cellars 31, 63, 84, 103
Chain Bridge 43, 44 **figure 14**, 73,
80, 100
Chain Bridge Farm 73, 80
chapels 20
Charles I,
   king of England 39, 88
Charlieu, abbot of 32
chert tools 13
Cheviot Hills 8, 9
Chiefswood 8

Christianity,
    introduction of   19
Chronicle of Melrose   24, 61, 103
churches   20
    barrel-vaulted   100
    St Cuthbert's   73
Cistercian abbey   *see* Melrose Abbey
Cistercian General
    Chapter   32
Cistercian life   26
Cistercian monks
    excommunication   29
Cistercian Order   23, 81
    relaxation   32
    Rievaulx Abbey   22
    trading rights   25
cists   14
Clairvaux   23, 59
clearance heaps   14
Clennan, John   38, 62
Clifford, Sir Robert de,
    justiciar and warden of
    Scotland   30
Cloisters, The   100
Cloisters Road   59, 60, 65, 67, 94, 107
Clyde
    Firth of   17
    River   15, 18, 22
Clydesdale   8
coal quarriers   32
Coat of arms, Haddington   36, 86
coffins, stone   59
coins, Roman   18
Coke, William,
    schoolmaster   37, 75
Coldingham   19, 20
Coldingham abbey,
    rental income   26
Coldstream   19, 26, 40
Colonisation,
    placename evidence   19
Columban church   19
Colville
    Alexander,
      commendator of
      Culross   34, 67
    Janet   25
Commendator's House   24, 34, 57, 59, 60, 62, 65
    built from Abbey ruins   68
Comslie   25
Comyn, John,
    third earl of Buchan   30, 83
Corbridge   17

corn exchange   91
Cornwall, earl of   30
Corse Rig   36
cotton looms   41
councillors   36
Coupar Angus
    abbey   27, 83
    abbot   32
courts   36–7, 87
Cowbyre   25
craftsmen   69
Crailinghall   40
cremation urns   14
cropmarks   13
Cross, the   10, 81
Cross Ridge   *see* Corse Rig
crosses   32, 36
Culross   67
Cumberland   7
Curle
    Dr James   7, 31, 74, 104
    James, Baron Bailie
      Depute   45, 91
customs   26, 36
    exemption   30

d
Da'l Riata Gaels   18
Dalriada   20
dam   24
Damnoni   18
Danzeltoun   24, 36, 37, 38, 39, 62, 87, 88
Darnick   5, 22, 37, 38, 40, 42, 75, 87
    hearths in 1691   39
    property of Melrose
      Abbey   25
Darnley, Lord Henry,
    king of Scots   35
David I, king of Scotland   7, 22, 25, 60
David II, king of Scotland   26, 30, 63
Defoe, Daniel   42, 69
Dere Street   17
Deuchar, Robert, Ltd   69
dice   63
Din Eidyn   19
Dingleton   *see also* Danzeltoun
Dingleton Mains   14
Dingleton Road   10, 45, 81, 90, 91, 92, 107
Dingleton Wynd   43, 91
ditches   20, 61
    defensive   18
Dod, The   20

doocot, dovecote 98
Doon Hill 19
Douglas
    second earl of,
        charter illustration
        of tomb 33 **figure 11**
    fourth earl 63
    fifth earl, Archibald 63
      sixth earl of Angus 32, 85
    James
      building of
        Commendator's
        House 68
    commendator 34
    family tombs 33
    Lord James' regiment 40
    Sir William,
      of Lochleven, later
      earl of Morton 34
Douglas Road 57, 81, 107
Douglas tombs,
    damaged in Rough
    Wooing 66
drains 41, 57, 61, 63
Dryburgh 14, 27, 83
Dryburgh abbey 7, 22, 60, 65
    burned by Richard II 30, 84
    fealty oath to Edward I 29
Dryburgh Mains Farm 13
Dumfriesshire 7, 17
Dunbar 8, 19
Dunfermline 61, 86
    Abbot House 87, 88
Dunfermline abbey
    drains 60
    gatehouses 75
    precinct walls 61, 74
duns 7, 40
Durham 22
Durie, Andrew, abbot 33, 66
dyeing 20

e
Earlston 14
Earlston Mains 14
East Lothian 15
East Port 10, 42, 43, 59, 61,
    81, 83, 88, 89, 90
    figure 24, 95,
    100, 103, 107
    terraced houses 99
Eata, abbot
    of Melrose Abbey 20
Eccles 26
Ecclesiastical History

of the English People 20
Eddy Pool 68, 78–9
Edgar,
    king of Northumbria 19
Edinburgh 19
    Castle Rock 18
Edward,
    prince of England 33, 66, 85
Edward I,
    king of England 27, 29, 30, 64, 83
Edward II,
    king of England 29–30, 64, 83
Edward III,
    king of England 30, 64
Eildon 14, 22, 37
    property of
      Melrose Abbey 25
Eildon Hill North 5, 10, 13, 15, 18
Eildon Hills 5 **figure 2**, 7, 8, 9,
    10, 22, 36, 48, 78,
    81, 87, 92
Eildon Mid Hill 10, 14, 59
Elginhaugh 17
Elleis, James 36, 86
enclosure wall 98
Esk, River 17
Eskdale
    disputed land 29
    teinds 25
Ettrick forest 29, 64, 83
    easements 25
Ettrick and Lauderdale
    District 5
Ettrick Water 8
Eure, Sir Ralph 33
    burned Melrose
      Abbey 66
Evers *see* Eure
Exchequer Rolls 26
Excise 41, 89

f
fabric 20
Fairnington, laird of 25
fairs 26, 36, 40, 48, 78,
    86, 87, 89
farmers 32, 35
farmlands 22
farms 9
ferms and customs 30, 64, 83
feu duties 39
feuars 42
field banks 14
fireplace 24
fishermen 32, 40

fishings 34
Flanders 29
    Count of, Melrose
        freedom from toll 25
Flavian 15
flax 41, 78
Fletcher, David,
    Bishop of Lismore
        and Argyll 37, 75
flint arrowheads 14
flint blades 14
flint tools 13
flood defences 38, 64
Floors Castle 7
footbridges 62, 75, 76
fords 22, 37, 43, 60, 80
forest rights 25
forestair 37, 87
foresters 22, 81
'forinsec' 25
Forrester, Thomas,
    minister 37
Forth, River 15, 18, 19
forts 5, 7, 15, 17 *see also*
        hillforts, Roman
        fort
France, Scottish support 30
Freemason lodge 42, 90
French ambassador 32
Friendly Society 42, 89
frontages 84, 86, 88, 93
fruit trees 24, 64

g
Gaedil 18
Gala Water 8, 22, 25
Galashiels 7, 8, 41, 78, 79, 89
Gallows Brae 57, 81
Gallows Hill 45, 88, 91
gaol 36, 87
gardens 24, 61
garrisons 15
Gattonside 22, 24, 35, 37, 42, 43,
        60, 63, 74, 80, 87
    hearths in 1691 39
    property of Melrose
        Abbey 25
Gattonside Haugh 22
    property of
        Melrose Abbey 25
geology 8–9
geophysical surveys 58, 65–6, 79–80, 94
George, Lord Seton,
    sons of 34
George Inn, later George

and Abbotsford Hotel 43, 90, 91, 99
Gibson Park 81
Gilbert,
    bishop of Whithorn 24
gilding 59
Glasgow 25
glass vessels, Roman 18
Glen App 8
Glenlochar 17
Glenluce 62
    abbot of 32
Gloucester, earl of 30
Gododdin 18
Golden Rose 24
golf course 32, 36, 84, 87
granaries 15, 20
granges 26, 31, 65, 84
graveyards 20
Gray, Thomas 27
Great Cause 29, 83
Green Knowe 14
Greenyards 28, 36, 39, 48, 73,
        74, 78, 80, 87, 94,
        107–8
greywacke 8, 9
Grove Priory, bakehouse 76
guesthouses 18, 20
gypsies 37, 87

h
Haddington
    earls of 40, 48, 78, 88
    Viscount *see* Hamilton,
            Thomas;
            Ramsay, John
Hadrian,
    Emperor of Rome 17
Hadrian's Wall 17
halls, timber 19
Haly Sing of St Waltheof 32, 84
Hamilton, Thomas,
    Lord Binning,
    later earl of Melrose,
        then of Haddington 35, 36, 39, 86, 88
Handball 45 **figure 16**
Harmony Hall 45, 73, 76, 77, 99
Hartside 25
Hassendene, church of 26
Hastie, John 36, 86
Hatley, Gibbie,
    of Gattonside 36, 87
Hawick 7, 14, 40, 41, 89
hearth tax 39
helmets, cavalry 17
henges 13

Henry, son of David I   25

Henry III,
  king of England,
  Melrose rights of
   passage   26

Henry VIII,
  king of England   33, 66, 85

Hepburn, James,
  fourth earl of Bothwell   35, 85

hermitage   7

Heron, R
  Scotland Delineated   42, 69

Hertford, earl of   33, 66

hides   63
  customs paid   26

High Cros   10, 32, 84

High Cross Avenue   13

High Cross Street   45, 91

High Road   10–11, 57, 59, 61, 81, 108

High Street   10–11, 37, 38–9, 62, 73, 74, 81, 83, 87–8, 90, 95, 103, 108

Highland Boundary Fault   8

hillforts   5, 13, 14–15 *see also* forts; Roman forts

hinterland   36, 39, 77, 86

Historic Scotland   57, 66

hoards   14

horse harness, Roman   18

hostelries   28

hotels   48

house-platforms, circular   14

Hugh, Abbot-Elect
  of Dere   24

Hunter
  Andrew, abbot and
   king's treasurer   24
  John   34

hunter-gatherers   13

Hunterian Museum,
  Glasgow   13

Huntly Burn   68, 79

Huntly Road   81

i

Ice Age   9

Improvements   *see* agricultural improvements

Inchtuthil   15, 17

infeftment, charters of   29

infirmary   59, 70–1, 75

inn keepers   40

inoculations   41

Iona monastery   19, 20

Iron Age   20
  sites   17

iron tools   14

Irvine   17

Isle of Man   24

Italians, trading with
  Melrose Abbey   26

j

James, commendator
  of Melrose   35

James I,
  king of Scotland   26, 63

James II,
  king of Scotland   26
  and Archibald
   Douglas   63

James IV,
  king of Scotland   27, 32, 63, 66, 85
  repair of Melrose
   Abbey   65

James the Stewart,
  Steward of Scotland   29

James V,
  king of Scotland   32, 33, 85

James VI,
  king of Scotland   35, 86

Jedburgh   7, 32, 33, 35, 40, 41, 43, 66, 85, 89, 90

Jedburgh Abbey   7, 22, 60
  fealty oath to Edward I   29

Joanna,
  queen of Scotland   27
   wife of St Waltheof   64

Jocelin, bishop of
  Glasgow   24, 26

Julius II, Pope   32, 85

k

Kalemouth   14

Keir Fair   36, 87

Kelso   7, 40, 41, 89

Kelso abbey   7, 22, 60

Kenneth II,
  king of Scotland   19

Kerrera   27, 63

kilns   61, 75, 90

King's Arms Hotel   38, 87, 91, 99

Kirk Session   41
  payments to poor   39–40
  records   40

Kirkcudbrightshire   20

Knitwear   8

Knox, John, minister | 34, 35, 68
Kylesmuir | 25

l

lambs, income from | 26
Lammas Fair | 36, 40, 78, 87
Lammermuir Hills | 8, 20
land grants | 25
land use | 9–10
Langshaw | 14
   house of | 39
latrines | 24
Lauderdale | 18
lay brothers | 24, 26, 28, 62
   choir | 31
lay settlement | 81
lead seals | 63
Leader Water | 5, 22, 25
leather tents, Roman | 18
Leith | 25, 34, 68
Leslie, General | 38, 87
Leslie House, West Port | 38 **figure 12**
letters of protection | 30
library | 48, 91
Liddesdale, lordship of | 35
Lindisfarne | 19, 20
linen | 41, 78, 79, 89
Little Battery | 73, 77, 94
Little Fordell | 37, 39, 75, 77, 87
Lockit Well | 24
lofts | 42
   church | 37
London | 41, 89
Long Knowe | 14
Longformacus | 14
Longhaugh | 37
looms | 41, 42, 78, 89
   power | 8
Lord Governor | 32, 66, 85
Lords of Council | 32, 66, 85
Lorimer, John | 38
Lothian | 19, 22
   archdeaconry of,
      incomes assess-
       ment | 26
      justiciar of | 30
Lucius III, Pope | 24
Lunnok, William | 25
Lythgow, Thomas | 37, 69

m

mac Alpin, Kenneth | 18, 20
MacLagan, Frederick,
   minister | 41, 76
Maeatae | 17

'Mailros' | 20
'Malchomisrode' | 22
Malcolm II,
   king of Scotland | 19
Malcolm III,
   king of Scotland | 22
Malcolm IV,
   king of Scotland | 24, 25
Malthouse Burn | 10, 22, 59, 81
Manderston | 7
Manse | 45, 71, 100
Marches, East, Middle
   and West | 5, 35
Margaret,
   queen of Scotland | 22, 29
Marion Ker
   fountainhead | 38
market cross | 36, 37, 39, 45, 48,
      77, 86, 88, 91,
      93, 98
market place | 10, 31, 63, 81
Market Square | 27 **figure 8**, 32, 45,
      48 **figure 18**, 90,
      91, 92, 99
markets | 36, 40, 48, 77, 86
Martin V, Pope | 22
Martinmas fair | 40
Mary, queen of Scotland | 33, 35, 66, 85
Mary of Guise,
   Queen Regent | 34
Mason, John, visitor | 45, 91
masons | 30, 32, 37, 40, 65, 84
Mauchline | 25
Mavisbank | 90, 99
medicinal plants | 63
Mein, Thomas, dean | 35, 68
Meldon Bridge | 13
Mellerstain | 7
Melrose
   16th-century admin-
      istration by abbot | 35
   aerial view | 10 **figure 5**
   archaeological
      potential | 93–5
   area location | 56 **figure 19**
   assessment | 72, 82
   hearths in 1691 | 41
   historic buildings | 97–101
   location | 4 **figure 1**
   origin of name | 19
   physical setting | 6 **figure 3**
   property of Melrose
      Abbey | 5
Melrose Abbey | 22–32, 57, 59–65,
      97–8
   abbatical court | 84

126

abbots
  Adam — 24
  ambassador to France for William Wallace — 29
  Andrew Durie — 33, 66
  Andrew Hunter — 24
  David Binning — 84
  Ernald — 24
  Jocelin — 24
  as lawyers — 25
  as money-lenders — 25–6
  Patrick Selkirk — 24
  Ralph — 24
  Richard — 23, 60
  St Waltheof — 24
  as Scottish commissioners at Westminster — 29
  William — 24
altars — 59
burials — 61
burned by Edward II — 64
burned by English — 15, 33, 66
burned by Richard II — 30, 64
cellars — 60
chapter house — 23, 26, 32, 59, 60, 61, 84
construction sequence — 66
church — 57
  altars — 23
  based on Rievaulx — 23
  chancel — 27
  chapels — 23, 31, 32, 59, 74, 84
  choir — 23, 34, 59
  floors — 23
  High Altar — 27, 64
  nave — 59
  nave piers — 23, 59
  roofs — 23
  tiles — 23
  transepts — 23, 30
cloister — 23, 57, 61
cross — 32, 84
deans
  John Watson — 35
  Thomas Mein — 35
dormitory — 23, 59, 61
drains — 60, 62, 74, 75
fealty oath to Edward I — 29
fruit gardens — 62, 74
gates — 31, 35, 74
graveyard — 57, 59
great, or main, drain — 62

kitchen — 62, 74
land holdings
  dispersal — 34
lands confirmation by Henry, son of David I — 25
latrines — 60, 62, 74
lavatorium — 24, 62
lead pipes — 24, 62, 75
lead roof removal — 34, 67–8
monks, trading in England — 26
precinct — 31, 45, 57, 73–4, 93
precinct walls — 24
presbytery — 23, 59
refectory — 23–4, 60, 61
rental income — 26
repairs — 34
restoration work 1822 — 43
roofs — 59
sacristy — 23, 61
site of south gate — 27 **figure 8**
stones reuse — 99
tiles — 59
transepts — 59
vestments — 23, 61
warming room — 23, 61
water supply — 23, 62
Melrose bypass — 43, 81
Melrose Grammar School — 81
Melrose Parish Registers — 104
Melrose Regality Records — 38, 62, 87, 103
Melrose Rugby Football Club and Ground — 11, 73–4
merchants — 40, 89
Merse — 7, 9
Mertoun, James, tailor — 36, 86
mesolithic
  settlements — 13
  tools — 13
metal workers — 32
metal working — 14
Methodists — 41
microburins — 13
microliths — 13
middens — 13, 40, 88
Middle Tweed Basin — 5
Midland Valley — 8
Midlothian — 7
millers — 40
mills — 24, 35, 61, 62, 63, 75
  corn — 74, 76
Moffat — 9
monasteries — *see* placename

monks   19, 33, 34
   disputes   24
Monksford   13
Mons Graupius, battle of   15
Moorfoot Hills   8
Moreville, Richard de   25
Morow, John,
   French master mason   30, 65, 97
mosses, uses   63
Mosshouses   14, 37, 63
Motor Museum   73
museum   59
Mutiny Stones, The   14

n
National Museum of
   Scotland, Edinburgh   13, 17
National Trust
   for Scotland   59
neolithic sites   13
Newbattle abbey   65
   burned by Richard II   30, 84
Newcastle   30, 64
Newcastleton   14
Newhouses   37
Newlyn Road   81
Newstead   5, 13, 15, 17, 22, 37,
                                          38, 42, 75, 84, 87, 89
   aerial view   7 **figure 4**
   hearths in 1691   39
Newton   37
Newtown St Boswells   5, 36
Ninestone Rig   14
Nithsdale   34
North British Railway   17
North Sea   7, 9
Northamptonshire   26
Northumberland   7, 22
   sheriff of   29
Northumbria   19, 20
Northumbrian church   19
notaries   40, 68, 89
notary public   68

o
Old Kirkpatrick   17
Old Melrose   20, 23, 37, 60
   abbey   5, 7, 19, 20
   abbot, Eata   20
   Cistercian establish-
      ment   22
   monks, St Bothan
      precinct   10–11, 13
   priors
      St Boisil   20
      St Cuthbert   20, 22

Old Statistical Account   37, 68
Orchard Fields   13
orchards   9, 24, 61, 62, 64, 74,
                                        75
Ordnance for the
   Governance of
   Scotland   29
Osbert, abbot of Kelso   24
Oswald, king of
   Northumbrian Angles   19
outlaws   32
ovens   76–7
Overhowden   13

p
Paisley abbey, drains   62–3
palisade alignment   19
palisaded enclosures   15, 20
Palma Place   81, 108
palstaves   14
pannage rights   22
property of
   Melrose Abbey   25
Pant Well   45, 48 **figure 18**, 91
papal legates   27
papal taxes,
   submitted to Melrose   26
parish   34, 67
parish church   37, 42–3, 68, 69, 70,
                                        78, 80
pasturage rights   22
   property of Melrose
   Abbey   25
pastures   9, 10
Patrick, third earl
   of Dunbar   25
Peebles   9, 13, 35
Peeblesshire   14
Perth   86, 87, 89, 90, 93
   provosts and bailies   25
Pictish placenames   19
Pictland   19
Picts   17, 18, 19
pilgrimage   26, 83
pilgrims   28, 32, 83–4
pits   13, 24
   Roman fort   18
placenames   19
plague   40
ploughgate income   26
Ploughlands Quarry   9
plum trees   24, 73
police station   81
Pont, James, minister   34
population   7, 45, 91

128

ports | 7, 93
Post-glacial period | 9
pottery | 14, 63, 88
  jugs | 28 **figure 9**
  Roman | 18
poverty | 39–40
prehistory | 13–15, 93
Prenteyse yairdis | 38, 62
Pringall, Robert | 37, 68
Prior Bank | 45, 71, 77
Prior's Walk | 59, 64, 108
Priorswalk housing estate | 57
Priorwood | 64
Priorwood Gardens | 59, 61, 67, 69, 73, 94
Priorwood Youth Hostel | 11, 59
Priory Cottages | 11, 73
Priory Farm | 11, 59, 61, 73
Priory Farm Cottages | 74
prisoner of war camp | 69
proclamations | 36, 88
prostitutes | 40
Protestantism | 34, 67, 74
provosts | 35, 36
Ptolemy's map of Britain | 15, 16 **figure 6**, 18
pulpitum | 23, 59

q
quarries | 34, 67, 85
Quarry Hill | 10, 40–1, 81, 88

r
radar | 65, 80
railway | 43, 81, 91, 101
  station | 43, 44, **figure 15**, 45
  viaduct | 5
Ralph, bishop of Down | 24
Ramsay
  John, first Viscount
    Haddington | 35, 85–6
  Sir George,
    of Dalhousie, later
    Lord Ramsay of
    Melrose | 35
Ratho | 19
Red Abbey | 20
Red Abbey Stead | 20, 22
red deer | 13
Red House | 20
Redpath, Brown & Co | 43
refectory, lay brothers' | 24
Reformation | 34, 36, 67, 78
refuse cart | 43, 80
regality, grant of | 30

regality court | 31, 34, 36, 84
Reginald de Roxburgh,
  abbot and royal
  ambassador
    to Norway | 24
Register of
  Disbursements | 40
Reinald,
  bishop of Rosemark | 24
Relief Church | 41
rentals | 35
  gifts of | 25
rents | 34
repletion | 89
resistivity | 65
Richard II,
  king of England | 30
    burned Melrose
      Abbey | 64, 84
    repair of Melrose
      Abbey | 65
Richmond, Professor,
  Sir Ian | 17
Rievaulx | 59
Rievaulx Abbey | 60
  Bishop Ernald | 24
Rievaulx Cartulary | 23, 61
ring-ditch enclosures | 15
ritual enclosures | 13
ritual offerings | 14
roads | 15, 22
  by-pass | 43, 81
Robert, earl of Carrick | 25
Robert I,
  king of Scotland | 29–30, 83
  heart of | 27, 59, 64
  rebuilding of
    Melrose Abbey | 64
Roman army | 18
Roman fort | 13, 17–18 *see also* forts
  aerial survey | 18
Roman period | 15–18
Romans | 5, 7, 8
Rome | 24
roofs, thatched | 42
Rosebank | 45, 81, 91, 100
Rough Wooing | 33, 35, 85
round houses | 20, 7
Roxburgh
  County of, Valuation
    Books | 42
Roxburghshire | 5, 7, 41
Royal Commission of
  Ancient and Historical

Monuments 68, 79
run-rigs 42, 69

s

St Abbs Head 8
    possible monastery 19
St Aidan 19, 20
St Andrews 61, 63, 87, 89
    barn 76
    Bishop of 29
St Andrews abbey
    drains 62
    gatehouses 75
    precinct walls 74
St Andrews Castle 64
St Boisel, prior
    of Melrose Abbey 20
St Boswells 8, 9, 20
St Bothan, monk
    of Melrose Abbey 20
St Bothan's nunnery,
    rental income 26
St Botolph's Fair 26
St Columba 19
St Cuthbert, prior
    of Melrose Abbey 20, 22
St Cuthbert's church 73, 79–80
St Dunstan's Park 81, 108
St Dunstan's spring 10
St Dunstan's Well 81
St Helen's 68, 78–9
St Helen's spring 10
St Mary's church,
    Berwick 22
St Mary's Road 73, 74, 76, 77, 78,
    94, 108
St Mary's School 11, 73, 74, 79–80, 94
St Mary's spring 10
St Ninian 19
St Waltheof 23, 24, 59, 61
    grave of 64
    grave slab 27
St William's spring 10
Salerno, John,
    papal legate 24
salmon 10
saltpan 25
sanctuary 20
Sandale, John de,
    chamberlain
    of Scotland 29
Sandilands, John,
    of Kelso 36, 77
Scare/Scarce Thursday
    Fair 36, 78, 87

Scheduled
    Ancient Monument 17, 57, 93
schoolhouse, repair 42, 75
schoolmasters 37, 40, 41
schools 37, 42, 48, 69, 75,
    87, 91
Scot, Thomas,
    tailor in Jedburgh 34, 68
Scoti 8, 20
'Scots, assured',
    fifth column 33
Scott
    John, notary 35, 68
    Sir Walter
        of Branxholm 34, 67
        novelist 43, 45, 70, 90
    Walter, of Branxholm
        and Buccleugh 32, 85
Scottish Border Council 5
Scottish Chancery 29
Scottish Guardianship 29
Scottish Tourism
    Town of 1992 Award 7
Scott's Place 81, 108
scrapers 13
Selgovae 15
Selkirk 8, 25, 30, 35, 40
    Patrick, abbot and
        ambassador to
        French court 24
Selkirk forest 29, 64, 83
Selkirk Museum 14
Selkirkshire 7
Septimius Severus,
    Emperor of Rome 17
settlements
    pattern complexity 18
    unenclosed 14
Severus,
    Emperor of Rome 18
sewage pipes 37
sewage works 57, 59
sheep 9
    Cheviot 8
    Melrose estimation
        in 1300 26
shellfish 13
Sheriffdom of Roxburgh
    and Berwick 36
Ship Inn 90 **figure 24**, 98–9
shoemakers 40
shoes, Roman 18
siege of Edinburgh 19
sieges 7
signal-tower, Roman 15

130

Simon, bishop of Moray	24
Simson, James, brewer	69
slates, inscribed	63
Smailholm	7
Smith, John, builder	43, 45, 48, 70, 77,
social elite	91
soils	14
Sorrell, Alan,	9–10
reconstruction of	
Melrose Abbey	
c 1500	31 **figure 10**
souterrains	15
Southern Uplands	7, 9
Southern Uplands Fault	8
Soutra–Kelso route	22
spearheads	14
Spittal	40
springs	10, 22
Sprouston	13, 20
Square, The	61, 75, 91, 99
stables	61, 75
stagecoach	43, 90
Station Hotel	37, 87, 92, 99
statues	37
steeple	78, 100
Stewart	
Francis, fifth earl	
of Bothwell and	
Commendator	
of Melrose	34
James, commendator	33, 34, 66–7
John, Duke of Albany,	
Lord Governor	32, 66, 85
stilts	43, 80
Stirlingshire	17
stone circles	14
stone tools	13
store rooms	20
storehouses	61
Stow of Wedale	29
Strang, James,	
schoolmaster	37, 75
Strathclyde	18
Strathearn	17
Strathmore	17
Sunday school	41, 76
sundial	42, 90, 99
Symon,	
Bishop of Galloway	22
Synod of Whitby, AD 664	19
t	
tailors	40
tannery	64
tanning	24

tanning pits	60, 63
taxes	32
Tay, River	15, 17
Teddy Bear Museum	31, 73, 74
teinds of Eskdale	25
temporary camps	17, 18
Teviot, River	7, 8
Teviotdale	7, 20
textiles	7
Thornholme Priory	
bakehouse	76
Threepwood	25, 37
tillers	22, 81
timber posts	13
timber rights	22
property of	
Melrose abbey	25
tolbooth	36–7, 86, 87, 88, 93,
	105
toll house	44 **figure 13**, 73, 80,
	100
tolls	43, 80, 101
tomb, monumental	59
tourism	7
tourists	43, 90
tower-houses	5, 9, 39
town clerk	40
town herd	40
town House	10, 48, 77, 99
town jailor	40
town piper	40
Toytown Fire Station	81
trade	7, 32, 77
links	14
trades	40, 88, 89
Traprain Law	15, 18
Traquair	7
Treasurer's Accounts	32, 66
Treaty of Perth, 1266	24
tree fellers	32
trees	9
tribes	14, 15
Trimontium	5, 15, 17, 22
tron	93, 105
troops	35, 40, 66, 85
trout	10
Turf Ford	37, 80
Turgot, prior of Durham	22
turnpike road	43, 90, 101
Tweed, River	5, 7, 8, 10, 11, 17, 19,
	20, 22, 23, 24,
	28, 34, 37, 57, 59,
	61, 62, 68, 73, 78,
	79
aerial view	7 **figure 4**

		131
level change	35	
rising	63	
Tweed Basin	9	
Tweed valley	13, 18	
Tweedale	5, 8	
Tyne–Solway line	17	
Tyninghame	19	

u

urinals, pottery	28 **figure 9**

v

vallum	20
vaults	71
vennels	81
Venutius	15
vintners	40
Votadini	15, 18

w

Wairds Cemetery	36
Walcher,	
bishop of Durham	22
Wallace, William	29
Walter the Stewart	25
Wars of Independence	7, 22, 29, 83
'waste'	22
Ettrick	25
Water Company	45
water power	22
water supply	22, 45, 75, 91
Watson	
John, dean	35, 68
John, minister	34
John, pensioner	34, 67
Watsoun, Agnes	38, 62
Waugh, Robert	45, 77
weavers	37, 40, 41, 42, 69, 78, 88, 89
weaving	20
Wedale	25
forest of	29
weight	87
Weirhill	10, 36, 38, 39, 41, 42, 43, 57, 70, 73, 77, 79, 80, 86, 88, 108

wells	10, 24, 37–8, 45, 62, 81, 88, 91, 93
Welwood	25
West Port	38, 42, 83, 87, 88, 89
Westhouses	37, 42
wheat	63
wheel wrights	32
wheels, Roman	18
White Hill	8
Whithorn	19, 20
Whittinghame	19
Wigtownshire	8
William,	
Bishop of Rievaulx	24
William I,	
king of Scotland	24, 25, 26, 63
Wilson	
John, minister	34
Robert, minister	39
Wishart, Alexander,	
schoolmaster	37, 75
Wood, John,	
Plan of Melrose and	
Gattonside	46–7 **figure 17**, 48, 69, 83, 91
woodlands	13
clearing tools	14
wool	
export	65
export grants	30
export to Flanders	25–6
manufacture	41, 76
Melrose freedom	
from toll in Flanders	25
trade	9, 26
woolfells, customs paid	26
Wordsworth, Dorothy	43, 71
wrights	40
writers to the signet	40, 89

y

y Gododdin	19
yarn	20
Yarrow, River	8
Yeavering	19, 20
York	17
Yorkshire, barons of	29